Contagion in Financial Markets

Friedrich L. Sell

Professor of General Economics, Macroeconomics and Economic Policy, Munich University of the Federal Armed Forces of Germany, Germany

Edward Elgar

Cheltenham, UK • Northampton, MA, USA

Published by
Edward Elgar Publishing Limited
Glensanda House
Montpellier Parade
Cheltenham
Glos GL50 1UA
UK

Edward Elgar Publishing, Inc.
136 West Street
Suite 202
Northampton
Massachusetts 01060
USA

A catalogue record for this book
is available from the British Library

Library of Congress Cataloguing in Publication Data
Sell, Friedrich L.
    Contagion in financial markets / Friedrich L. Sell.
        p. cm.
    Includes bibliographical references and index.
    1. Financial crises. 2. International finance. I. Title.

HB3722 .S45 2001
332'.042--dc21

                                                            2001031366

ISBN 1 84064 564 4

Printed and bound in Great Britain by Biddles Ltd, *www.biddles.co.uk*

Contents

Figures

Tables

Abbreviations

AMF	Asian Monetary Fund
ASEAN	Association of Southeast Asian Nations
BEF	Belgian franc
BIS	Bank for International Settlements
CEPR	Centre of Economic Policy Research
DEM	German mark
DKK	Danish krone
EBRD	European Bank for Reconstruction and Development
ECB	European Central Bank
ECU	European currency unit
EMS	European Monetary System
ERM	exchange rate mechanism
ESP	Spanish peseta
FDI	foreign direct investment
FIDF	Financial Institution Development Fund
FRF	French franc
FSF	Financial Stability Forum
GATT	General Agreement on Tariffs and Trade
GDP	gross domestic product
GRD	Greek drachma
IBRD	International Bank for Reconstruction and Development
IEP	Irish pound
IFIAC	International Financial Institution Advisory Commission
IMF	International Monetary Fund
ITL	Italian lira
LST	pound sterling
NAFTA	North American Free Trade Agreement
NBER	National Bureau of Economic Research
NIFA	new international finance architecture
NLG	Netherlands guilder

OECD	Organization for Economic Cooperation and Development
OPEC	Organization of Petroleum-Exporting Countries
PPP	purchasing power parity
PTE	Portuguese escudo
SSC	South Sea Company
THB	Thai baht
UNCTAD	United Nations Conference on Trade and Development
URR	unremunerated reserve requirement
USD	US dollar
WTO	World Trade Organization

Symbols

$\ldots^{c}$	cheating
$\ldots^{f}$	fixing
$\ldots^{f\,or\,c}$	fixing and cheating strategy mix
$\ldots^{f\,or\,ac}$	fixing and anticipated cheating strategy mix
$\ldots^{r}$	regaining reputation
$\ldots^{t}$	taking the medicine
$\ldots^{t\,or\,r}$	taking the medicine and regaining the reputation strategy mix
$\ldots^{t\,or\,ar}$	taking the medicine and anticipated regaining the reputation strategy mix
α	a constant
α_i	a constant with $i = 1, 2, \ldots, 9$
β	transmission coefficient
γ	per capita rate of leaving the infectious class
δ	per capita rate of movement out of class M
ε	rate at which immunes 'regain' susceptibility
η	a constant
θ	a constant
ι	a constant
κ	a constant
λ	a constant
μ	natural per capita mortality rate
ν	a constant
π	actual rate of devaluation/inflation
π_t^{e}	expected rate of devaluation/inflation
ρ	expected return on a bank
σ	defines the per capita rate of leaving the latent class
τ	per capita disease-induced death rate
υ	a constant
ϕ	difference between domestic and foreign interest rates
χ	a constant
a	a proportional constant
A	value of commercial banks' foreign(er) deposits

b	inherited stock of net foreign liabilities of the consolidated government
BL	non-performing or bat loans
BL_{NT}	non-performing or bat loans on non-tradables sector
BL_T	non-performing or bat loans on tradables sector
C	costs which accrue after 'engineering' a surprise devaluation
CI	finance capital inflows
CO	capital outflows
CRR	relaxation of credit rationing
df	a discretionary widening of the exchange rate target zone corresponding to a devaluation well above 10 per cent
dfl	the target zone is given up and the domestic currency is being floated
D	realized and/or expected rate of devaluation
D^F_{Sp}	speculators' demand on forward market
D^S_{De}	dealers' demand on spot market
e	real exchange rate
E	nominal exchange rate
E^F	nominal exchange rate on forward market
E^S	nominal exchange rate on spot market
E^T	target exchange rate
$E(...)$	expected value of ...
E^e_{Sp}	expected spot rate
EC	equity capital
EO	exaggerated optimism
$f(...)$	function of ...
f	a narrow exchange rate band with a *fixed* central parity towards the US dollar – a fixed exchange rate system
F	effective reproductive rate of a parasite
F_0	basic reproductive rate of a parasite
FER	foreign exchange reserves (of central bank)
$g(...)$	function of ...
G	share of guaranteed private debt in total private debt
GL	good loans
$h(...)$	function of ...
H	number of infected, but not yet infectious, individuals
i	hypothetical patient
I	infected country
j	hypothetical patient
J	first-victim country
k	assets hold by investor in the domestic banking system

K	total capital
l	a constant
L	welfare loss
LB	lending boom
LI	liquidity injection through a central bank
m	a composite of main medical indicators
M	number of infants with maternally derived immunity
N	number of ...
p	probability
P	ratio of domestic to foreign price level
q	probability
r	domestic interest rate
r^*	foreign interest rate
r_m	market-clearing interest rate
$\tilde{r}$	equilibrium interest rate
R	world real gross rate of interest which emerging markets have to afford
s^*	fraction of the host population that is susceptible in equilibrium
S	number of susceptibles
S_{De}^F	dealers' supply on forward market
S_{Sp}^F	speculators' supply on forward market
S_{Sp}^S	speculators' supply on spot market
t	a time period
T	length of time that primary case is infectious to others
TLO	total loans outstanding
$U(...)$	utility of ...
v	proportion of the population successfully immunised by a vaccination
w_t	total number of commitments faced at time t
x	amount of tax revenue
Y	number of infectious individuals
z	random flow of government spending
$\bar{z}$	exogenous government income
Z	number of immunes

Foreword

This is the right place to thank a number of people who made this book possible. Francine O'Sullivan, Julie Leppard and Christine Gowen from Edward Elgar Publishing Ltd (Cheltenham, UK) gave invaluable help and assistance and their enthusiasm for this project was sincere and fresh right from the beginning. I also thank two anonymous referees chosen by the editor, whose reports added useful comments from which I benefited considerably.

I also want to thank Silvio Kermer, whose research assistance in Munich was extremely accurate and useful, especially during the last six months of 2000. Marcus Mittendorf and Christine Barth helped me with some of the diagrams and tables, Silke Münzner provided me with some of the economic literature, and Dr Peter Nunnenkamp generously put at my disposal a number of illustrative graphs. I also appreciated the help of Dr David J. Nokes from the Epidemiological Group at the Faculty of Biological Sciences of the University of Warwick (Coventry, UK), who guided me through the eloquent simulations which he and Professor Roy M. Anderson from the University of Oxford (UK) had produced in several papers.

To understand key models of epidemiology was an extraordinary experience for me. It was the first time since I had studied economics and political science at the University of Freiburg in the mid-1970s that I have felt the need to make use of a natural science and to study the relevant textbooks and papers. I warmly recommend such an experience to many of my colleagues in the fields of economics.

Last but not least, I should thank my wife, Heidi, and my two beloved daughters, Marie Jeanne and Caroline. I made them suffer by spending many extra hours working on this book. My wife assisted me in some of the basic terms of medical science (she comes from a family of doctors of medicine and is herself a nurse) and discussed with me a number of working hypotheses. I should also not forget my father, the poet and novelist Hans Joachim Sell; he has always encouraged me to write and he has done so in this particular case with vigour.

I hope that readers of this book may feel some 'contagion' with the emphasis, enthusiasm and the passion I felt when working on this subject. If not, then it will have been my fault because the cause deserves all our attention.

Friedrich L. Sell
Munich, Germany
July, 2001

1. Introduction

1.1 WHY THIS BOOK?

For about 12 years my main interest in the vast field of economics has been development economics. Like others at that time, I took a great interest in the theoretical debate of the mid-1980s among people like R.I. McKinnon, E.S. Shaw, B. Kapur and M.J. Fry on the one hand and C.D. Alejandro, L. Taylor and S. van Wijnbergen on the other. The discussion was on the short- and long-term (beneficial or not) effects of liberalizing domestic financial markets in developing countries. This debate was followed by a second one on the liberalization of the current the capital accounts in the balance of payments, and in particular on the order, timing and pacing of such a deregulation. In the early 1990s, when Mexico was apparently doing fairly well with its 'growth and stability pact', I can remember that the majority of my colleagues were convinced that Mexico – and perhaps also New Zealand – were basically implementing an optimal strategy of 'liberalization and stabilization', designed by economists from the International Monetary Fund (IMF), the World Bank and a group of brilliant professionals.

Then my interest switched to European questions, with the European Monetary System I (EMS I) figuring prominently. We were told in 1992 that this exchange rate system had functioned well since 1987 as measured by the lack of realignments which were so abundant between 1979 and 1986. We were astonished to see in 1992, but also in 1993, how fragile EMS I was and how many fierce speculative attacks almost brought down the whole system. When the margins around the central parity were widened to ± 15 per cent in 1993, we professors had problems explaining to our scholars why this was still a kind of fixed exchange rate system. Paul Krugman's paper of 1991 – written in the late 1980s – had provided with analytical elegance a theoretical proof of when and under what conditions target zones for exchange rates can succeed. Obviously, the referees who prevented the paper from being published for so long had little concern for reality. Who really cared about Krugman's fine results after the severe financial turmoil in the summer of 1992?

During the crisis of EMS I and the observed waves of speculative attacks, 'big' individual speculators like George Soros were blamed for their 'irresponsible', profit-orientated behaviour which – it was alleged – contributed to the occurrence of the several realignments. Such charges even intensified after the Mexican crash of 1994–95. About six months after the crash, in June of 1995, I had the opportunity to get acquainted with the then Mexican ambassador to Germany, Juan José Bremer. He was invited by the Dresden (Saxonia) law firm, Voigtländer-Tetzner & Partner. The purpose of his visit was not primarily to talk about the financial turmoil in his country. Indirectly, he had to, given that his purpose was to raise the interest of foreign (that is, East German) investors in direct investment in Mexico. He was surprised to learn that the business community in Dresden was more keen to hear about Mexico's plans to invest in the 'New *Länder*' rather than the other way around. Also, he was questioned about the role that domestic Mexican politicians had played during the severe crisis his country had been experiencing since December 1994. I can remember well that he was inclined to blame 'irresponsible speculators' from foreign countries as the main source of the crisis.

Two years later, in the summer of 1997, a colleague of mine, Helmut Wagner (Fernuniversität Hagen), invited me to submit a short paper on 'Issues in Monetary and Exchange Rate Policy of Developing Countries' for a conference on 'Current Issues in Monetary Economics' to be held in Castroprauxel in mid-September 1997. I intended to give a survey outlining the successful experiences of developing countries which had employed sound liberalization and stabilization strategies. During my holiday on the Portuguese Algarve coast, however, I noticed that something significant and alarming was going on in Thailand and its major partners in ASEAN (Association of Southeast Asian Nations). Today we know that the collapse of the Thai baht exchange rate regime on 2 July 1997 was the beginning of what we nowadays tend to call the 'Asian Flu'. The paper I was preparing for Wagner's conference got a new focus; instead of reporting on success stories I switched to a different topic. Equipped with the daily newspaper reports outlining the financial turmoil in Thailand, the ASEAN countries and some of the 'tigers', I tried to find common factors and a similar sequence of events in the Mexican crisis of 1994–95 and the Thai crisis of 1997.

In both the Mexican and the Thai cases, extensive liberalization measures in the respective domestic financial sector and in the capital account preceded the crisis. Alba et al. (1998, p. 34) have given an excellent synopsis of the interrelated forces at work which affected into the balance of payments and the overall economic crisis (see Figure 1.1). A major missing piece in the diagram is perhaps only the exchange rate regime which in both cases was seemingly fixed ('crawling peg, adjustable peg') and led to immense unhedged exposure to foreign creditors. Strong capital inflows contributed to the significant overvaluation of the respective currencies.

Figure 1.1 Financial liberalization and external vulnerability

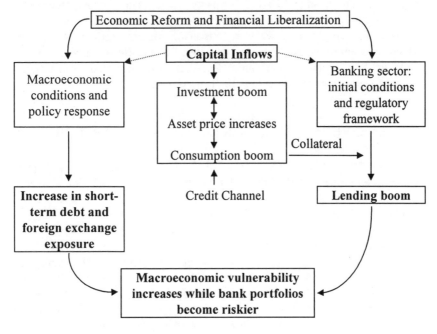

Source: Alba et al. (1998, p. 34).

Ever since the Thai crisis spread to other ASEAN countries and to South Korea, Taiwan and Hong Kong in 1997, the economics profession has begun to explore the phenomenon of 'contagion'. Although the term was not a new one – Gerlach and Smets (1995) had successfully introduced it into the literature dealing with the EMS I crisis in 1992 and 1993 – it now became widely used and was also applied 'backwards' to the Mexican crisis of 1994– 95. The 'Asian Flu' on the one hand and the 'Tequilazo' or 'Tequila effect' on the other, were the folkloric and euphemistic notions which economists began to apply with increasing enthusiasm. I must confess that I had played with the notion of 'epidemic economics' during the intellectually refreshing talks with my assistants when I held a Dresden chair between autumn 1996 and spring 1997. Now that this term was obviously becoming popular, I found myself accepting it on the one hand. On the other, I was somewhat discomfited; how could the economics profession use a notion from medicine in general and from epidemiology in particular? How could we be sure that by making use of borrowed terms we would find an appropriate analogy with the phenomenon of contagious diseases?

The idea of writing a book was born then and was given an additional impetus by the ensuing 'Russian Virus' which caused so much trouble to Brazil and to other emerging economies. For the first time, it seemed to us, the scientific community, we were observing 'pure contagion'. Countries which were not in the geographic neighbourhood, and did not have important trade links or exchange substantial financial flows with the 'first-victim' country, were strongly affected by the financial crisis.

1.2   AN OVERVIEW OF FORTHCOMING CHAPTERS

The main body of the book consists of Chapters 2 to 6; this first chapter serves as an introduction, and Chapter 7 draws some brief and – most likely, given our subject – rather preliminary conclusions. In this section we present an overview of the forthcoming chapters.

Chapter 2 first investigates historical (recent and less recent) episodes of financial market crises which either effectively or only latently spread from the 'country of origin' to other economies. After defining the nature of financial market crises, we recall some of the major financial turmoils which primarily affected industrialized countries during the last centuries (between 1630 and 1930). We present three not so good and three quite good examples. Then we proceed to report on the more recent banking and currency crises in Chile (1982), the Czech Republic (1996–97), Mexico (1994–95), Thailand (1997–98), Russia and Brazil (1998–99) as far as developing countries/economies in transition are concerned. With regard to the more advanced economies we focus on the main aspects of the exchange rate mechanism (ERM) crises of 1992 and 1993. This section also explains the nature and functioning of speculative attacks. The aim is to identify common causes for the onset of such crises while also addressing some hypotheses on the factors that made an 'international propagation' (Kindleberger 1978) of these crises more or less likely. In the summary of the chapter, we address the question whether similar action should be taken if similar causes existed for the crises we reported on. Also, we discuss the important matter of how financial wealth is affected and possibly redistributed in the course of financial market crises. As Aghion et al. (2000, p. 730) have argued, entrepreneurs' wealth is the fundamental variable that determines investment and output.

In Chapter 3, a model is developed which incorporates in an eclectic way several different hypotheses on the causes of financial crises in emerging markets. Before presenting our own model, we briefly survey existing approaches to the problem of the onset of financial market crises. In doing so, we do not follow strictly the recent taxonomy of Krugman (1998b) who distinguishes between 'first generation', 'second generation' and 'third generation' models. The subject we are dealing with has no 'dynastic' aspects! The basic model we start with is taken from Sachs et al. (1996b) which is a portfolio decision-based approach of financial panic with the possibility of multiple equilibria. At the centre of the authors' reasoning is the occurrence of a 'lending boom'. However, the lending boom remains an exogenous event in their paper. Therefore, we add to this model insights from the theories of credit rationing (Stiglitz and Weiss 1981) and of limited liability (Sinn 1997) in the financial sector. A combination of both of these approaches helps to endogenize the lending boom, which is to be understood as a relaxation of credit rationing on the condition of existing government bailout guarantee schemes. As in Schneider and Tornell (1999, p. 4), we assume that bailout guarantees 'allow more leverage and also, encourage firms to not hedge currency risk'. Thereby, adverse selection problems in underdeveloped financial markets and moral hazard aspects of financial crises are combined with speculative attack motivations of investors.

Recent papers have put forward similar explanations for the onset of financial market crises. Huang and Xu (1999) argue about overinvestment under the condition of 'soft budget constraints' – a term which goes back to Kornai (1986) – in a highly concentrated domestic financial sector, and Eichengreen and Rose (1998) find that banking crises in developing countries are strongly correlated with changes in the external conditions (above all, interest rates). This effect is embedded in our model as we postulate low interest rates in the world economy during the phase of strong external capital inflows which reduce portfolio discipline in emerging-economy banking systems (ibid., p. 6), but (first domestic, then foreign) rising interest rates (which precipitate banking problems) and increasing devaluation expectations in the phase of financial panic preceding the crash. Schneider and Tornell (1999) stress, among other things, the fact that a lending boom is associated with a gradual increase in credit to the non-tradables sector (ibid., p. 3). Our model also emphasizes the special role of the non-tradables sector during the crisis. At the end of the chapter, we 'reformulate' the original contribution of Sachs et al. (1996b) formally, and provide selective empirical evidence for our analytical results. Our indicators are related to the cases of Mexico (1994–95), the Czech Republic (1996–97) and Thailand (1997–98).

Chapter 4 investigates in the first place the different aspects or categories of 'contagion' put forward in recent contributions on the spreading of financial crises in the world economy in general and among emerging markets in particular. All in all we find at least nine different channels of contagion. Among them, 'herding' figures prominently. Herding has become a key notion in the modern theory of finance (see Nofsinger and Sias 1999). In order to find a well-founded definition of susceptibles and infectious processes in economics, the chapter then draws extensively on the results available from the analysis of highly infectious diseases in epidemiology. Following the standard contributions of Anderson and May (1991), and Anderson and Nokes (1996, 1997), we clarify key terms such as the 'transmission coefficient', the 'force of infection' or the existence of an 'endemic equilibrium'. The process of infection and transmission is modelled by differential equations and simulated. We are able to demonstrate when infectious diseases cause (i) no epidemic, (ii) a transitory epidemic or (iii) persistent of an infection among the population. Illness and recovery is reproduced in a stylized two-agent setting.

Based on these insights, we intend to reinterpret 'contagion' as a useful term in economics. A systematic categorization leads to six basic forms of contagion in economics. All of these forms are identified (in the econometric sense) and emerge from different sources of shocks (events, new information, new interpretation of old information) at the beginning of the transmission process and the types of contagion channels (direct versus indirect) activated. The most important transmission channels we found are *trade links*, the *financial or investment channel* and the repercussions of *competitive devaluation*. At the end of this chapter, we discuss whether there are economic means of prevention and/or immunization against 'contagion'. A summary and some conclusions complete the chapter.

In Chapter 5, we build a model capable of explaining contagion in a decision-making framework. First, we formulate a 'contagious setup' in which the susceptible country follows a strategy conditional on the strategy chosen by the first-victim country. The first-victim country has an incentive structure in the vein and tradition of the contributions of Kydland and Prescott (1977) and of Barro and Gordon (1983). Hence we model the crisis scenario in a game-theoretic approach. Here, we follow in many, but definitely not in all aspects, the paper of Sachs et al. (1996b). After discussing the first-period problem, we assess the losses associated with four distinct strategies (fixing the exchange rate, cheating, taking the medicine, regaining reputation) in the two-period problem, following the example of Maaß and Sell (1998). This seems to be quite appropriate as credibility issues – towards the domestic public, but also towards the rest of the world – should be discussed in a multi-period framework.

Thereafter, a second country, symmetric to the first one, is introduced into the analysis. Both countries are now linked with each other through two channels: the interest rate and the exchange rate. If the second country is aware of the first country's situation it will decide upon its own action depending on the strategies chosen by the first country. We calculate alternative situations in a simulation exercise first by raising the common interest rate (specific to emerging markets) and second by varying the likelihood for a devaluation. We find that a 'compound strategy' which is associated with a devaluation in the first period and which leaves room for a possible second devaluation in the next period is the more likely for the second, susceptible country, the higher the default risk in the first-victim country, the higher the international interest rate which applies to industrialized countries, the higher the exchange rate risk in the first-victim country, the higher the share of the first-victim country in the explanation for the emerging markets' real rate of interest and the higher its own 'commitments of the past'.

Empirical evidence for key parts of the model is provided by the example of the crises in Russia (1998) and Brazil (1998–99), but also with regard to Brazil and its Latin American partners in 1998–99. Finally, we report the evidence of Asian Flu available in the recent literature. Interestingly, 'contagion' can be clearly observed in the case of Russia and Brazil though there are obvious diverse 'distances' between these two countries. As opposed to this, key variables of Brazil and its major partners in Latin America, such as the exchange rate and short-term interest rates, do not show increased correlation at the time of the real crash. The 'Asian Flu' seems to resemble more the 'Tequilazo' of 1994–95 than the 'Russian Virus' of 1998–99.

Chapter 6 is dedicated to the so-called 'new international financial architecture' (NIFA). Like Eichengreen (1999a), who chose the subtitle 'A Practical Post-Asia Agenda', we are not interested in a wide-ranging, comprehensive discussion, but we do want to address the question which national and supranational (new/reformed?) institutions, economic instruments, prudential/supervisory standards, national and international contracts/ coordination schemes and financial market surveillance arrangements have been most successful (efficiently and effectively), to date, in predicting, preventing and (risk) managing contagious financial crises. The main existing proposals are examined to see whether they can contribute to the achievement of those goals on the one hand and – at the same time – respect the constraints imposed by several 'impossible trinities' (exchange rate regimes, financial market regimes, domestic financial sector regime).

In Chapter 7 we draw some final conclusions. Also, we intend to establish a continuing link between the earlier chapters and to formulate working hypotheses for future research. Do the increased international capital mobility and the quick reactions of investors news make more countries susceptible to 'contagion' in the future? Can long-term engagements of pension funds from the developed countries bring more stability and less volatility into the capital flows of emerging economies? Did the crises in Asia break down a special sort of corporatism? What mechanisms exist by overvaluations are corrected by means other than precipitous nominal devaluations? Can a dollarization of emerging markets' economies make these less vulnerable to capital flow reversals? Do we overlook country-specific weaknesses when we identify robust cross-country early warning indicators?

1.3 ON THE INCAPABILITY OF MAKING AN APPROPRIATE DIAGNOSIS AND PROGNOSIS OF FINANCIAL MARKET CRISES

Thus far, most of the literature on the leading indicators of financial crises is interested only in the deterioration of economic variables which – if it occurs fast enough, strongly enough and above the threshold – should signal an imminent financial crisis. Looking from different points of view, this type of early warning approach can be conceptually misleading. One reasoning (which is not ours) is that early warning indicators can exacerbate the crisis (if available to the public) as markets would take them into account, and, by anticipating crises, precipitate them earlier, and push up the herding effect. Some of us believe instead that traditional early warning indicators are obsolete because they are intrinsically *late*!

Some claim that a decrease in the stock market index increases the probability of a crisis. This statement demonstrates how traditional early warning systems operate. It could well be just the opposite! A substantial decrease in the stock market index perhaps only signals *ex post* that a price bubble has ended, more or less drastically. The likelihood that a new crisis could result *now*, may – on the contrary – be quite low! Capital inflows into countries which are candidates for a financial crisis are accountable for the observable real exchange rate appreciation, the latter causing the balance of the current account to deteriorate (increase of imports/decrease of exports). However, not all real appreciations are the consequence of something wrong happening! On the contrary: there are a number of benign real appreciation cases which in no way signal a danger to the domestic economy.

Once the reversal of the capital flows has begun, we observe – late (one should say too late) – poor figures concerning the *terms of trade*, *international reserves*, the *real interest rate* or, likewise, the *real interest rate differential*. Here, the performance of domestic and foreign (nominal and real) interest rates is of special importance. But what do these changes in interest rates signal? Is there a policy of preventing capital outflows by pushing up interest rates? If so, this signal is late. Is the signal coming from the bond market, where the pulling back of foreign investors in the consideration of a higher country risk raises the effective interest rate? This signal would, of course, be coming late, too. Or do the higher interest rates reflect an increase in inflationary expectations, perhaps because of a price explosion in the bubble sector? Such a signal would be an early one, and important as well.

For all of this, we have to understand the roles of globalization and of human expectations. Why? Essentially, globalization has made it possible for capital owners to place their money whenever and wherever they want. Globalization has also changed the tasks of banks; in their normal domestic operations, banks engage in maturity transformation, borrowing short term and lending long term. With the modern globalization of capital markets, banks increasingly engage also in currency transformation. The so-called 'emerging markets' attract foreign capital in as far and in as much as there are good *promises* to earn a rate of return which is significantly above the return elsewhere.

Various changing financial conditions in the world economy of the industrialized countries, such as a fall in interest rates, may have important consequences for the allocation of financial capital, that is, it will tend to push more capital into the economies of emerging markets. Also, the creditworthiness of externally indebted emerging market countries benefits from lower interest rates. Large capital inflows coupled with a high propensity of domestic governments to guarantee private debt may reflect an *exaggerated optimism*. The latter can lead to an excessive relaxation of credit rationing, which later explains the vulnerability of the domestic financial sector at the onset of the crisis. A reversal of capital flows is already under way when the poor figures (mentioned above) show up! In this sense, any early warning system fashioned in the old way must be late by definition. It is then a sharp correction of (exaggerated) optimism downwards which leads to a revision of decisions by capital owners. Poor macroeconomic figures show up (and therefore, they also fulfil low expectations) later. We may even go one step further: early warning implies the detection of *exaggerated optimism*. Because expectations were excessive, they will have to be revised.

What can lead to deceptions and/or sharp corrections of an earlier (exaggerated) optimism? As the case of Thailand (1997) shows, asset price inflation – in a specific sector like real estate – can be a good example. As long as the bubble rose – the increasing risk of the bubble bursting was (over)compensated for by peaking return expectations – optimism was still in crescendo, but when the risk of a bubble bursting became overwhelming, expectations were revised downwards and contributed to the occurrence of the bubble bursting. Note that the bubble itself was not at the core of the problem, but the attitude of investors and of lending institutions towards the bubble sector was causal, because the prices of risky assets were raised above their appropriate level, and investors/financial intermediaries acquired a false appearance of solvency, allowing them to continue their operations.

Contagion in Financial Markets

What does all of this mean for the construction of early warning systems? These systems should be able to identify situations where the domestic economy becomes too attractive for a large inflow of (short-term) foreign capital, which is steered by the domestic commercial banking system into booming sectors. Moreover, some explanation should be provided as to what motivates the domestic banking system to engineer a relaxation of credit rationing. If banks have fuelled a price bubble by giving extensive loans, it should not come as a surprise that their balance sheets reveal (*ex post*) a severe exposure to risky loans. What made the banks become *too* enthusiastic would be the more interesting question! It is this *shift* in expectations which tends to throw the economy into disequilibrium. Early warning system indicators should detect the likelihood of such an expectation shift long before the results of disequilibrium are reflected in the macroeconomic figures of the respective country!

It seems, however, that not only leading indicators of crises – manufactured by economists – but also *markets* are unable to foresee 'exchange rate crises or devaluation' (Goldfajn and Valdés 1998, p. 873). As Figure 1.2 and 1.3 tend to demonstrate quite impressively, both in the case of the Mexican peso and that of the Thai baht, forecasters were surprised.

Figure 1.2   Mexican peso: actual exchange rates and forecasts

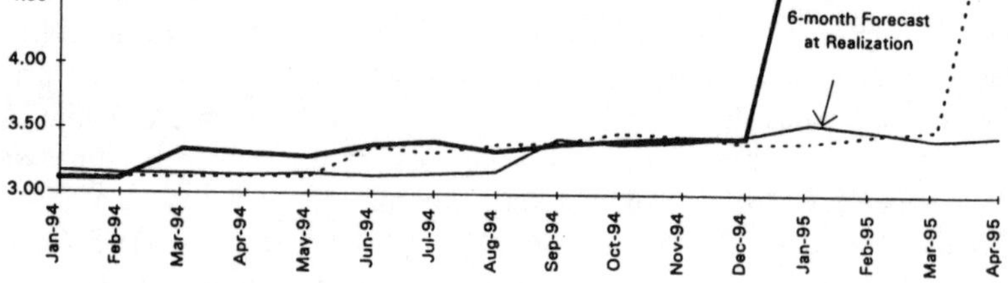

Source: Goldfajn and Valdés (1998, p. 874).

In both countries, neither six nor three months before the respective currency crises, were forecasters able to predict the exchange rate correctly. As opposed to economists, we are talking here about market participants, that is, about people who bet. It is surprising to see that it does not make a big difference whether we look at three- or six-months forecasts. Hence, additional information which could be gathered during the sixth, the fifth and the fourth months before the crisis occurred has not been used.

Figure 1.3 Thai baht: actual exchange rates and forecasts

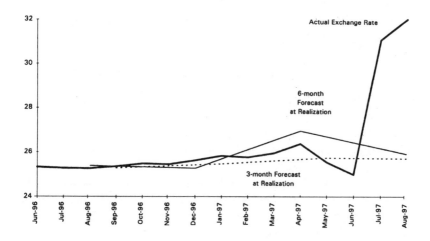

Source: Goldfajn and Valdés (1998, p. 874).

Expectations of market participants should under normal as well as under unusual circumstances incorporate all information available, 'including other leading indicators, when predicting crises' (ibid., p. 885). In no estimated regression – with a crisis dummy being the dependent variable – could a proxy for expected devaluation contribute significant coefficients, that is, expectations failed completely to anticipate crises (ibid., p. 883).

Are exchange rate crises in particular and financial crises in general then largely unpredictable, as Goldfajn and Valdés presume? As Berg and Pattillo correctly state, 'the key test is not, however, the ability to fit a set of observations after the fact, but the prediction of future crises' (1999a, p. 562). Econometricians tend to call this type of test the 'out-of-sample predictive power of a model'. Recent contributions in this field, such as those of Kaminsky et al. (1998) and of Berg and Pattillo (1999a, 1999b) raise more questions than they can answer.

2. Contagious Financial Crises in Economic History and in the Recent Past

2.1 INTRODUCTION

The phenomenon of financial market crises – whether on issued external debt, in the banking sector, on the foreign exchange market or in all of these at more or less the same time – which have their origin in one particular country and tend to spread to other countries, is not a new one. In his 'classic' of 1978, *Manias, Panics, and Crashes*, Charles P. Kindleberger had his own terminology to deal with this phenomenon: he spoke of 'international propagation'. Modern literature on financial markets, however, has found a new notion to describe this phenomenon: 'contagion'. At this stage of our analysis it is not necessary yet to clarify this apparently new notion in depth. That task is confined to a later chapter. For the moment, we limit ourselves to a rather neutral term like 'spreading' which symbolizes by and large what Kindleberger already had in mind.

The aim of this chapter is to have a look back into the history of financial market crises which tended to spread, either because they effectively did spread or because they were strong candidates to spread but did not do so for reasons that will have to be elaborated. In this vein, we shall discuss issues that relate not only to the recent exchange rate and capital market crises in developing countries/economies in transition – by recent we mean since the mid-1990s – but also to financial market crises in industrialized countries which spread to other countries much earlier in previous centuries and, last but not least, to the currency crises which affected members of the EMS in the early 1990s.

I consider it a rewarding task to analyse those developments that despite extensive existing research, alleged existing early warning indicators and the 'supervision/surveillance watch' of international institutions, have 'routinely' surprised national as well as international policymakers. It happened in the past and possibly will also happen in the future in spite of the dramatic experiences in economic history in general and with Mexico's financial market turmoil in 1994–95 in particular. Moreover, the developments in

1997–98 have shaken a group of newly industrializing countries in East and Southeast Asia, which were previously regarded as the most challenging competitors to the Organization for Economic Cooperation and Development (OECD) group. The crises of the Czech krona in 1996–97 and of the Russian rouble/Brazilian real in 1998–99 have impressively demonstrated that the occurrence of speculative attacks is an experience that economies in transition cannot avoid. So what is the structure of this chapter?

In the first place, we shall recall 'early' financial market crises in economic history which can help us to understand more about the functioning of the 'contagion' processes observed in more recent years. In the following section, our aim is to portray the important events which occurred in Chile in 1982. These are important primarily for two reasons: on the one hand because the Chilean crisis displayed so many of the characteristics of the turmoils on financial markets which occurred in developing countries and in countries in transition in the late 1990s, and on the other hand because the Chilean crisis – in contrast to the aforementioned cases – barely spread at all to other economies. This observation will be helpful for the detection of significant factors responsible for a crisis that may or may not spread.

The severe crisis of the ERM during the early 1990s serves to give a better understanding of two important issues. One is the mechanics of the so-called 'speculative attacks' on currencies which were supposed to be overvalued or weak in substance and to be strong candidates for a devaluation. Another is the interesting fact that during the crises of 1992 and 1993, additional currencies came under attack where it was a matter of debate whether they had similar 'fundamental' weaknesses as those first attacked. Here, the spreading of speculative attacks was remarkable.

The analysis of the 1994–95 crisis in Mexico will be undertaken against a background of a full academic discussion of this event. The focus is on a diagnosis of the currency and banking crises and the specific role that monetary and exchange rate policy played. As far as I know, by that time there were no comparable cases of exchange rate cum capital market crisis in transformation countries. The 'first case' observed among this group of countries was the deep crisis which affected the Czech Republic in 1996–97. It will be shown that many of the characteristic features of the Mexican crisis were present here as well.

In the following, I shall then try to provide a chronicle of the more recent crisis of 1997–98 in Thailand and the subsequent turmoil in many Asian economies. These events had the most severe consequences for the world economy ever observed among crises stemming from outside the group of the industrialized countries. The discussion of the Czech krona crisis and also the insights gained from the analysis of Mexican and Thai crises could be very helpful for the group of transformation/developing countries in the future.

Finally, we record the sequence of events/occurrences in Russia and Brazil and the strange correlation between them: the Russian rouble crisis which had its beginnings in July 1998 and apparently 'spread' to the Brazilian real and to the Brazilian economy in August–September 1998. As these two economies tend to have many more differences than similarities and have few trade or financial linkages, this seems to be a very interesting case for what possibly may be termed 'pure contagion' later on. The chapter ends with a summary and conclusions.

2.2 EARLIER CONTAGIOUS FINANCIAL MARKET CRISES IN THE HISTORY OF INDUSTRIALIZED COUNTRIES

2.2.1 The Nature of Financial Market Crises

Financial market crises can be defined according to Hoffmann (1999, p. 73) as more or less lasting disturbances of capital markets. Such crises can take the form of banking crises, of (external) debt crises and of currency crises. In many cases, these different forms are interlinked with one another. For example, a currency crisis is often preceded by a banking or by a(n) external debt crisis in the country in question, as both tend to undermine the trust of foreign creditors/depositors in the domestic currency and in the sustainability of the exchange rate system. The opposite may occur as well: if the currency is victim of a speculative attack, and if in the course of the crisis the domestic currency suffers a substantial devaluation, the equivalent of external debt in domestic currency will rise. In the case of private debtors, equity capital will be reduced; in the case of governmental debt, the budget deficit will increase making it more difficult to finance (ibid.).

Hence, we shall not, or at most indirectly, touch on the stock markets and their legendary crashes of 1929 and 1987, primarily for the reason that there already exists a large body of literature on this subject but also because we are mainly concerned with the spreading of financial market crises in the above sense. As we shall show below, the possibility of an international propagation of financial market crises does not hinge upon the existence of a well-functioning stock market in the respective countries. On the contrary, the existence of such stock markets is neither a necessary nor a sufficient condition for whether financial market crises spread.

In the history of financial market crises in industrialized countries – not only in developing economies/countries in transition – the so-called 'twin crises', that is the joint occurrence of banking *and* currency crises, deserve special attention (Miller 1998; Kaminsky and Reinhart 1996). In principle, both chains of causation exist: one runs from a balance of payments (or foreign exchange rate) to a banking crisis, the other from a banking to a balance of payments (foreign exchange rate) crisis (Miller 1998, p. 439).

In the first case, one can think of a fixed exchange rate system under an incomplete gold standard. If there is a loss of gold reserves not sterilized by the monetary authorities this may result in a credit crunch – triggered by the 'leverage effect' of a monetary base not fully backed by gold – accompanied by abnormally high interest rates or followed by bank runs that 'give rise to increased bankruptcies and financial crisis' (Kaminsky and Reinhart 1996, p. 2). In the second case, it may well be that a government has taken rescue measures for the bailout of the banking system by printing new money and/or issuing new debt. Then the exchange rate system may soon become unsustainable either because of the government's inability to raise interest rates in defence of the exchange rate parity or because expansionary monetary and fiscal policies (fuelling an import boom and a deterioration in the current account) turn out to be inconsistent with the exchange rate target (Krugman) or, last but not least, because self-fulfilling expectations of private agents – who do not believe in the government's promises with regard to the servicing of the debt – trigger a crisis in the foreign exchange market (ibid.).

2.2.2 A Few Remarkable Experiences (Three Not So Good and Three Quite Good Examples)

In his admirable survey, Kindleberger (1978) reviews financial market crises in past centuries and questions whether there was already 'international propagation' or 'contagion' (as we would say in modern terms) among financial centres of the world at that time: 'financial crises tend to be international, either running parallel from country to country or spreading by one means or another from the centers where they originate to other countries' (ibid., p. 118).

Three famous events are often cited as 'archetypes' of international financial market crises; these are the Dutch 'Tulip Mania' (1634–37), the French 'Mississippi Bubble' (1716–20) and the English 'South Sea Bubble' (1717–20). While it is true that they were international in that agents from various countries were involved, in the first case, the crisis remained by and large a Dutch experience, whereas in the second and third cases, they originated in France or England, but instead of spreading to the respective other country, it seemed that both crises rather had a number of characteristics in common and were also connected with each other in a number of ways (see below).

As Garber (1990) has pointed out, the Dutch Tulip Mania was one of the first bubble experiences on futures markets (for tulip bulbs); the bubble burst in February 1637 as a consequence of huge sale orders by important (domestic and foreign) speculators who wanted to realize the price peak achieved by the end of January and the subsequent 'herding behaviour' of other speculators (see below). Bulb cultivators had not participated in the speculation but remained locked in the spot market. Trading on the futures market was vetoed for several months while trading on the spot market continued as before.

Both the Mississippi Bubble and the South Sea Bubble (for the following, see Aschinger 1995, pp. 61–83) were very much the result of John Law's 'original' way of dealing with the government's debt. His main idea was to create a company (Compagnie d'Occident, later Compagnie des Indes) which would acquire large amounts of government bonds from the portfolios of private agents in exchange for shares in the new company. Thereby, John Law became one of the most important creditors to the government. He promised the (French) government that he would reschedule short-term papers with medium interest rates to long-term papers with low interest rates. The French government in turn gave John Law's company special rights (tobacco monopoly rights and so on) and exclusive trade permission which should enable his Compagnie to earn those profits in international trade necessary to pay significant dividends (quite above the interest earned from the government bonds) on the shares issued. By 1719 the 'Compagnie des Indes' had bought the right of coinage and the right to collect all sorts of French direct and indirect taxes.

The second pillar of John Law's financial emporium was the Banque Générale (later Banque Royale) founded in 1716. This bank was allowed to issue bank notes and shares, the latter to be paid by government bonds and coins. It was guaranteed that bank notes could be converted into (gold and/or silver) coins at any point in time. The Banque Royale issued notes almost in parallel – with regard to timing and size – with the increase in the equity stock of the company. This was a means of creating the necessary liquidity for the absorption of the new shares by the market.

Between October and December 1719 euphoric purchases by the public pushed up the share prices of the Compagnie, but this development came to a sudden end when in January 1720, because of excess liquidity in the market, explicit quotas were introduced for the conversion of bank notes into coins. The public reacted quickly by selling Compagnie shares and even more so by trying to convert – whether legally or not – bank notes into (domestic or foreign) coins. The Banque itself had to issue new money in order to buy shares and stabilize the share prices of the Compagnie, but at the price of doubling the circulating bank notes. Inflation soared, and the French government decided to devalue the circulating notes and shares temporarily by almost 50 per cent. The government pulled back on recognizing the rising panic among investors. Confidence among the public, however, could not be restored.

The linkage to the English financial market is easily explained: since May 1719 thousands of foreigners, mostly Englishmen, had poured into Paris to subscribe in person to the Compagnie. This temporarily revaluated the French denier to the detriment of the English penny. When inflation began to soar in France, the denier began to lose value against the penny and this tendency was strengthened when the share prices of the Compagnie fell and foreign investors sold their stocks. The penny did appreciate further *vis-à-vis* the French denier when foreign capital was attracted by the fact that the South Sea Company (SSC) took over large parts of the domestic government debt in England (March 1720). The price of SSC equities climbed and John Law himself (!) became one of Europe's largest new investors buying 30,000 SSC shares. The English penny came under pressure during the summer of 1720 when the SSC plunged into crisis, too.

The SSC had acquired from the English government – much in the vein of the Compagnie – the monopoly of trade in the South Atlantic, including the right to exploit newly discovered isles on behalf of the government. As the largest holder of government bonds (by virtue of the 'refunding act'), the SSC was provided with the right to collect indirect taxes on behalf of the government. Contrary to earlier expectations reflected in peaking share prices and fuelled by false or at least overoptimistic information, the South Sea trade did not perform as promised to the stock holders. When the stock prices began to fall, the English parliament forced the SSC to sell a large part of its bonds to the Bank of England. On December 1720, the SSC share prices recorded an all-time low.

But there are three other historical examples of financial market crises which seem to fit better to the notion of 'contagion'. To Kindleberger, the crisis of 1847 could be regarded as the first spreading international financial crisis. It first occurred in England and France, and from there it spread to the Netherlands, to Germany and even to New York. In January financial distress developed in London, when calls for further payments on railroad subscriptions were made. The banking sector was deeply involved in merchandise trade in general and in grain trade in particular. Also, the portfolios of the banks had a large share of owned land and loans to single builders (Kindleberger 1978, p. 126). There was strong speculation both on grain prices and on real estate in London. The grain speculation peaked in May, collapsed in August, and led to panic in November 1847 (ibid., p. 105). Due to bad weather and storms in May which ruined the crop, wheat prices went up in England by 100 per cent. The price fell in July due to French shipments in June and July, but also to the coming of fine weather and 'the prospect of a good crop' (ibid., p. 108). As a consequence, a large number of houses (firms, banks) connected with the corn trade were brought to bankruptcy. These bankruptcies spread to the 'merchant banking network of London–Antwerp–Hamburg–Bremen–Le Havre–Marseilles' (ibid., p. 128). As social unrest built up in the course of the turmoil in merchant banking, there was a run on deposits which led many banks to disengage from real estate financing and/or to raise the credit costs to the borrowers. This in turn removed the biases in the real estate and housing sectors. D. Morier Evans (1969, reprint of 1849), deserves the credit of having collected highly interesting data on the number of failed banks and firms (unfortunately, Evans did not report on the volume of failed assets) involved in the crisis of that time. Table 2.1 gives an excellent impression 'of how the shock wave of a crisis spreads', in the words of Kindleberger (1978, p. 128). Could anybody give a more sensible description of what we nowadays tend to call 'contagion'?

A second historical example of a 'significant international crisis' (ibid., p. 132) with a spreading virus is the crisis of 1873. It first occurred in Austria and Germany in May, and then spread to other European countries (Italy, Holland, Belgium), crossed the Atlantic in September, and leapt back again to Europe (England, France, Russia). Speculation was again the main driving force of the subsequent crash. Excess liquidity, which so often (see below) prevails at the beginning of a boom and bust cycle, was present as well. Curiously, the source of excess liquidity in Germany was the Franco-Prussian indemnity which France was obliged to raise as a consequence of the 1870–71 war. The gold standard was a useful vehicle to enable German liquidity to spread: the Reichsbank obtained substantial sterling claims from France that could be converted into gold, thus draining the reserves of the Bank of England and destroying part of the monetary base (ibid., p. 103). The converted gold, in turn increased the German monetary base and provided the banking system with the means of financing a speculative bubble. But how could the German speculation cross the Atlantic? The main reason for this phenomenon, given by economists and historians, is that German investors financed American railroads and western lands. When the speculative bubble burst in Germany, foreign direct investment from Germany to the US came to an abrupt halt (ibid., p. 132).

More than 20 years ago, Kindleberger identified main channels of transmission of 'boom, distress, and panic' (ibid., p. 118): economies were and are connected to one another by markets of commodities and securities, by the respective goods prices and interest rates, but also by exchange rates. An interesting case for the latter is the crisis of 1930:

> Depreciation of the Argentine, Uruguayan, Australian, and New Zealand currencies in early 1930 helped push down wheat prices in the United States. Falling prices of grain were communicated to corn and other feeds, sowing

Table 2.1   Reported failures in the crisis of 1847–48, by cities (number of failures)

City	1847					1848								
	Aug	Sept	Oct	Nov	Dec	Jan	Feb	Mar	Apr	May	Jun	Jul	Aug	Oct–Dec
London	11	19	21	25	7	3	7	3	1	8	2	1	1	1
Liverpool	5	4	28	10	4		3						1	
Manchester		6	11	8	1				1					
Glasgow	2	4	6	9	7	6				1				
Other UK	2	4	16	7	7	2		1	1			1		1
Calcutta					1	11	5		1	2				1
Other British Empire											1		1	4
Paris		1				2	1	14	2		1	2		
Le Havre				1			1	5	2					
Marseilles		1			1	1		2	13					
Other France			2			1		1		1	1			
Amsterdam				3	1	1		14	4		1			
Other Low Countries	1		1	4				4		1	1			
Hamburg	1			2		1			7	4	3			
Frankfurt					3	1			1			1		
Berlin								3	4	1				
Other Germany		2			1		1		6					
Italy		3		7	1									
Other Europe		1		3	2	1	1		1	1				
New York		1		3	1	1			1	5				4
Other US														7
Elsewhere		1			1					2	1			2

Sources: Derived from names of firms and banks listed by D. Morier Evans (1969, pp. 69–127). Cited from Kindleberger (1978, p. 127).

19

bankruptcies among farmers, as well as failures among banks in farm communities (which were severely exposed to the farm sector and recorded an increasing number of bad loans, the author), particularly in Missouri, Indiana, Illinois, Iowa, Arkansas, and North Carolina. (ibid., p. 120)

The exchange rate channel will be of particular interest in the following. In the modern context of 'contagion', exchange rates seem to play (at least) a threefold role in the transmission of financial market crises: one is the case put forward above by Kindleberger where, 'in a world poised on the brink of deflation' (ibid.), depreciations of main importing partners' currencies drag domestic goods prices down, with negative repercussions for the involved banking sector. A second example holds for countries which compete on third goods markets, where unanticipated and possibly even unintended devaluations of competitors may put the domestic economy under pressure to counteract with an own strategic devaluation which may harm its own financial sector if it is highly indebted towards foreign countries. A third aspect is at stake when speculative attacks on individual currencies lead to a strong devaluation, a subsequent floating of the exchange rate and then tend to spread – for reasons we shall discuss later – to other currencies.

2.3   THE CHILEAN CURRENCY AND BANKING CRISIS OF 1982

About 15 years ago, Carlos Díaz-Alejandro (1985, reprinted 1991) described the Chilean exchange rate and banking crisis in detail in his famous seminal paper 'Good-bye Financial Repression – Hello Financial Crash'. Re-capitulating the stylized facts presented by him begs the question why the later cases of Mexico in 1994–95 and of Thailand in 1997–98 have been received with such surprise. From 1974 onwards the Chilean authorities began to liberalize their capital account. This development was accompanied in the field of exchange rate policy by a crawling peg (1973–77), organized since December 1977 in the form of a '*Tablita*', that is, by a preannounced schedule of exchange rate devaluation over a specific horizon (Blejer 1984, p. 7), which in this case was two months (Sjaastad 1984, p. 93). The average rate of devaluation was 2.7 per cent. The rate of devaluation was changed twice, before in June 1979 the parity towards the US dollar was again fixed – the level that was to be reached at the end of December – and it was announced that there would be no further devaluations. But this shift in the regime turned out to be unsustainable. Rising capital inflows – given a tremendous spread between domestic and foreign interest rates – created a deficit in the current account in 1981 of about 15 per cent of GDP. The capital inflow was absorbed into the system with domestic inflation above international levels, and the Chilean economy ended up with a booming non-tradables sector and a large deterioration in the real exchange rate (Corbo 1984, p. 57).

The amount and size of foreign capital inflows had a policy reform aspect. While capital account restrictions were important before, June 1979 marked a fundamental change in policy:

> Global limits on external borrowing were eliminated. The only limit which was retained was the overall borrowing limit, including both internal and external borrowing. ... In June 1980, commercial banks were granted permission to lend their own resources abroad. Monthly restrictions on capital inflows were eliminated in April 1980 and in September 1980 commercial banks were authorised to invest in foreign financial assets. (Haggard and Maxfield 1993, p. 73)

The large and fairly stable spread between nominal domestic and foreign interest rates in Chile throughout the period from June 1979 to June 1982 is somewhat puzzling. As Sjaastad (1984, p. 98) argues, 'that spread was not affected systematically by either international capital movements or by the volume of peso assets and loans (which increased in real terms by more than 200 per cent from the end of 1979 to June 1982)'. While Sjaastad attributes the spread to fairly high and stable costs of arbitrage, market imperfections and credit rationing in the domestic credit market along the lines of the model of Stiglitz and Weiss (1981) could provide an alternative explanation (see below).

As Edwards (1984, p. 66) correctly stated, expectations of devaluation developed quickly during the first half of 1981. In June of 1981 the Chilean peso was in fact devalued drastically and – as in the case of Thailand, above – a period of widespread destruction of asset values followed. Towards the end of 1981 net capital inflows from the rest of the world started to decrease drastically and domestic inflation came down – in part because of the strong appreciation of the US dollar on international foreign exchange markets and the direct peg of the peso to the US dollar. As a consequence, *real* domestic interest rates soared – from a level of about 5 per cent a year – to levels of close to 30 per cent. At that time, the central bank had already had to increase domestic credit to rescue small financial institutions. In spite of this, the Chilean banking sector was – voluntarily or not – still fuelling a lending boom: domestic credit rose by 41 per cent between December 1981 and June 1982 (Díaz-Alejandro 1985, p. 226).

The real estate and construction sectors which had profited so much from low real interest rates and domestic credit expansion, now, with high real interest rates, accounted for a substantial accumulation of inventories. Houses were not selling, and real estate prices dropped substantially, perhaps by 25 or 30 per cent in real terms (Corbo 1984, p. 62). In Chile, from the 1970s to the 1980s, asset prices increased eightfold in real terms (Lüders 1984, p. 69). Most owners purchased when prices were up, and the purchases were primarily financed with debt. It came as no surprise that when prices were forced down either companies or the owners of these assets incurred losses or eventually went broke.

Similar to Mexico, the domestic financial system had funded a significant part of the credit expansion through foreign borrowing. A second drastic devaluation of 18 per cent took place in June 1982. In the second half of 1982, the authorities sought to avert the bankruptcy of numerous financial institutions, so that by the end of 1982 they assumed the responsibility for almost the entire foreign debt. This confirms the rule of thumb – said to have been identified by the Japanese – that for developing countries a distinction between private sector and public sector external debt is irrelevant (Díaz-Alejandro 1991, p. 231). But a 'nationalization' of private debt can never be a substitute for proper supervision and regulation of the banking sector. This is especially true when the private sector anticipates the government's acceptance of private debt. Then the problem of moral hazard in private borrowing will be particularly accentuated. In later theoretical chapters we shall develop this point carefully.

Chile was a case for a perhaps premature integration of internal with external capital markets which would have required that local financial institutions were in good health. As they were not, domestic financial weakness had a devastating effect on domestic interest rates because, among other things, uncertainty caused individuals to flee the domestic currency.

2.4   THE CURRENCY CRISES OF EMS MEMBER COUNTRIES IN THE EARLY 1990s

2.4.1 The Nature and Functioning of a Speculative Attack

Speculative attacks on currencies – no matter whether these are currencies of industrialized, of developing or of transition economies – have a number of common characteristics worthwhile presenting and discussing in the overall framework of this book. As Steven Hanke (1999, p. 3) has often maintained and as many empirical investigations tend to support, a currency can only come under attack if the exchange rate regime in question is neither fully flexible nor (really) fixed. This means that all types of exchange rate regimes 'in between', such as (crawling) pegs, managed floatings, target zones around a central parity and so on, are prone to speculative attacks. Currency boards *are* fixed exchange rate regimes and hence in principle they are not candidates for speculative attacks. There is one case for qualification, however. If there are huge capital outflows from the domestic economy which runs a currency board and this puts enormous pressure on domestic interest rates and thereby on the public budget – because of interest rate payments on domestic government debt – this may give rise to a situation where it may be welfare improving to give up the currency board regime in favour of a flexible exchange rate regime.

In order to illustrate the simplest case of a speculative attack situation, think of a central bank which defends a parity *vis-à-vis* the US dollar and assume for reasons of simplicity that there is no exchange rate band, but just a central parity so that there is an 'empty target zone'. Let – as depicted in Figure 2.1 – the exchange rate E_0 represent this central parity which in the initial situation is associated with equilibrium in the balance of payments, that is, where the curves D_0D_0 and S_0S_0 intersect. As in Paul Krugman's seminal paper (1979), we assume in the following that the government decides upon expansive measures of domestic fiscal and monetary policy which shift the demand curve in the foreign exchange market outwards to become D_1D_1. This creates an excessive demand on the foreign exchange market. The fixed parity can hence only be defended by giving in, that is, by selling foreign exchange from the reserves of the central bank amounting to R_1. The alternative, to let the exchange rate depreciate to its new hypothetical level E_1, is not an option for the domestic government in this case as it would *uno actu* symbolize the '*forfait*' with regard to the earlier chosen central parity.

Now let the speculators enter into this picture. They are, in the first place, market observers, so they will have noticed in the first period the depletion of central bank reserves by the amount – for example – R_1. If they see 'that the course of action is unsustainable, then, if they are rational, they will anticipate a realignment or the abandonment of the [almost] fixed exchange rate regime' (Gibson and Tsakalotos 2000, p. 19). Hence they will anticipate more or less correctly that in the second period the remaining official reserves amount to R_2 and if they also anticipate that the government will face in the next period – because of its own actions – another excess demand on the foreign exchange market tantamount to R_1, their calculus should be the following. If they are able to *force* the government to sell not just R_1 but R_2 in that second period – in Figure 2.1 this result can emerge if the speculators themselves cause a further shift of the demand curve (equivalent to the horizontal distance ΔR) to the position D_2D_2 – the central parity will collapse and the exchange rate will, once floated, depreciate to levels in the neighbourhood of E_1'. This is so, because speculators will sell the same amount of foreign exchange after the collapse of the exchange rate targeting policy of the central bank as they purchased earlier, thus causing the supply curve to shift into its new position S_1S_1! Speculators will take this action provided it is profitable. In our simple case the profit would amount to $\Delta R\,(E_1' - E_0)$. Note that speculation is stabilizing as the exchange rate volatility (the targeted exchange rate would have collapsed in the next period anyway) is reduced: $(E_1' - E_0) < (E_1 - E_0)$.

Figure 2.1   Speculating against a central bank on the foreign exchange market

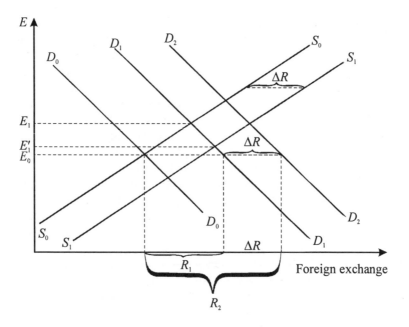

Source: Own compilation.

When will it be profitable? Let us first make the very simple case of a spot market speculation with no forward market transaction involved.[1] Speculators – as is well known – must not invest their own money to make money. On the contrary, they will usually borrow domestic currency and promise an interest rate r on a credit to be paid back after a period t. If the interest rate is not fixed but variable and varies according to the fluctuations in the money market rate, the central bank may itself influence the interest to be paid by speculators, making their speculation more costly and possibly unprofitable. This effect comes more so into play if the speculators borrow directly from the central bank. Speculators will exchange the credit sum extended in domestic currency into foreign currency at the official central parity (by selling assets denominated in the domestic currency to the central bank). This causes a fall in the foreign exchange reserves. If the attack on the domestic currency should be successful, the necessary amount of foreign exchange for the speculative action must at least equal ΔR (see Figure 2.1), which is just enough to deplete official foreign exchange reserves. The fixed exchange rate system breaks down as the central bank is no longer able to defend its parity (ibid.). In order to be profitable, the gain from the depreciation of the domestic currency (when foreign exchange is sold again at the new flexible exchange rate to market participants on the foreign exchange market, see the curve $S_1 S_1$ in Figure 2.1) must exceed the interest rate payments – if we disregard a maturity mismatch – due when the credit expires. Hence, it is the aim of the central bank to discourage speculators from borrowing large amounts, 'converting them to foreign currencies and waiting for the devaluation to occur' (ibid., p. 22). However, rises in interest rates may spread to loan rates, 'thus hitting the real economy' (ibid.).

Instead of borrowing domestic currency and selling foreign exchange on the spot market, speculators can make use of the forward market. Forward rates imply some estimate, but seldom an accurate one of future spot rates. Speculators should be convinced that they are better predictors of future spot rates than forward rates are. At the same time, speculators must have – as the credit sum plus interest rate payments are due at a specific date – a forward contract so that they can deliver domestic currency from the point of view of the attacked currency to the creditor bank at that specific date. To make a profit, speculators have to combine their transactions in such a way that the net outcome outweighs the interest rate payments on the credit.

Let us first examine the less dramatic case where speculators attack the domestic currency, but only enforce a realignment in the parity of the domestic currency – a case which occurred several times in the EMS (see below) – and not the collapse of the exchange rate system as a whole. We also disregard credit transactions of speculators. Instead, we assume that their partners on the foreign exchange market depend upon the domestic credit market. Those will in principle be foreign exchange dealers who want to – let the domestic currency be, say, the French franc – buy francs (sell foreign exchange) forward from 'those who want to speculate against the franc' (Kenen 1995, p. 183). These foreign exchange dealers will

> typically cover their positions by borrowing Francs and selling them/buying foreign exchange spot (which, by the way, they have to if they want to fulfil their forward contract). When the supply of Franc credit is inelastic, so that dealers must pay high interest rates to cover their positions, the dealers must quote large discounts on their offers to buy Francs forward. (ibid.)

Thereby, high interest rates will make it more expensive for their customers – the speculators – to sell francs forward. If speculators were right they will see the franc devalue, buy francs on spot and fulfil on maturity their debit in the forward contract. Let us examine this in detail by assuming the foreign currency to be the German mark and painting a picture of the speculators' and the dealers' decision problem in Figure 2.2.

In the upper part of the graph, we have depicted the transactions of foreign exchange dealers and of speculators on the forward market. According to conventional theory, D_{Sp}^F and S_{Sp}^F stand for the curves representing speculators' demand and supply on the forward market, respectively. If the expected spot rate, E_{Sp}^e, is above the forward rate, E^F, only the left parts of the upper (and of the lower diagram) are important. The dealers' supply curve of DEM on the forward market is upward sloped and may intersect the speculators' demand curve either at point 0 or at point 1. If foreign exchange dealers can get credit extended in francs at a low interest rate, then $S_{De,0}^F$ is relevant, otherwise, with a high domestic interest rate, $S_{De,1}^F$ becomes relevant. In the lower part of the graph, we first identify on the ordinate the old exchange band with the edges $\bar{E}$ and $\underline{E}$. If the monetary authorities allow the spot rate to spring out of the band to a value of $E^S = E_{Sp}^e$, a realignment may consist in defining the new edges $\bar{\bar{E}}$ and $\underline{E}$. Spot supply curves (here drawn vertically for reasons of simplicity) of the speculators, $S_{Sp,0}^S$ and $S_{Sp,1}^S$, intersect with foreign exchange dealers' demand curves, $D_{De,0}^S$ and $D_{De,1}^S$, respectively.

In the more severe case, where speculators intend to bring the total exchange rate regime to a state of collapse, they will enter a forward contract with the central bank of the currency to be attacked. They will first buy foreign exchange (sell domestic currency) on the forward market (short position) and later on sell foreign exchange (buying domestic currency) on the spot market (long position). On the day of the expected depreciation of the domestic currency the central bank has to submit the foreign exchange to the speculators, thereby getting rid of its last reserves while speculators can wait for the collapse in the exchange rate regime before making their profitable spot market transaction. The effects on the spot market for foreign exchange are analogous to those depicted in Figure 2.1.

In a game-theoretic framework, Maurice Obstfeld (1996, pp. 1039–41) has shown how the results of a speculative attack depend on the number or likewise the endowment with foreign exchange of the speculators on the one hand but also on the disposable reserves of the central bank on the other. Suppose we want to analyse the possible payoffs in a one-shot non-cooperative game considering as players two traders and one monetary authority. In Figure 2.3, each trader has domestic resources of six units which can be sold to the government for reserves or held. Committed government reserves are variable: they can be high (case a), low (b) or intermediate (c).

Figure 2.2   Agents and transactions involved during speculative attacks

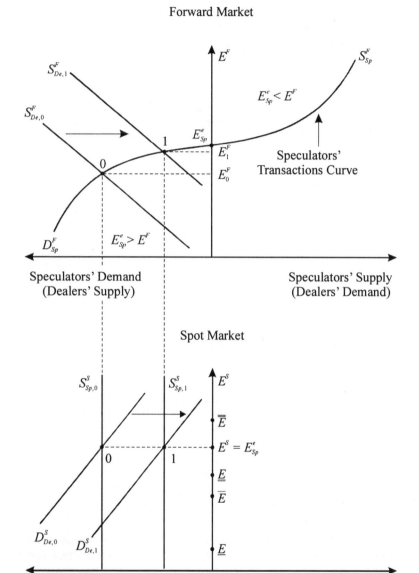

Forward Market

Spot Market

Source: Own compilation.

*Figure 2.3 High, low and intermediate government commitments in a
            speculative attack*

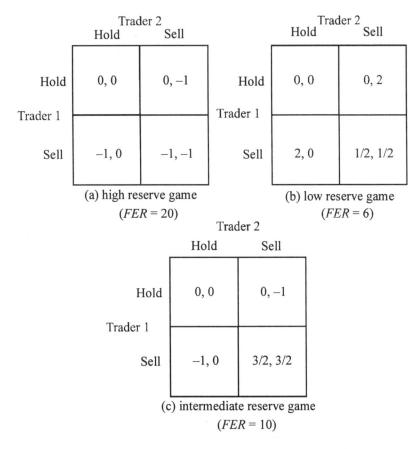

(a) high reserve game
(FER = 20)

(b) low reserve game
(FER = 6)

(c) intermediate reserve game
(FER = 10)

Sources: Obstfeld (1996, p. 1039); own compilation.

If traders attack the domestic currency they have to bear costs of 1. What
are the likely outcomes in the three differing scenarios depicted Figure 2.3?

1. When the authorities have reserves (20) in excess of the maximal sum
    traders can invest altogether (12) to attack the currency, speculation
    (sell) is a strictly dominated strategy and the Nash equilibrium is in the
    northwest corner of the payoff matrix. A trader who attacks the currency
    (regardless of what the other one does) receives a negative payoff of −1.
2. When the authorities are short of reserves (six units), one trader could
    take out the currency peg alone. Suppose one of the traders invests all of

his/her domestic money in attacking the currency and does so with success. Assume the domestic currency devalues by 50 per cent. This would imply a gross gain for the trader of three units of the domestic currency. After paying for transaction costs, a net gain of two units remain. If both traders do so simultaneously, the net gain for each of them would reduce to $3/2 - 1 = 1/2$. In this case, holding is a strictly dominated strategy. The unique Nash equilibrium is in the southeast corner and the collapse of the exchange rate regime is inevitable.

3. The intermediate case is the most interesting: with official reserves amounting to ten units, no single trader could attack the authorities alone. Moreover, if one of them attacks the currency (sell) he/she must fail if the other (hold) does not so and on top of that he/she has to bear the costs of -1. But if both attack, each has a net gain of $5/2 - 1 = 3/2$. Hence, the southeast corner can be a Nash equilibrium, provided that both traders are confident that everybody will attack the currency. The attack thus has a self-fulfilling element in that the exchange rate collapses if everybody is convinced that it will collapse and vice versa. If both traders, however, believe that the other one will not attack, then the northwest corner will be a Nash equilibrium. 'The intermediate state of fundamentals makes a collapse possible, but not an economic necessity' (Obstfeld 1996, p. 1041).

2.4.2 The Crisis of the Italian Lira and the English Pound

After a period of about five years (1987–92) without realignments, several currencies came under severe speculative pressure in the late summer of 1992: the Italian lira had to be devalued by 7 per cent against its EMS partner currencies on 13 September (Noorlander 1992, p. 4). Only a few days later, on 17 September, not only the Italians but also the British suspended their membership in the ERM. Basically two factors were said to be responsible for this remarkable EMS crisis. On the one hand, when Germany's reunification occurred, it was accompanied by a significant budgetary impact as well as by an accelerating domestic demand. 'The Bundesbank sticking to its monetary orthodoxy, substantially increased interest rates to 8.75 per cent on July 16 1992, which contributed to the strengthening of the German mark against the remaining EMS currencies' (Muns 1997, p. 23).

In the same vein, Salvatore argues that 'high interest rates in Germany to contain inflationary pressures made the German mark strong against other currencies' (Salvatore 1996, p. 606). This argument, however, serves at best to explain why the British government, which was at that time fighting a strong recession at home, was unwilling to follow the restrictive monetary and interest rate policy of the Deutsche Bundesbank as a consequence of its own exchange rate target in the ERM. More convincing is the argument that both the Italian lira and the British pound had already for some time been considerably overvalued. This impression is backed by data contained in Figure 2.4.

Figure 2.4   PPPs of EMS currencies, over- and undervaluations against the DEM in 1992

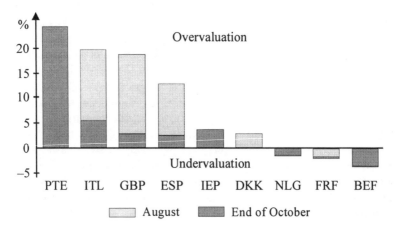

Source: Noorlander (1992, p. 4).

When the British pound entered the ERM in November 1990 with an unusually, large band of ± 6 per cent around its central parity, a number of observers found this 'start-up' central parity too high in comparison to its fundamentals. In spring 1991, massive capital outflows were recorded in Great Britain which were taken as a strong sign that the exchange rate band lacked credibility. By the end of August 1992 the current account balance revealed a deficit of 2 per cent of GDP. This information fuelled the impression of an overvalued British pound.

As far as the Italian lira was concerned, even some months before the ERM crisis of September 1992, the implicit lira–German mark forward exchange rates 'were far outside the narrow band even for short maturities. The Italian lira slid to its lowest level during the September crisis but the following recovery in forward premia indicated that stabilisation of expectations had not been achieved' (Masera 1994, p. 257).

Figure 2.4 also shows that not only the pound and the lira, but also the Spanish peseta and the Portuguese escudo were 'overvalued to the extent that their eventual realignment was unavoidable' (Noorlander 1992, p. 4). The overvaluation of the Irish pound showed up later by the end of October 1992.

2.4.3 The Crisis of the Spanish Peseta, the Portuguese Escudo and the Irish Pound

The abandonment of the ERM by Great Britain and Italy was followed by 'six other devaluations (of the Spanish peseta later in September 1992, the peseta and the Portuguese escudo in November 1992, of the Irish pound in January 1993, and the peseta and the escudo again in May 1993)' (Salvatore 1996, p. 606).

From the beginning Spain found it difficult to liberalize its capital account according to European guidelines from 1 July 1990. High domestic interest rates gave Spanish companies the incentive to incur debt in foreign countries while the restrictive monetary policy stance was imposed to dampen the expansion of domestic absorption. The deficit in the current account kept rising until summer 1992. Several speculative attacks preceded the devaluations of November 1992 and May 1993. Newly organized capital account restrictions were, however, unable to contain the pressure on the exchange rate. In August 1993 the exchange rate band of the peseta around its central parity was widened from 2.25 to 6 per cent on both sides.

As with Spain and Portugal the Irish economy is very much interlinked with the British. Hence, it was a surprise neither that the escudo followed the devaluations of the peseta – not only with regard to the size, but also to the timing of the devaluations – (see above) nor that the Irish pound could only maintain the fluctuations on the foreign exchange markets within the band around its central parity only for a short period. Despite large interest rate increases, on 30 January 1993 a 10 per cent devaluation against all countries participating in the ERM became inevitable (SVR 1993, p. 138).

2.4.4 The Crisis of the French Franc

On Monday August 2, 1993 a new EMS crisis erupted, this time involving the French Franc. After massive interventions in foreign exchange markets, especially by the Bank of France,[2] in concert with the Bundesbank, failed to put an end to the speculative attack, EU finance ministers agreed ... to allow fluctuation for their currencies in favor of the much wider band of 15 percent on either side of the parity. ... During the crisis, the Bundesbank sold more than $35 billion worth of marks in support of the Franc and other countries, and the total spent on markets by all the central banks involved exceeded $100 billion. (Salvatore 1996, p. 607)

In the case of the French franc, the currency's short-term forward rates re-entered the band limits after the crisis (Masera 1994, p. 257).

Table 2.2 summarizes the experiences of all of the affected countries, the dates of the decisions taken and the percentage values of the (re)devaluations implied in the realignments.

Table 2.2   Realignments in the ERM (percentage values)

Dates[a, b]	DEM	FRF	ITL	DKK	BEF	NLG	IEP	LST	ESP	PTE
Phase I										
24 September 1979	+2.00			-3.00						
30 November 1979				-4.80						
23 March 1981			-6.00							
5 October 1981	+5.50	-3.00	-3.00			+5.50				
22 February 1982				-3.00	-8.50					
14 June 1982	+4.25	-5.75	-2.75	+2.50	+1.50	+4.25				
22 March 1983	+5.50	-2.50	-2.50	+2.50	+1.50	+3.50	+3.50			
22 July 1985	+2.00	+2.00	-6.00	+2.00	+2.00	+2.00	+2.00			
7 April 1986	+3.00	-3.00		+1.00	+1.00	+3.00				
4 August 1986							-8.00			
12 January 1987	+3.00				+2.00	+3.00				
8 January 1990[c]			-3.68							
Phase II										
14 September 1992	+3.50	+3.50	-3.50	+3.50	+3.50	+3.50	+3.50	+3.50	+3.50	+3.50
17 September 1992[d]									-5.00	
21 November 1992									-6.00	-6.00
Phase III										
30 January 1993							-10.00			
15 May 1993[e]									-6.50	-6.50

Notes:

[a] Effective dates of new central exchange rates; data refer to bilateral exchange rate charges with respect to the reference currency in the realignment.

[b] The ERM started on 13 March 1979. The peseta joined the ERM on 19 June 1990, the pound on 8 October 1990, and the escudo on 6 April 1992.

[c] The Italian lira entered the narrow fluctuation band; no changes have been made in the lower margins of the lira *vis-à-vis* other ERM currencies.

[d] The Italian lira and the British pound temporarily withdrew from the ERM.

[e] Fluctuation bands are widened to 30 per cent on 1 August 1993, without changes in central rates.

Source: Masera (1994).

2.4.5 Did the Crisis of the Aforementioned Currencies Spread to other European Currencies?

Gerlach and Smets (1995) have emphasized that the ERM crisis of September 1992 not only involved countries from the centre or the south of Europe, but also Nordic countries. In fact, the Finnish markka was attacked by speculators in early September 'which led to the floating ... on 8th September' (ibid., p. 45). What is more interesting for the main subject of this book is the observation that the attack on the Finnish markka also triggered speculation against the Swedish krona (nevertheless, in September 1992 Sweden allowed the interbank rate to reach 500 per cent) which in turn – after the abandonment of the Swedish krona's parity to the European currency unit (ECU) on 18 November – 'spread' to the Norwegian krone, and also (albeit later) and less so to the Danish krone.

Interestingly, in both Finland and Sweden a crisis in the banking sector preceded the turmoil in the foreign exchange market. In the case of Finland, a large bank (Skopbank) collapsed on 19 September 1991 and the government intervened. On 15 November the currency was devalued by 12.3 per cent. That was about one year ahead of the discontinuation of the peg to the ECU (Kaminsky and Reinhart 1996, p. 20). In the case of Sweden, the domestic government rescued Nordbanken, the nation's second-largest bank, on November 1991.

Gerlach and Smets measure the 'pressure' on the currencies by detecting phases of rising interest rates in the immediate aftermath of the floating of the Finnish markka and, later on, of the Swedish krona, in the other Nordic countries (Gerlach and Smets 1995, pp. 47–8). The authors deduct devaluation expectations for the single respective currencies from the assumption of a fulfilled uncovered interest rate parity among three-month interest rates. It is a matter of debate and policy analysis whether strong movements (volatility) and peaks in short-term domestic interest rates on bonds are dominated by high devaluation expectations (in the sense of Kindleberger's 'elastic expectations') and changes in realignment expectations[3] (see below) or rather action taken by the respective governments to alleviate the pressure on their currencies. 'With inelastic expectations – no fear of crisis or of currency depreciation – an increase in the discount rate attracts funds from abroad, and helps provide the cash needed to ensure liquidity' (Kindleberger 1978, p. 11). In the case of the EMS, during a speculative attack or currency crisis, 'the central bank of the weak currency must either (i) instigate a policy to repel a speculative attack restoring confidence in the currency, or (ii) consider a realignment of the target zone' (Dahlquist and Gray 2000, p. 403). When choosing the first option, central bank interventions have to keep the exchange rate inside the bands, and if they *are* to fight off the speculative attack successfully, a switch in the interest data which reflects a further change in realignment expectations should be observed (ibid., p. 418): 'if the potential realignment is averted, the interest rate may switch back to the low-volatility (of interest rate) regime' (ibid., p. 408). That is, we observe a switch in interest data that is not evident in exchange rate data (as there was no realignment).

The most interesting aspect of the Gerlach–Smets paper is to raise the question whether the speculative attack on one currency can trigger a speculative attack on 'another parity that otherwise would not have occurred' (ibid., p. 59). As we shall see in later chapters, this insight leads in the first place to the investigation of 'how a speculative attack spreads once it has started' rather than to the question of its initial cause (ibid., p. 51).

2.5   THE FINANCIAL MARKET CRISES IN MEXICO, ASIAN COUNTRIES AND THE CZECH REPUBLIC IN THE MID-1990s

2.5.1   An Outline of the Exchange Rate Crisis in Mexico

Since the Mexican crisis in December 1994 we have known (see above) that speculative attacks are not only directed against established capital market currencies, for example, the British pound in the ERM crisis in 1992, or against more or less 'soft' currencies that belong to an established ERM, for example, the Italian lira and the Spanish peseta during the ERM crisis in 1992 and 1993 (Sell 1993a, p. 70). Currencies of the so-called 'emerging markets' – a term that is assumed to include developing and transformation countries as well as the ASEAN countries and the OECD economy of Mexico – are also prime targets for speculative currency attacks. In the case of Mexico the United States assumed, as did Japan in the case of Thailand (see below), the role of foster parent contributing a lion's share of $12 billion to the rescue package.

In the following a brief outline of the development culminating in the crisis is provided. On 1 January 1993 Mexico introduced the so-called 'new peso' with a conversion rate of MexN$1 = Mex$1000 coupled with an exchange rate intervention band *vis-à-vis* the US dollar. This occurred after a decade of preannounced crawling pegs which alternated with short periods of managed floating, a free floating exchange rate, a fixed exchange rate system and earlier attempts to install exchange rate intervention bands. Economic prospects appeared to be excellent given Mexico's imminent accession to the North American Free Trade Agreement (NAFTA). In the period from 1990 to 1994, Mexico attracted $95 billion of foreign capital of which the main component were $43 billion of portfolio investment into high-yielding *teso bonos*. Foreign direct investment and equity investment attracted only $24 billion and $28 billion, respectively.

Before the exchange rate crisis, Mexico's government debt consisted mainly of short-term, peso-denominated bonds (*cetes*), most of which were held by foreign investors. However, after the guerrilla insurrection in Chiapas in January and the assassination of the most likely presidential candidate Luis Donaldo Colosio in March 1994, foreigners began to withdraw invested capital for the first time. Foreign exchange reserves dropped from a level of $30 billion to a new level of $18 billion. The government reacted through an expansionary sterilization of capital outflows on the monetary side, and through an increasing substitution of peso-denominated *cetes* bonds through dollar-denominated *teso bonos* on the fiscal side. This had an ambiguous effect on investor confidence. On the one hand, the *teso bonos* insured investors against capital losses from a possible devaluation of the peso. On the other hand, the increasing use of *teso bonos* eroded confidence as investors saw that the outstanding total was not covered by foreign exchange reserves and there seemed to be little opportunity for a roll-over of the liabilities. On 20 December 1994, a 15 per cent devaluation of the new peso's band ceiling was decided. The pressure on the currency, though, could not be stopped and on 21 December 1994 the central bank lost in one single day reserves totalling $6 billion in an attempt to stabilize the exchange rate. One day later the authorities abolished the intervention band and switched to free floating. Almost instantly, the new peso devalued by another 15 per cent. By the end of 1994 the new peso had depreciated by no less than 71 per cent for the year as a whole! Liabilities caused by outstanding *teso bonos* stood at $30 billion, while foreign exchange reserves had fallen to $5 billion.

Since the end of 1994 and the beginning of 1995, a consensus on the causes can be identified among experts who have analysed the peso crisis. These causes bear a remarkable resemblance to those responsible for the later crisis in Thailand to be discussed below. Of relevance are at least three domestic factors and one global factor:

1. Not a fiscal deficit, as described in the standard analysis of balance of payments crisis (Krugman 1979), but a past lending boom 'caused by poorly managed capital inflows led to a banking-system bail out' (Calvo and Mendoza 1996, p. 237). It is important to understand not only how the central bank manages capital inflows but also how commercial banks invest these funds on the micro-level, for example, increased lending as a result of abolished minimum reserve requirements, accelerated privatization, insufficient supervision of banks[4] and so on. In fact Mexico's crisis is seen in part of the relevant literature as deriving from a

liquidity crisis in the banking system. It is argued that, as in the later case of Thailand, there was a severe problem of term mismatch in Mexico: 'the banks' increased reliance on short-term financing such as certificates of deposits from non-residents' (Griffith-Jones 1996, p. 17). Comparisons were made with the banking crisis in the US at the end of the 19th century. The approach emphazises the liability side of the banks' balance sheets. Even mildly negative news, let alone the assassination of Colosio, led to a significant withdrawal of funds from banks. This train of thought is compatible with the sterilization policy of the central bank. In addition, aspects pertaining to the asset side of banks' balance sheets are considered. In the period from the end of 1992 to the end of 1994, the proportion of non-performing loans in the commercial banking sector rose from 5.6 to 8.3 per cent. The proportion of assets classified as 'risky' rose from 51 to 70 per cent in the same period (Gruben 1996, p. 23).

Another perspective on the pivotal role of the banking sector for the Mexican crisis was developed by Sachs et al. (1996a, p. 190). Financial market reform in Mexico was accompanied by an aggressive borrowing and lending policy. To attract deposits banks offered high interest rates that were invested in high-yielding but risky investment projects to finance the return on liabilities. On one hand, the larger the capital inflows during the reform programme, the more likely are lower interest rates as long as the central bank refrains from sterilizing measures. But this is precisely what the Banco Central de Mexico did not do. On the other hand, with increasing capital inflows the danger of a lending boom manifesting itself in explosive credit growth coupled with a deteriorating average risk assessment rises. The ability and also the willingness of banks to screen for marginal projects is reduced (ibid., p. 161). In the end, banks administer portfolios with a high proportion of under-performing assets (but not necessarily riskier assets in the sense of Stiglitz and Weiss 1981).

2. Even before the crisis actually broke the financial vulnerability of Mexico was visible. The vulnerability derived from the discrepancy between the amount of foreign exchange reserves on one side and on the other side: (a) the outstanding total of government debt (in particular the dollar-denominated proportion) and (b) the quantity of money in circulation, for example, M2. The money aggregate M2 is of importance because it relates to the problems of the banking system on the liability side. It includes sight and savings deposits by non-residents that can be quickly exchanged into foreign currency. In times of crisis not only the high-powered monetary base but total money supply M2 becomes the liability of the central bank (Sachs et al. 1996a, p. 189). In this context,

the sterilization attempts of the central bank as a reaction to capital outflows after the assassination of Colosio also play an important role. This is because with fixed or quasi-fixed exchange rates, continued capital outflows (outflows that were wrongly deemed temporary) are reflected in a one-to-one reduction of the money supply. The effect was compensated through an expansive discounting policy to commercial banks. Importantly, this funding helped the banks to survive the withdrawal of deposits by foreign investors (ibid., pp. 150–51). Chances of a devaluation rise with a lower proportion of foreign exchange reserves to M2.

3. The crawling peg policy (agreed with the unions in the so-called '*pacto*' with the purpose of limiting the effect of imported inflation on domestic wages) led to a massive real appreciation of the peso (there were estimates of 20 to 40 per cent). In the framework of the Australian dependent economy model, this should have reduced the demand for non-tradables and led to lower prices or at least to a lower rate of price increases in the sector under normal circumstances. However, prices in the real estate and construction sectors continued to move upward, reducing profit margins in the tradables sector which uses non-tradable output as an input. This adverse effect was enhanced by the fact that because of higher output prices, employers in the non-tradables sector were able to offer higher wages than employers in the tradables sector in the competition for skilled workers.

4. Similarly to Thailand (see below), which is also considered as an emerging market from a capital market perspective, Mexico experienced the effects of globalization during the crisis. There are two important effects. First, there is a trade-off for investors between the gains from diversification and the cost of information gathering. Consequently, the more diversified a portfolio is, the less a representative investor will collect and process information on an individual asset. But even 'small' negative news will then provoke a radical reaction from the investor, that is, a 'fire-sale' of the asset. This first effect is magnified by the tendency of investors to mimic the behaviour of other investors, so that sales by individual investors will quickly translate into a stampede of sales, giving rise to speculative attacks (Griffith-Jones 1996, p. 3). Sachs et al. (1996a, p. 158) stress the role of domestic factors in the case of Mexican crisis. Bad fundamentals in the form of an exchange rate overvalued in real terms, a weak banking system and a low level of foreign exchange reserves made the country a prime target for speculative attacks in 1994.

The financial rescue operation of 1995 for Mexico amounted to $50 billion. Of this amount, $12 billion were credits extended by the US government. In January 1995, the Mexican government announced a 'stability pact' – 'in exchange' for the financial rescue operation. Its main ingredients were a cut in public expenditures by 1.3 per cent of GDP and a significant curtailment in the credit expansion of the central bank. The response to the latter measure could be felt intensely on the domestic money market: in March 1995 nominal interest rates on *cetes* rocketed to a level of 80 per cent. Throughout 1995 the Mexican economy cooled down enormously: while inflation – due to the strong credit expansion in earlier years – rose to 52 per cent by the end of the year, real GDP dropped by 7 per cent *vis-à-vis* 1994, and unemployment went up to 7 per cent. A collapse in domestic demand by 20 per cent helped to improve the balance of trade and to reduce the deficit in the current account to 0.3 per cent of GDP. However, 1996 and 1997 brought the Mexican economy back on a growth path with a declining inflation rate and moderate deficits in the current account.

2.5.2 Some Observations on the 'Tequilazo'

'Tequila' is best known as the national drink of Mexico. Historically, the term was already commonplace to Bernal Díaz, an associate of the Spanish conqueror Hernando Cortéz. Some Mexicans even call Tequila the holy water of the Aztec god-kings. Its basic source is an agave plant, the so-called '*Maguey Tequilero*' and the most popular way to drink the final strong liquor is with salt and a piece of lemon. However, there are also a number of famous cocktails which have Tequila as their main ingredient, the 'Tequila Sunrise' figuring prominently. What we report in the following had more of a 'Tequila Sunset' for those who were 'shaken' by the Mexican economy's turbulences and it has become known in the literature as 'Tequilazo' or the 'Tequila Hangover'!

There is agreement among economists that Argentina was the country most affected by the turmoil in the Mexican financial markets. 'Between December 1994 and March 1995, prices of Argentine bonds and stocks [the latter suffered a cumulative decline of only 24.8 per cent between December 1994 and February 1995; Agénor 1997, p. 4] traded on domestic and international markets fell abruptly' (Agénor and Aizenman 1998, p. 207). Moreover, during the same period, the central bank lost about one-third of its liquid foreign exchange reserves, domestic interest rates increased from about 10 per cent to levels between 30 and 40 per cent, while bank deposits and bank credit dropped dramatically (ibid., p. 208). There is a remarkable similarity between the course of real GDP and the interest rate spread between US dollar-denominated bonds issued by Argentina and Brazil, respectively, on the one hand and US treasury bills on the other during the whole of 1995.

This means that Argentina was not only temporarily hit by the Mexican turbulence, but was also thrown into a 'full-fledged economic crisis' (Agénor 1997, p. 4): industrial output fell by 6.7 per cent, real GDP by 4.6 per cent while unemployment had a peak of 18.5 per cent for 1995 as a whole. All of this was triggered by the Tequila effect which in its narrow sense was meant to account for the massive capital outflows (or the drastic reduction in net foreign borrowing) in conjunction with a massive loss of confidence of investors in the country's economic prospects and the 'perception that the exchange rate regime was about to suffer the same fate as Mexico's' (ibid., p. 7). More precisely, Uribe identifies the heart of the issue when he states:

[T]he Argentine crisis of 1995 was caused by the reluctance of foreign investors to renew their loans to the country, resulting from the fear that it would soon follow in Mexico's footsteps. According to this hypothesis the change of confidence of foreign investors was exogenous to the country and, moreover, completely unrelated to domestic economic fundamentals. (Uribe 1996, p. 2)

After Argentina, Brazil was the Latin American economy most affected by the Mexican crisis. Like Argentina, Brazil had to bear a considerable drain on its foreign exchange reserves. 'In the height of the crisis, Brazil implemented measures to stimulate capital inflows, by reducing or eliminating existing taxes on foreign purchases of stocks and bonds' (Calvo and Reinhart 1995, p. 1). Interestingly, neither of the two countries had large deficits in their current account at the time of the crisis, but both countries were equipped with a more (Argentina) or less (Brazil) fixed exchange rate system.

Speculative attacks were not limited to Argentina and Brazil. Peru and Venezuela were also attacked but to a lesser extent. However, not all Latin American countries were attacked – 'Chile being the most visible exception – and not all economies attacked were in Latin America (Thailand, Hong Kong, the Philippines and Hungary also suffered speculative attacks)' (Glick and Rose 1998, p. 3).

2.5.3 An Outline of the Crisis of the Czech Krona in 1996–97

Clearly differences between transformation and developing countries are not all due to the fact that the former still have to grow into their role as emerging markets. Transformation countries generally suffered from a significant monetary overhang which they sought to reduce through price liberalization. With accommodating monetary policy, inflation increases sharply and the authorities are soon under pressure to reduce inflation without limiting the budget deficit to ensure that the recently gained signalling effect of the price system is not destroyed. Importantly, transformation countries are frequently partially rationed on international capital markets. This provides an incentive for the authorities to increase seigniorage through the introduction/increase of minimum reserve requirements in the banking system. With constant money supply this increases the share of the central bank in total credit expansion at the cost of reducing the lending possibilities of commercial banks. The drawback of this strategy is that while a limited success in terms of stabilization is achieved, an additional distortion in terms of interest rates is introduced or increased. The cost of this distortion and the seigniorage revenue obtained by the authorities is borne by the users of the commercial banking system, on the liability as well as on the asset side.

The Czech Republic is a very recent nation, as it was (re)founded after its separation from Slovakia only in 1993. In May 1993 the authorities decided to fix the rate of the krona to a basket of two currencies, the US dollar and the German mark, with an alleged share of 65 and 35 per cent, respectively. The intervention band was set at a range of ± 0.5 per cent. In the subsequent years the Czech Republic went along the unstable growth path which is so typical for countries in transition. In 1995, however, one could observe strong capital inflows into the country which amounted to 17 per cent of GDP. Economic growth achieved a rate of 4.8 per cent, the deficit in the current account reached a level of 4 per cent of GDP and the money aggregate M2 rose by 19 per cent (!). Therefore, the central bank did not attempt to sterilize the capital inflows. In the banking sector there were strong signs of a lending boom as the share of bad loans increased and insolvencies rose overall by 11.6 per cent and by 78.2 per cent in the construction sector.

The authorities reacted on February 1996 when they widened the target exchange rate band to ± 7.5 per cent with the purpose of actively increasing exchange rate uncertainty and thereby reducing the speed of foreign capital inflows. At the same time the central bank started to sterilize the decreasing but still large foreign capital inflows, and raised the prime rate and the minimum reserve requirement, resulting in a sharp increase in the real interest rate to a level of 10 per cent. The share of bad loans which the banking sector had to face rose to 25 per cent (from 6.2 per cent in 1994!).

Despite these attempts to reduce the pace of the economy, economic growth in 1996 was still at 4.4 per cent while inflation – fuelled by the strong expansion of the monetary base in the previous periods – was at 7.4 per cent and the current account deficit deteriorated to an unprecedented high of 8 per cent of GDP. By the end of 1996, and much more pronounced in the first quarter of 1997, the domestic currency came under pressure of speculative attacks. By 15 May 1997 the krona fell by about 5 per cent below the lower target band. Central bank interventions were unable to bring the exchange rate back into the band again. However, these costly though useless actions brought foreign exchange reserves down by $2 billion in only ten days. Ultimately, the central bank stopped selling foreign exchange and announced a 'managed floating' *vis-à-vis* the German mark on 26 May 1997. Although the Prague Interbank Offered Rate (PRIBOR) was raised to 26 per cent in June, the krona continued to depreciate against major currencies.

From July 1997 onwards there was some relaxation in the level of interest rates (PRIBOR came down to 17 per cent) and the Czech currency recovered relatively, that is, the exchange rate *vis-à-vis* the German mark stabilized somewhat. The disaster in the financial markets, however, had already occurred: ten banks lost their licence to operate and another four were put under direct government control. Restrictive fiscal and monetary policies tended to exacerbate the crisis. In 1997 economic growth fell to a low of 1 per cent, unemployment rose to 5.2 per cent along with only small reductions in the inflation rate (8.5 per cent) and the current account deficit (6 per cent of GDP). In the following year, major economic variables deteriorated further as economic growth became negative (–2.7 per cent) and inflation rose again to 9 per cent.

If one compares in broad lines the Czech crisis with the Mexican case, despite a lot of differences it is possible also to identify a number of important similarities. As in the case of Mexico, it seems worthwhile to distinguish between 'home-made' and 'global factors' responsible for the crisis:

1. A lending boom – preceding the crisis – could be observed in the Czech Republic quite as much as in Mexico. This lending boom was fuelled last but not least by considerable external capital inflows. Foreign private investment, for instance, tripled in 1995 in comparison to 1994. All in all, foreign capital inflows reached a share of 17 per cent of GDP in that same year.
2. Within the banking sector, short-term credits amounted to a share of 42 per cent in total outstanding credits of banks in 1995. This ratio points to a significant maturity mismatch. Bad loans accounted for 6.3 per cent in 1995, but at a share of 25 per cent in June of 1996. The most affected sectors were, as in other countries, construction and real estate. Banking supervision worked poorly, if at all. In 1996 a withdrawal of foreign deposits could be observed. Meanwhile, the financial sector was left with a number of risky assets.
3. The ratio between M2 and net foreign exchange reserves developed in the period preceding the eruption of the crisis as unfavourably as it did in the case of Mexico. Only short-term debt compared to net foreign exchange reserves did slightly better.
4. The pegging of the krona against the US dollar and the German mark led to an accumulated real appreciation of the Czech currency of no less than 80 per cent between 1991 and 1996. It was only a matter of time before a

speculative attack against the currency could be expected. Surprisingly, this fact was not taken into consideration by many experts for a long time. Moreover, as late as in June 1996 the OECD defended the opinion that the krona was at the time undervalued (OECD 1996, p. 155).

5. Global factors – in the sense that assets of this country had already entered the portfolios of global players – may have had a role in the case of the Czech crisis as well, given that the country was already considered to be an advanced economy in transition, hence an 'emerging market' (United Nations 1998, p. 45).

2.5.4 Did the Crisis of the Czech Krona Spread to Other Countries?

In contrast to the Mexican case (and more so to the Thai case, see below) the crisis of the banking sector and the collapse of the exchange rate regime in the Czech Republic 'spread' neither to other emerging markets in general nor to economies in transition located in Central and Middle Europe in particular.

2.5.5 An Outline of the Exchange Rate Crisis in Thailand

During the summer of 1997, newspaper reports frequently described the strong capital market and exchange rate turbulences which affected the ASEAN countries in general and Thailand in particular. I had the chance to visit the five founding member countries of this rather loose supranational organization as part of the fieldwork for my habilitation thesis (Sell 1988b) in 1985–86. The thesis analysed the progress made by the ASEAN countries in removing the effects of 'financial repression' – a term that had just been coined by E.S. Shaw (1973) and R.I. McKinnon (1973) in the 1970s. Like many of my colleagues I then read the famous contribution 'Goodbye Financial Repression – Hello Financial Crash' by Carlos Díaz-Alejandro (1991, see above). The author died prematurely (a neostructuralist would add: especially for his intellectual adversaries). I also forgot about his contribution too soon – because, as we have seen above, many of the issues raised in his seminal contribution are not confined to the Chilean crisis of 1982, but are still of relevance today. As a result of the baht crisis in 1997, even Thailand, the show-case country for the export-led growth strategy in the ASEAN group, had and still has lost some of its shine. In a pertinent newspaper article, Paul Krugman (1994) – who had already coined the term 'the myth of Asia's miracle' in 1994 – proposed that the East Asian economic miracle was occasioned more by transpiration than inspiration. Can we really go that far?

Nicholas Crafts's recent study (1999) on East Asian growth before and after the crisis provides an illuminating though preliminary assessment: for the long period between 1960 and 1994, he finds that 'the tendency for Asian countries to have substantial growth from capital accumulation is clearly shown ... [and also a] much stronger contribution made by labour force growth in Asian countries than in Europe' (Crafts 1999, pp. 149–50). Hence, it seems that 'the evidence has been broadly supportive of the position taken by Krugman' (ibid., p. 150). Between 1994 and 1996, however, total factor productivity growth was considerably more impressive than that of the early years of rapid economic growth, a fact which according to Crafts could lead to more optimism than Krugman's pessimism would allow (ibid.).

Crafts attributes the main reasons for Asia's severe crisis in 1997–99 to the fact that 'without adequate regulation of the banking system, severe disruptions to economic growth are very possible' (ibid., p. 158). 'Asymmetric information, implicit guarantees for depositors, and weak balance sheets ... are a serious risk of financial crisis as liberalisation proceeds unless regulators with incentives and powers to take prompt corrective action are available' (ibid.). A positive consequence if the crisis described below may have been the identification of the areas/issues where microeconomic reforms, not only macroeconomic ones, are necessary in the future.

The Thai currency crisis had been imminent for more than a year. In 1996, GDP and export growth dropped significantly. On 14–15 May 1997, a first speculative attack hit the Thai baht. Both the Monetary Authority of Singapore and the Bank of Thailand intervened on the foreign exchange market to defend the parity with the US dollar. These transactions depleted the reserves of the Thai central bank – which at that time stood at $32.4 billion – by $5 billion. At the same time, existing capital controls were reinforced. Later in the month, on 23 May, rescue actions taken in favour of Thailand's largest finance company, Finance One, failed. In June 1997 a budget deficit began to emerge for the fiscal year 1996–97 for the first time. After the resignation of the minister of finance and trade on 16 June, the exchange rate for the baht rose to the upper boundary of its target zone, but the prime minister categorically refused to devalue the baht. No less than 16 finance companies lost their licence to operate. Up to now, the government had spent about 200 billion baht subsidizing the domestic financial sector. The stock exchange continued its tendency – known for almost two years – to produce sudden gyrations downwards. At this stage the government still ruled out a devaluation. However, in the face of continued speculative activity against the baht, the government was forced to abandon the peg to the US dollar on 2 July. As a consequence, the Thai exchange rate fell by 30 per cent against the dollar, massive capital outflows ensued and equity prices on the Bangkok stock exchange continued their downward trend. Between January and September 1997 total capital on the Bangkok stock exchange fell by 41 per cent. The Thai authorities then asked the IMF for 'technical assistance'.

What had happened? Most observers emphazised the collapse of the Thai real estate sector in their analysis of the crash. The sector had previously enjoyed a boom that by many critics had been identified very early on as a speculative bubble supported by mostly non-performing loans from domestic banks and so-called finance companies (Sell 1988b, p. 124). An estimate of 1997 put the total of non-performing loans to the real estate sector at $36 billion. During the last five years before the exchange rate collapse, Thai banks advertised growth rates of 25 per cent annually for their lending activities. But these loans – principally funded through capital borrowed abroad in US currency – were not supported by an adequate risk assessment. Towards the end of 1996, 29 per cent of all loans by commercial banks went to the real estate sector. At first the government refused to let financial institutions declare themselves bankrupt and tried to shore up their operation through subsidies.

The second problem was Thailand's finance companies. Abundant capital allowed many finance companies to offer loans to firms and households imprudently without paying enough attention to the solvency of their debtors. This in fact (see Chapters 3 and 5) represented a moral hazard problem, 'since these financial intermediaries implicitly assumed a government guarantee of their liabilities, being that they were exposed to only negligible regulation' (Aschinger 1998, p. 12). As part and in advance of the IMF stabilization programme launched on 11 August, an additional 48 finance companies in trouble were closed during the summer of 1997 for at least 60 days. This came on top of the closure of 16 finance companies in June 1997 (see above) and the loss of licence by about half of the registered banks in Thailand. This increased the proportion of finance companies closed by the authorities to 51 out of a total of 91, that is, 64 per cent. Sources in Bangkok put the proportion of lending by finance companies that went to the construction and real estate sectors in the relevant period at about one-quarter of total assets.

In 1996 the total capital inflow into Thailand was 10 per cent of GDP. The flood of foreign capital was directed primarily at the real estate sector, causing rapidly rising prices. When the bubble nature of these price increases became more and more obvious given limited basic demand, confidence in the baht collapsed and speculative attacks against the currency followed. Thailand had a gross foreign debt of about 43 per cent of GDP or $89 billion by mid-1997, when the net value of these foreign liabilities was reduced by foreign exchange reserves of $32.4 billion. Half of the gross outstanding loans were owed to Japanese banks and 82 per cent of these loans were owed by Thai nationals or companies. The strong devaluation of the baht had increased the vulnerability of Thai banks and companies further, since the nominal value of outstanding liabilities in domestic currency had gone up.

We can identify the following stylized facts. Foreign capital was absorbed principally by the non-tradables sector. The central bank showed extreme neglect in its duty of supervising the lending activities of Thai banks. It is very likely that the speculative activity by financial institutions was also fed significantly by sources in the informal capital market. These sources routinely require very high rates of return combined with an extremely short-term investment horizon. This almost automatically presents with problems of term matching and provides a strong incentive to invest in high-risk–high-return projects in the spirit of the Stiglitz–Weiss hypothesis (Stiglitz and Weiss 1981).

On 11 August a multilateral emergency package giving Thailand access to $17.2 billion – of which the IMF funded $4 billion – was agreed in Washington, DC. Thailand promised to reduce its current account deficit to 3 per cent of GDP, to conduct a restrictive fiscal policy and to hold foreign exchange reserves equivalent to the costs incurred by imports for four months. After the financial rescue operation of 1995 for Mexico amounting to $50 billion, the emergency support for Thailand was the second package prepared by the IMF to avoid major disturbances in global capital markets. In the case of Thailand, Japan had assumed a leading role by providing $4 billion of the $17.2 billion in non-conditional loans. This commitment came as no surprise given that Japan was Thailand's largest single creditor and had a strong interest in the stabilization of the country's capital markets and economy. But particularly in Japan there were doubts as to whether the rescue package was sufficient: through interest payments and repayments on mostly short-term foreign debt and additional needs to support the baht in the near future, a capital outflow of about 25 billion until the end of 1997 was more likely. Japan's banks then found themselves in the dilemma well known from previous debt crises: should good money be thrown after bad, or was it necessary to provide fresh loans to maintain the value of outstanding ones?

It is remarkable that in its emphasis the IMF rescue package did not follow the capital market approach to currency crises (Sachs et al. 1996a; Calvo and Mendoza 1996) but rather the goods market/balance of payments approach proposed by Dornbusch and Werner (1994). In addition to higher government revenue (through value added tax) and a reduction in expenditure, it was the aim of the IMF programme to reduce the current account deficit from 8 per cent of GDP to 5 per cent in 1997 and to 3 per cent in 1998. Foreign exchange reserves were to be stabilized at a level that covered four months' worth of imports. Even after the magnitude and the content of the IMF package was announced at the end of August/beginning of September 1997, pressure on the baht remained. This was because problems of credibility persisted: on the one hand the domestic value of Thailand's foreign debt continued to increase; on the other, the terms of trade between tradables and non-tradables had not reached a level that rendered the necessary real outward transfers on the foreign debt sustainable in the long run.

2.5.6 Some Observations on the 'Asian Flu'

It should be kept in mind that as a knock-on effect of the crisis in Thailand, other Southeast Asian countries including Indonesia, Malaysia, the Philippines and others were also affected. Most of these countries also had high current account deficits and high foreign debts and 'were subjected to destabilising speculation in the construction and in the real estate industries' (Aschinger 1998, p. 13). The currencies of other ASEAN countries have come under pressure since July 1997: the Malaysian ringgit (after intensive interventions, the authorities ceased to defend the parity with the US dollar on 14 July 1997), the Singaporean dollar (the central bank defended the exchange rate with particular vigour), the Indonesian rupee (the authorities decided to stop their intervention in the foreign exchange market and let the currency float on 13 August 1997), the Philippine peso (the authorities had already decided on a widening of the exchange rate band *vis-à-vis* the US dollar on 11 July) and even the Hong Kong dollar since the end of August. However, in contrast to the South Korean won whose value had declined significantly against the US dollar since the end of August, the Hong Kong dollar managed to retain its previous rate on international capital markets.[5] Although these countries had – as mentioned above – some problems similar to Thailand, most experts believe that if the Thai baht had not collapsed in early July 1997, the other exchange rates may have stayed more stable as well.

In early September 1997, all currencies in the ASEAN group continued their decline against major capital market currencies. The South Korean won reached an 'all-time low' in early November: finally, the South Korean authorities had to float their currency on 17 November 1997. On 3 December the baht, the won, the rupee and the ringgit reached an unprecedented all-time low of their parities with regard to the US dollar. In July (Philippines), October (Indonesia) and December (South Korea), the countries most affected by the financial market turmoil in Asia – which has had its origins in the collapse of the Thai baht – agreed with the IMF on rescue packages of considerable size.

Obviously, investors had downgraded the growth prospects of the ASEAN countries and, as a logical extension, their companies. Drastic increases in interest rates aimed at shoring up the value of the respective currencies had been met with little success. In most of the countries, domestic governments launched programmes for better bank supervision and capitalization, and for more competition in the domestic banking sector, and promised to liberalize trade. But once standing is lost it is hard to recover: by December 1997 Thai securities were classified by the rating agency Moody's as 'junk bonds'.

Hong Kong is an interesting exception, but it may have been no exception after all. What happened there? As Aschinger reports (1998, p. 18), the Hong Kong dollar withstood the pressure exerted by soaring interest rates. However, The Hang Seng Index plummeted on 23 October 1997 and this was 'partly due to bad news about the local economy and fears concerning the Southeast Asian crisis, which became apparent in summer 1997' (ibid.). The reasons for the earlier peak of the Hang Seng Index were quite familiar from the boom in Thailand: 'Hong Kong's real estate prices soared because of excessive lending and the lack of resale limitations' (ibid., p. 14). The rise in interest rates which preceded the stock exchange crash was, however, intimately linked to the fear 'that the peg of the Hong Kong dollar to the US dollar might be abandoned' (ibid.). Hence, many firms hedged their US-denominated debt by buying forward US dollars and selling Hong Kong dollars. In reaction to that, short-term interest rates in Hong Kong rose sharply and this primarily affected highly indebted firms, especially in the real estate sector, where of many of them were in danger of insolvency.

So we get the interesting result that the Asian Flu spread less to the Hong Kong foreign exchange market but more to the Hong Kong stock exchange. But this is not the end of the story: as Aschinger describes, the crash of the Hang Seng Index did have repercussions! There was a 'rapid spill-over ... to other stock exchanges' (ibid., p. 16) and these stock exchanges were located in industrialized countries! On 23 October 'European stock exchanges experienced share index reductions of between 3% and 5%, while the Nikkei 225 fell by 3 % and the DJIA lost 2.3%' (ibid., p. 12).

2.6 THE CRISES OF THE ROUBLE AND THE REAL IN THE LATE 1990s: A CASE OF 'PURE CONTAGION'?

2.6.1 Russia's Moment of Truth

Russia's financial markets, which had faced considerable volatility since October 1997, had been under intensified pressure since May 1998. Capital outflows had led to steep increases in interest rates, undermining fiscal consolidation and the nascent economic recovery. Real GDP had fallen slightly in the first months of 1998, compared with the same period in 1997, and while inflation had declined faster than projected, the balance of payments was in deficit during the first half of the year because of lower oil and gas prices, and the reversal in market confidence. The government had responded and had geared monetary policy towards defending the exchange rate, allowing domestic interest rates to rise substantially.

The real turmoil in Russian financial markets began at the end of June 1998: at the time, the rouble was supposed to move in a target band *vis-à-vis* the US dollar. But as the rouble weakened outside its target range, the Bank of Russia raised its prime rates to 80 per cent. The news of a tentative agreement between Russia and the IMF on a new loan package predicated on the condition of the adoption of a government's austerity programme arrived by mid-July. This news had an – albeit short-lived – effect on financial market prices and bolstered the rouble for a few days.

The IMF package was finally approved on 20 July 1998. But the originally promised initial outlay of $5.6 billion was reduced to $4.8 billion as neither the government nor the Duma approved and/or executed the measures (cut in government expenditures, higher tax revenues, restrictive monetary policy and so on) agreed with the IMF. Almost in parallel, rescue actions for one of Russia's largest banks, the Tokobank, aiming at restructuring its liabilities, did not make significant progress. By the end of the month, the Russian central bank lowered its refinancing rate from 80 to 60 per cent, but the move failed to calm the markets. In an effort to protect foreign exchange reserves, the Russian central bank increased the daily fluctuation margins on the rouble's external value.

In early August, Russia's external debt situation raised doubts about the imminent future as the international rating agency Fitch IBCA lowered its rating on Russia's long-term foreign debt from BB to BB–. On 13 August the central bank moved to increase liquidity in the banking sector as rumours abounded that even some of the country's biggest banks were in severe trouble. More insecurity invaded Russia's economy when the finance minister cancelled his week's bond auction on 14 August and the international financier George Soros called for the immediate devaluation of the rouble, the introduction of a currency board, and a serious infusion of Western aid to stabilize the Russian economy. According to Soros, without a currency board, the rouble would find no anchor. Then there would be the danger that the population would again start to withdraw funds from savings accounts. Neither a World Bank loan for reforms in the energy sector and in the military nor 'good news' on a slowing inflation rate (5.6 per cent on a 12-month perspective) brought relief to public expectations.

The 'bomb' exploded on 17 August, when the authorities announced that (i) the rouble would be allowed to fluctuate within a wider fluctuation band between 6.0 and 9.5 roubles to the US dollar (which was equivalent to a 34 per cent devaluation!), (ii) its overnight lending rate would be raised to 250 per cent, (iii) a 90-day moratorium on the foreign debt servicing by Russian firms (mostly Russian banks that had borrowed extensively from abroad),

(iv) the imposition of capital controls and (v) debt-restructuring measures (a debt-swap programme, among other things). With the announcement of the programme, the rouble fell appreciably. The moratorium was supposed to give banks time to restructure their loan portfolios, but its immediate and main impact was to further weaken investor confidence in Russia. Standard & Poor's downgraded its long-term foreign currency issue rating for Russia from B– to CCC. The moves of the Russian government knocked stock markets across Europe. They started trading about 2 per cent lower but recovered more than half their losses by the close of trading. Michel Camdessus, managing director of the IMF, expressed his hope that the government's economic programme would continue to be implemented in full, allowing the second tranche of the $11.2 billion programme agreed on 20 July to be disbursed. Yet, the principle purpose of that programme was to prevent what then later happened.

Russian officials argued that the package was intended not only to address the budget deficit but also to help the Russian banking sector, which was suffering a severe liquidity squeeze and appeared to be on the verge of collapse. Not only the Tokobank but nearly 25 per cent of Russia's banks were in trouble: from the 1600 banks listed in August 1998, about 400 held many bad assets in their balance sheets. Russia's finance minister publicly predicted that the number of banks in Russia would fall to 30 if the rouble was devalued (further). The 12 largest banks planned to form a lending pool to discuss means of easing the liquidity crisis in the interbank market. By the end of August SBS-Agro Bank, Russia's third largest deposit bank, announced it was closing its doors so that its depositors could not withdraw roubles or US dollar from their accounts. The Russian central bank promised to guarantee those deposits.

After all, it was a political crisis which triggered the collapse of the rouble: on 23 August, President Boris Yeltsin dismissed Prime Minister Sergei Kiriyenko and his five-month-old government and appointed former Prime Minister Viktor Chernomyrdin to his old post. Since then, the rouble has continued losing value. The central bank could not stop the precipitous fall although trading on the foreign exchange market was halted several times. Russia appeared desperate to accelerate the release of the next tranche of the IMF's $11.2 billion support loan – which was due in September – before its hard currency reserves evaporated. On 28 August the central bank ceased to sell foreign currency at any price and then cancelled all trading in US dollars on the Moscow foreign exchange market. Instead, it moved to lower the reserve requirements for commercial banks on 3 September. The freed reserves, however, were used by the commercial banks to buy foreign exchange, thereby contributing to the further fall of the rouble. Trading continued in other currencies and the rouble lost 41 per cent against the

German mark. The depreciation of the rouble quickly fed into consumer prices and raised the inflation rate to more than 20 per cent. After five months in temporary administration, Russia's central bank revoked Tokobank's licence and the European Bank for Reconstruction and Development (EBRD) divested its stake in Tokobank.

After the Duma had voted down for the second time the nomination of Chernomyrdin to the post of prime minister, Yeltsin offered the Duma a compromise – Acting Foreign Minister Jevgeni Primakov. By 8 September the rouble had recovered slightly *vis-à-vis* the US dollar. Meanwhile, restructuring of the banking sector continued and the central bank agreed to let large deposits of assenting depositors at private Russian banks be transferred to the state-owned bank, Sberbank, in order to protect depositors. Foreign currency deposits would be converted into roubles at the official 1 September rate, which was a rather unfavourable rate to the depositors.

The heated climate on financial markets cooled down somewhat after Primakov received overwhelming approval from the Duma on 11 September. Viktor Geraschenko returned to his post as chairman of Russia's central bank. He announced the plan to bail out favoured domestic banks by giving them new credit (de facto this meant a freeing of reserves) worth $1.65 billion. Freeing the reserves would, according to the government, ease the payments system and get financial activity moving again. However, Russian banks could just as well use the roubles to buy US dollars. Furthermore, Geraschenko argued that a currency board was not appropriate to Russian circumstances, a message which – in contrast to some fears – did not weaken the rouble further. Instead, some strengthening of the rouble could be observed. But this was more the consequence of some special circumstances than of an increased confidence in Russia's currency. One was the falling due of rouble–US dollar forward contracts on 15 September, which raised the demand (supply) for (of) roubles (US dollars) on the spot market. Other reasons for the rouble's brief burst of strength may have been the demand for roubles from banks seeking to pay off local debts, huge withdrawals by depositors and a temporary lull in the importers' demands for US dollars.

By the end of September 1998 the crisis was not over but the over-whelming impression was that a 'back to business' attitude had returned to the markets. On 23–24 September, Russian finance ministry officials met with representatives of several foreign banks to discuss the terms of the government's debt-restructuring plans. Also, that week finance ministry officials discussed measures to calm sovereign creditors of the Paris Club, as Russia had already defaulted on $400–600 million in interest payments on its restructured Soviet-era debt.

2.6.2 The Russian Virus Leaps to Brazil

The story, however, does not end here. Moreover, the 'contagious' part is yet to tell: several Latin American countries – Colombia, Mexico, Chile and in particular Brazil – were affected by the Russian Virus by early September 1998. In all of these countries, interest rates shot up to percentages in the neighbourhood of 50, and the stock markets recorded severe losses. On 3–4 September officials from these countries – plus representatives from Peru, Argentina, Venezuela, Ecuador and Uruguay – were invited by the IMF to participate at 'urgent talks' with managing director Michel Camdessus in Washington, DC. Devaluation of the respective currencies – beyond extending existing exchange rate bands (an option used by Colombia and Chile) – was not a very appealing alternative given that the 14 major Latin American countries accounted for no less than $640 billion of external debt (see above). In a common declaration, the countries mentioned promised to continue their policies of an open capital account, and of liberalized trade-based economic growth. Only two days later the so-called 'Rio Group' (the above countries plus Panama, Paraguay and Bolivia) published a resolution demanding the intervention and support of the IMF and action by the G7 countries in order to stabilize international financial markets and to enforce the preconditions for economic growth in the world economy.

As the major economy on the South American continent, Brazil's response to the spreading Russian Virus was regarded as crucial. If Brazil goes, it was said, much of Latin America will go and this could push the already slowing world economy into recession. By 8 September the monetary authorities in Brasilia had already spent $10 billion out of $70 billion to defend the band around a crawling parity of the real *vis-à-vis* the US dollar on the foreign exchange market (see below). According to Brazil's minister of finance, the huge sales on the stock market of São Paulo were nothing but a reflex of the intent of international investors to match the large losses on other financial markets in the world economy. Due to the sharp interest rate increases (on 11 September the central bank took the headline rate to 49.75) – not only in nominal but also in real terms because inflation was running at only 4 per cent – the government's expenditures on debt servicing rose significantly and this cost factor forced the government to announce a reduction of the public deficit. The stock market's reaction was far from enthusiastic. On the contrary: 10 September became a sort of 'black Thursday' for the Brazilian economy as the stock market experienced the second largest ever recorded losses. The Bovespa Index fell by almost 16 per cent. Market specialists said that this event was triggered, among other things, by a negative Standard & Poor's statement on the perspectives of the Brazilian economy, the stumbling quality of Brazilian bonds and the unconvincing measures of the government to put a halt to the loss of confidence by virtue of its monetary, fiscal and exchange rate policy.

The Brazilian exchange rate peg (which had let the real devalue against the US dollar by 7.5 per cent a year, maintaining a narrow band around the central parity within which trade was permitted) had worked well for years after it was put in place as a central piece of the 'real plan' in 1994 by President Fernando Henrique Cardoso. The 'real plan' had played a crucial part in bringing inflation down (hyperinflation of 2000 per cent was wiped out in four years), overcoming in the process one of the world's most deeply entrenched pro-inflation cultures. But now, investors seemed in no mood to compromise. The worst outcome was felt to be if Brazil followed the example of Thailand, South Korea and Russia by defending the currency, and then being forced to devalue anyway. According to Pedro Malan, Brazil's finance minister, there was an irrational herd instinct at work which lumped all emerging markets together. However, it is fair to say that the crisis in Russia focused attention of investors on the very real problems of the Brazilian economy, notably the large public sector (8 per cent of GDP) and current account (4 per cent of GDP) deficits.

On 4 October 1998, President Cardoso was re-elected for a second term. He was under pressure by his own party (Brazilian Social Democracy Party, PSDB) to hold off (with an austerity programme) until after the second round of voting in elections for state governor on 25 October, so as not to damage his allies. But the results of these elections for state governors strengthened the hand of leftwing opponents of the government. Cardoso supporters lost the electoral race in three wealthy and populous southern states: Rio de Janeiro, Minais Gerais (see below) and Rio Grande do Sul. By the end of the month, Cardoso had tailored a three-year fiscal adjustment programme including projections on the reduction of the public deficit. The intention was to raise fresh taxes and to cut spending by 2.6 per cent of the country's output in 1999 in order to save 28 billion reals from the budget. Civil servants would have to pay higher pension contributions and public service pensioners would receive lower benefits.

In November the IMF entered into talks with the fiscal and monetary authorities on a stabilization programme for the Brazilian economy. By the middle of the month the IMF and governments led by the IMF announced that they would stake a large credit to stave off an economic crisis in Brazil. The final agreement on a $41.5 billion package was reached on 2 December. The Bank for International Settlements (BIS) participated with an amount of $14 billion, co-ordinating the support by the central banks of 20 industrialized countries. According to the package, the real was not to be devalued. The IMF released $5.3 billion in early December, with the next instalment due in February 1999. Brazilian interest rates began (but only began!) to come down from their earlier levels of 40 per cent to levels experienced before September 1998 and the turmoil on the foreign exchange market seemed to be over or at least interrupted. Another heavy storm, however, was yet to come.

International financial market actors were sorely troubled when on 6 January 1999 the government of Brazil's third largest state, Minas Gerais (see above), announced the suspension of its external debt payments ($15 billion) for 90 days. Other governors threatened to follow suit. The federal government was keen to assure the international community that Brazil would continue to fulfil all of its debt service obligations. The credibility of that promise, however, was not judged 'too high' by financial markets: the Bovespa Index fell by 5.14 per cent on the next day. Moreover, during the week, confidence in the ability of Brazil's politicians to afford the crisis eroded further. On 12 January the Bovespa Index fell by 7.62 and on the next day by another 5.05 per cent. On top of this, on 13 January the real – which had been in a narrow band of 1.12 and 1.22 reals per US dollar – was effectively devalued by 8.6 per cent when the authorities decided to broaden the band to a 1.32 parity at the upper bound. The central bank said it would contain the devaluation to 8.6 per cent. But many financial market observers were sceptical regarding the April 1999 futures contract for reals to be traded at about 18 per cent below the new central parity.

Central bank governor Gustavo Franco resigned and was replaced by Francisco López – one of Brazil's most prominent advocates of 'heterodox stabilization' policies in the 1980s – on the same day when the real's exchange rate *vis-à-vis* the US dollar was realigned. Brazil's currency devaluation sent the US market into a tailspin. The Dow Jones industrial average lost 354 points in two days. Would the 'Samba effect' leap to the US? The international rating agency Standard & Poor's reacted quickly by downgrading Brazil's bonds denominated in US dollars from a B+ to a B–.

The novelty of the Russian moratorium half a year earlier and of the partial Minais Gerais moratorium was that – some argue for the first time since Mexico's case of 1982 – sovereign default in the international community of autonomous states was no longer the unthinkable. As with Russia, a latent vicious circle of the following kind emerged: high interest rates on new bonds were necessary to compensate for the rising country risk. Those high interest rates induced a higher debt service burden and, at the same time, increasing expectations of devaluation – Kindleberger would say because of 'elastic expectations' (1978, p. 11) – but those exchange rate expectations also negatively affected the credibility of the government's ability to fulfil its future debt obligations. But would the latent vicious circle become effective once the exchange rate either fell outside the band or was floated?

Not necessarily, as the occurrences in the following days demonstrated impressively. On 15 January Brazil's government finally decided to give up the defence of the real's target zone *vis-à-vis* the US dollar and let its currency float. The domestic stock market reacted positively as the Bovespa Index rebounded 40 per cent at its peak, while the yield on Brazilian bonds fell. IMF authorities, together with US treasury officials, were initially dismayed by Brazil's move to floating rates. After all, the whole premise behind the $41.5 billion loan package arranged for Brazil in November 1998 was to provide conspicuously sufficient reserves to intimidate speculators from making a run on the real. After a weekend of meetings in Washington, DC, the IMF's managing director, Michel Camdessus, declared he was 'satisfied' with Brazil's Finance Minister Pedro Malan's 'useful clarification' of Brazil's objectives – despite the 22 per cent decline in the value of the real since 13 January. In the next weeks the real lost even more value on the foreign exchange markets. Yet, Brazil did not follow the path of the Asian crisis.

Contrary to many other examples surveyed above, Brazil had – on the negative side – to fight a high budget deficit of 8–9 per cent of GDP. If things go well, falling interest rates will soon ease the debt burden; if they go badly, it could become unmanageable. At the same time Brazil had and has some important advantages. Even at sky-high interest rates its banks were relatively sound. For six months there had been constant rumours of imminent devaluation, so many banks and companies had hedged their foreign exchange liabilities. Brazil's monetary authorities did not fritter away all of their reserves before floating the real. And, what is important for our main topic, the contagion effects of Brazil's devaluation have been remarkably limited compared with those that followed the meltdown of Mexico's economy in 1995, and the Asian crisis of 1997–98.

2.7 SUMMARY AND CONCLUSIONS

2.7.1 Similar Causes – Similar Action?

The occurrence of spreading financial crises is not a new one. As major events in economic history reveal, signs that turmoil in domestic financial markets could be contagious where already apparent in the mid-19th century. Investment, liquidity, trade and exchange rates were important channels of transmission.

Bypassing the exceptional case of Mexico in 1992, when this Latin American country defaulted on its external debt, we find interesting hints on the causes of modern financial market crises in the Chilean turmoil of the same year. Chile liberalized its trade and its capital account much earlier than other Latin American countries. Given the rather unstable and volatile domestic financial market, large capital inflows not only brought down the crawling exchange rate regime, but also led to a lending boom with deteriorating domestic banks' portfolios. Large devaluations were accompanied by a reversal of capital flows and a destruction of monetary and non-monetary wealth. The latter was triggered by a credit crunch pushing up real interest rates. The Chilean crisis did not spread to other Latin American countries, not so much because those other governments were pursuing 'wiser' economic policies, but more because they were – in comparison – closed economies with no free movement (internal or external) of capital.

Surprisingly, the spectacular attacks on EMS member countries' currencies in 1992 and 1993 showed some similarities with the Chilean case. Unrealistic central parities along with unsuccessful attempts to curb speculation via increasing interest rates and/or intervention on the foreign exchange market forced several governments into realignments/reintroduction of capital controls. Prominent banks – albeit never the whole commercial banking sector – suffered liquidity crisis and asked to be bailed out by the government. In the case of the Nordic countries (Finland, Sweden, Norway), the speculative attacks on their currencies had clear aspects of 'contagion'. Partly, this was attributed to their political, cultural/sociological and economic similarities, but also, it was argued, to the strong ties between these countries.

What conclusions should policymakers in emerging markets draw with respect to monetary and exchange rate policies from the experiences in Mexico, the Czech Republic and Thailand? As far as monetary policy is concerned, the authorities have to extend their policy coverage to monitoring and supervision of the banking system. When the time has come for capital market liberalization in emerging markets then minimum reserve requirements can be reduced if previously the budget deficit has been reduced as well. The liberalization of the banking system must be accompanied by strict banking supervision and one should bear in mind that large capital inflows can quickly become outflows.

A strong lending boom – as well illustrated by the examples analysed – is rarely accompanied by solid asset portfolios in the banking sector. Moreover, attention should be paid to the monetary aggregate M2 as an important early warning indicator of an impending speculative attack. If private agents are assumed to hold domestic currency more or less voluntarily, then the reduction in the real value of the currency will be dramatic following a fall in foreign exchange reserves. Sterilization policy that causes a strong expansion of M2 is highly problematic in fixed or quasi-fixed exchange rate systems since non-sterilization provides the anchor for this type of regime.

How early and how much Mexico or the Czech Republic or Thailand should have devalued their respective exchange rates in a discretionary manner (Dornbusch and Werner have discussed these questions extensively and publicly in 1994 for the case of Mexico) to avoid or reduce the risk of a speculative attack is probably not the core issue of exchange rate policy. The principal question seems to be whether any form of fixed exchange rate system is only optimal for a while and needs to be replaced by a floating exchange rate. As Sachs et al. (1996b, p. 281) argue, pegging regimes might by very sensible at the beginning of a reform programme, for example, to stabilize inflationary expectations and to re-monetize the economy, 'but just as important is to get out of the fixed exchange rate system in time' (ibid., p. 282). On the other hand, it should be borne in mind that the commitment of the Mexican authorities convinced private investors that there was no plan to devalue the currency. But dwindling currency reserves and a fast-growing government debt must have made it clear to the public that if a devaluation was to take place it would have been large (ibid., p. 281). From the experience of Thailand and the other ASEAN countries during the past years, some analysts have concluded that not only the policy of exchange rate pegging but also the choice of anchor currency needs to be re-examined. This line of argument evolves against the background of the longstanding dollar peg in this area of the world economy in contrast to a growing importance of the yen, for example, for trade factoring, in the ASEAN region.

The IMF has contributed to the economic consequences of the spreading financial crises in Asia by the design of its programmes. The initial approach of the IMF to Thailand's crisis was to promote a limited devaluation, counsel raising taxes, cut government expenditures and hope for the best. This strategy was tested in Mexico in 1994 – before the exchange rate collapse – with disastrous results. Thereafter, Thailand, South Korea and Indonesia all devalued; in consequence there was inflation, and massive destruction of their business and financial systems (see below) and social upheaval – which in Indonesia's case led to rioting, destruction of property and bloodshed. Thailand's per capita income fell from $3000 in 1996 to $1800 in 1998.

The Korean approach included a devaluation, a floating exchange rate backed by impossibly high interest rates, rosy IMF economic forecasts, the false hope of export-led growth and a heavy dose of patience. The result: Korea's living standard dropped by 42 per cent from 1996 to 1998. The trouble with the then imposed IMF stabilization plans was that the action needed to cure a banking crisis (controlled liquidity injection to re-monetize the economy, legislation for banking supervision and for equity capital standards in the banking sector and so on) is at least in part diametrically opposed to the action for dealing with a public budget crisis. China, Hong Kong, Taiwan and Singapore have stood by their currencies, reeling in money supply as needed, despite the pain. They have been rewarded with far gentler fallout than those who made themselves into devaluation blast zones.

When the IMF had to face the Russian crisis it was confronted with an economy largely running on barter. By rough estimates, Russian money supply, measured as M2, came to about 12 per cent of GDP in 1998, compared with 25 per cent for Brazil. Against the background of the devastating experiences with falling exchange rates, it was the IMF's conviction from the beginning that Russia (and also Brazil) should defend their respective currencies on the foreign exchange market. Moreover, the largest parts of the IMF tranches were meant to serve as a means of manoeuvre at the foreign exchange markets. The IMF bolstered the central bank reserves to inject more confidence into Russia's financial stability and hoped the debt markets would work the problem out by themselves. In the light of this philosophy, the 17 August measures decided by the Russian government were just the opposite of the programme agreed with the IMF earlier on 20 July.

The 34 per cent effective devaluation of the Russian rouble quickly hit the Brazilian economy: the stock market in São Paulo was nearly 2 per cent lower on the very same day. And the contagion effect from Russia was felt throughout much of the developing world. Argentine par bonds were down 0.75 basis points. Perhaps Brazil might have softened the consequences of the leaping Russian Virus if President Cardoso had already been elected by July or June 1998. Presidential and state elections only served to postpone necessary governmental action. As with Russia, the IMF was initially totally concentrated with a stabilization of the real either by interest rate policy or by foreign exchange market interventions.

It seems that Russia and Brazil had to face the biggest problems in comparison in that they were stuck (apart from external debt which applies to all the reviewed emerging economies) in a triple crisis: an exchange rate, a banking and a public budget crisis. To the best of my knowledge there does not yet exist an economic policy that can meet all these challenges simultaneously. However, from the various experiences with financial crises we have reported on it seems that one clear-cut consequence emerges: given the greater underlying volatility, there is a strong argument that emerging markets need stricter banking sector regulations than their G10 counterparts whatever monetary policy is adopted. As far as the latter is concerned, two serious alternatives are available: either a currency board – which, however, presupposes a number of institutional, legal and behavioural conditions – or inflation targeting in combination with a floating exchange rate.

2.7.2 The Impact of Financial Market Crises on Monetary Wealth[6]

One last point is worth considering. In our exposition, we have so far stressed the role of flows in the balance of payments, in domestic GDP and so on. We have admittedly neglected some important stock aspects such as the impact of financial market crises on wealth, primarily monetary wealth in the affected countries, but also on monetary wealth distribution in the world economy. A wealth perspective is much easier to perceive when we take into account that stocks result from the accumulation of flows.

If the accounting identity approach that regards savings deficits/surpluses as the force determining the direction of medium- to long-run capital flows is correct, then the countries that fall victim to financial market (including an exchange rate crisis) crises would be justified in suspecting that the rescue packages only partially re-patriate capital that had left the country in haste some weeks or months before. The 'only' difference being that the return of the capital is achieved at a much higher cost from the perspective of the recipient country, because its ratings on international financial markets have deteriorated in the meantime and it has to face much larger risk premia now. This, of course, has a negative net wealth effect on the domestic economy as the same stock of new (in comparison to the old) external debt is associated with higher debt service. The latter is a drain on domestic savings and hence prevents a higher domestic wealth accumulation.

When banks and firms which have deposits/shares of private agents on the liabilities' side of their balance sheet go bankrupt, private wealth is destroyed. This is no 'exception to the rule' in a market economy, however. The idea that economic crises serve to trigger a 'cleansing storm' and thereby produce new opportunities of growth in the economy goes back to Schumpeter's view of 'creative and destroying competition' (1934). In this sense, it may be that regional financial market crises have – notwithstanding the severe negative consequences on output and employment – the positive aspect of detecting deficiencies in the institutional framework of domestic financial markets, in the consistency of government's policies (Donges 1999, p. 144), and in the (underdeveloped) perception of risks by more or less well-informed (foreign) investors. It remains an open question, however, how far this argument goes. Can it be extended to economies when financial market turmoil leaps to them from third countries although market participants would have felt that the domestic economy was in good shape in the first place?

If government guarantees with central bank liquidity infusions are used to save domestic banks and firms from bankruptcy, this is no final safe haven: rescue actions must be financed by government bonds/ordinary taxes or by the inflation tax.

A bailout intervention can take different forms, but ultimately has a fiscal nature and directly affects the distribution of income and wealth between financial intermediaries and taxpayers: an implicit system of financial insurance is equivalent to a stock of contingent public liabilities that are not reflected by debt and deficit figures until the crisis occurs. (Corsetti et al. 1998a, p. 3)

In either case, net private wealth of the aggregate economy suffers. We then also have a wealth transfer from shareholders/owners of healthy firms/ depositors in sound financial institutions and from owners of non-monetary wealth to the aforementioned shareholders/depositors in firms/ banks with bad assets.

There is another wealth aspect, related to the new exchange rate after the collapse of the old exchange rate regime. If the collapse was due to a speculative attack, the extent of the subsequent currency's devaluation depends on how price stabilizing the speculation has been. This is essential because the domestic value of the inherited old debt rises according to the percentage devaluation of the domestic currency. As stated above, in the case of private debtors, equity capital will be reduced, and in the case of government debt, the budget deficit will increase. What are the determinants for profitable speculation to be price stabilizing, thereby reducing the volatility of the exchange rate? As Aschinger (1995, pp. 23–31) puts it, complete stabilization – that is, when the floating rate after the exchange rate collapse equals by and large the managed exchange rate before the attack – emerges when speculation renders no profit at all, or even losses. The likelihood for such an outcome increases, the more speculators gamble with money they have to pay back to domestic financial institutions (the latter, in turn, is inversely related to the interest rate charged by domestic banks and to the transaction costs involved), and the more they misjudge the (unknown) development of future foreign exchange demand and supply of non-speculators. The risk of suffering losses is the higher, the more speculators overestimate the future demand on the foreign exchange market (ibid., p. 30).

Summing up, we can say that the wealth effects of (contagious) financial crises are a serious item which should be taken into consideration. It is hardly conceivable that in market economies there would exist 'social agreements' or 'transcendental belief systems' capable of revaluing stocks independently from the devaluation of flows. If so, then some sort of wealth illusion would be in place. Moreover, during economic development, portfolio/expected cash flow considerations tend to become familiar to all economic agents, a fact which should not be surprising given that economic rationality is indivisible.

In Chapter 6, we shall address the questions of the (re)distribution of wealth in the world economy caused by (contagious) financial market crises and how a participation of banks/investment funds/private investors from the industrialized countries can be organized. The ongoing discussion seems to favour the view that against the background of the sometimes tremendous monetary wealth losses occurring in emerging economies, much responsibility rests on those institutions/agents as well.

NOTES

1. In reality, a spot market speculation can be broken down into two separate transactions: a combination of a speculation on the forward market with an interest rate arbitrage deal.
2. As the report of the economic advisers to the German government states, the French authorities lost literally all of their foreign exchange reserves in an attempt to avoid any devaluation of the franc (SVR 1993, p. 138).
3. In a target zone regime, interest rate differentials can be divided into expectations of realignment and expectations of depreciations within the band (Dahlquist and Gray 2000, p. 410).
4. The seigniorage aspect of minimum reserve requirements will be analysed below.
5. However, as will be discussed below, the Hong Kong Stock Exchange suffered a severe setback on 23 October 1997 when the Hang Seng Index plunged by more than 10 per cent (Aschinger 1998, p. 12).
6. I owe the inclusion of the following aspects to the thoughtful comments of one of the anonymous referees.

3. Explaining the Onset of Financial Market Crises in Emerging Markets

3.1 INTRODUCTION

In two recent papers, Radelet and Sachs (1998a, 1998b) have provided an excellent overview on the causes and consequences of the Asian financial crisis. Also, they have made the most admirable attempt to put some order into the many different theoretical approaches which aim to explain the onset and the course of speculative attacks on currencies combined with banking crises in emerging markets. In essence, they find the following five main strands of analysis (1998b, pp. 3–4; Alba et al. 1998, p. 9):

1. *Macroeconomic policy induced*: Basically, financial crises are here the result of the pursuit of a set of inconsistent macroeconomic policies. This includes the case of a Krugman-type (1979) ('first generation') balance of payments crisis, where the exchange rate collapses as domestic credit expansion by the central bank is inconsistent with the exchange rate target, as well as the type ('second generation') of self-fulfilling crises of Obstfeld (1986, 1996). This explanation presumably also includes the presence of some structural weaknesses (for example, declines in competitiveness as a result of poor labour upgrading, weak financial systems) which make macro policies more likely to be inconsistent to begin with. Calvo (1998b) has made the remarkable effort of putting 'under one roof' these two generations of balance of payments crisis models. Recent contributions (Morris and Shin 1998a, 1998b) come up with a game-theoretic analysis of what speculators think other speculators will do and can also explain self-fulfilling currency attacks. Here, even very small differences in information lead to great uncertainties about the beliefs of others. If such disparities cannot be removed, they form a constant backdrop to market participants (Morris and Shin 1998a, 1998b). Also, the role of prospective, rather than actual government deficits (as in Krugman's seminal paper), associated with implicit bailout clauses to failing banking systems has deserved recent

attention for the explanation of collapsing exchange rate regimes (Burnside et al. 1998).

2. *Financial panic*: The country in question is subject to the equivalent of a run on a bank (Diamond and Dybvig 1983) where creditors, particularly those with short-term claims, suddenly withdraw from the country, leaving it with an acute shortage of foreign exchange liquidity. The withdrawal may be rational for each creditor as there is a lack of co-ordination among creditors and each individual's incentive is to withdraw first, as he/she fears that others will withdraw before him/her. One should add here the contributions of Sachs et al. (1996a, 1996b) which formulate a decision algorithm for the foreign investors involved: to hold or to withdraw their assets from the economy at stake.

3. *Collapse of a bubble*: The collapse of a stochastic speculative bubble as in Blanchard (1979) or in Blanchard and Watson (1982) and others which was itself a rational equilibrium, but nevertheless was *ex post* irrational and had a positive probability of collapse all along. The bubble burst approach is quite appealing for the case of Asia as it could be observed a price bubble there in the sectors of real estate/housing and construction on the eve of the financial crisis. Consequently, Edison et al. (1998) argue with a bubble burst when there are highly leveraged, credit-constrained firms which have to face a fall in asset prices which reduces the value of their collateral, induces them to sell assets and, so, causes prices to fall further.

4. *Moral hazard crisis*: Here we detect excessive, overly risky investment by banks and other financial institutions which were able to borrow as they had implicit or explicit guarantees from the government on their liabilities and were undercapitalized and/or weakly regulated (Akerlof and Romer 1993). Foreign as well as domestic creditors went along with this risky behaviour, as they knew the government or international financial institutions would bail them out. Krugman (1998a), applies this model to the East Asian crisis. Moral hazard (implied by implicit guarantees on bank deposits) is also at the heart of the 'overborrowing syndrome' hypothesis of McKinnon and Pill (1997) where 'falsely optimistic signals' sent by domestic banks resemble our own approach (see below). The overborrowing syndrome describes the 'sudden transition from [a] repressed to [a] liberalized state, and the resulting surge of optimism or euphoria' (McKinnon and Pill 1998, p. 326), a term which in our approach is called 'exaggerated optimism'.

5. *Disorderly workout*: This refers to the equivalent of a grab for assets in the absence of a domestic bankruptcy system in the case of a liquidity problem of a corporate (Sachs 1994a, 1994b; Miller and Zhang 1997). Since there is no means of reorganizing claims in the case of an

international liquidity problem a disorderly workout would result, which in turn will destroy value and create a debt overhang (Alba et al. 1998, p. 9).

In this chapter, we shall draw on a number of aspects discussed in the approaches surveyed above; on the one hand, we shall combine these aspects in an eclectic manner and, on the other hand, we shall add important insights from the theory of credit rationing which goes back to Stiglitz and Weiss (1981): it seems that major assumptions of their model, asymmetric information of market participants figuring prominently, are extremely well suited to the issue of financial crises in emerging markets. Also, any sensitive approach in this field should be able to cope with the issue of imperfect credit markets in emerging markets (see also Aghion et al. 1999) and of credit rationing relaxation as a precondition for the 'lending booms' (or overlending by banks) observed. Combining insights from Stiglitz and Weiss (1981) with the theory of limited liability as put forward, among others, by Sinn (1980, 1982, 1997) can help to explain why some sort of exaggerated optimism switches into financial panic, a phenomenon whereby (see Sachs et al. 1996a, 1996b) foreign investors are inclined to withdraw their assets in the domestic economy in a 'run on banks', but where also multiple equilibria exist. In our terms, financial panic arises when exaggerated financial optimism turns into its opposite. The reasons for exaggerated optimism are to be found in huge capital inflows (overshooting effects) pushed by low interest rates elsewhere which go along with generous state guarantees for private foreign debt which, in turn, lead to a relaxation of credit rationing. The behaviour of foreign investors is fully rational before, during and after the crisis and corresponds to optimal portfolio decisions (see, for a similar reasoning in a different model, Bacchetta and van Wincoop 1998). The role of state guarantees in our model is in the same vein as in Krugman's moral hazard of financial intermediaries approach (1998a).

3.2 THE BASIC MODEL (FOLLOWING SACHS, TORNELL AND VELASCO)

In the following, we analyse a government that pegs the nominal value of its currency to a foreign anchor currency. The nominal exchange rate is E_0 and the real exchange rate is E_0/P. Here P represents the ratio of the domestic to the foreign price level. For the short term, this ratio is assumed to be equal to one and constant. The nominal peg is maintained by the government as long as foreign exchange reserves, FER, are sufficient to finance capital outflows, CO. Hence as long as the condition

$$CO \leq FER \tag{3.1}$$

is fulfilled there is no devaluation or floating of the exchange rate. If

$$CO > FER \tag{3.2}$$

there is always a devaluation. In this case the government establishes a new (nominal) peg rate E^T to achieve a target real exchange rate. Consequently, the exchange rate of the following period is

$$E_1 = E_0 \text{ for } CO \leq FER \tag{3.3}$$

$$E_1 = E^T \text{ for } CO > FER. \tag{3.4}$$

The extent of devaluation is measured by D so that

$$D = \frac{E_1}{E_2} - 1 \tag{3.5}$$

$$D = \begin{cases} 0 & \text{if} \quad CO \leq FER \\ \dfrac{E^T - E_0}{E_0} & \text{if} \quad CO > FER. \end{cases} \tag{3.6}$$

Note that D stands both for realized as well as for expected devaluation. Implicitly, the authors assume rational expectations. The target exchange rate E^T reflects a large number of structural variables, for example. the terms of trade, the extent of current and capital account liberalization, expectations about long-term capital flows and so on. In addition, the target exchange rate must take into account the 'health' of the banking system. If the banking system is in 'good health' then the government chooses the target exchange rate of

$$E^T = e \tag{3.7}$$

where e represents the long-term real exchange rate. If there is a crisis in the banking sector (see below), then the government will choose an exchange rate that is higher, that is, more depreciated, than e. This is because the government will try to avoid high interest rates that are necessary to defend a lower exchange rate but increase the chances of bankruptcies in the financial system. The vulnerability should be assessed on the basis of whether there is a *lending boom* (*LB*) with banks being committed to a large amount of short-term foreign capital on their liabilities side and having a high proportion of their portfolios locked in a bubbling sector with the risk of a bubble bursting on their credit side. The banks will then most likely suffer from non-performing loans immediately after the period analysed. For the target exchange rate we have:

$$E^T = e\, f(LB) \tag{3.8}$$

with $f'\,(LB) > 0$ and $f(0) = 1$.

The options for devaluation are

$$D = \begin{cases} 0 & \text{if} \quad CO \le FER \\ \dfrac{e}{E_0}\, f(LB) - 1 & \text{if} \quad CO > FER. \end{cases} \tag{3.9}$$

This implies the following. The devaluation is larger the larger the extent of overvaluation of the exchange rate in relation to its long-term equilibrium value, so that e/E_0 is high; or there has been a preceding boom in bank lending, so that $f(LB)$ is large (Sachs et al. 1996a, p. 157). Next we look at the N small investors who each hold assets amounting to k in the domestic banking system. If in a speculative attack all investors withdraw their assets, then there will be a capital outflow of magnitude

$$CO = Nk \;. \tag{3.10}$$

As long as the expected devaluation is smaller than/equal to $\phi\,(= r - r^*)$, hence as long as the advantage in terms of return of holding domestic assets exists, investors will not withdraw their assets. Thus

$$k_j = \begin{cases} 0 & \text{if} \quad D \le \phi \\ k & \text{if} \quad D > \phi. \end{cases} \tag{3.11}$$

Because of symmetry we also have

$$CO = \begin{cases} 0 & \text{if} \quad D \le \phi \\ Nk & \text{if} \quad D > \phi. \end{cases} \tag{3.12}$$

For scenario 1 we assume that fundamentals are pointing in the right direction

$$\frac{e}{E_0} f(LB) - 1 \le \phi. \tag{3.13}$$

Under theses circumstances every possible devaluation is smaller than the threshold that needs to be exceeded for capital flight to set in. Condition (3.13) can be fulfilled for an exchange rate that is only mildly overvalued and a moderate lending boom if ϕ is very small. Even if a devaluation does take place, CO remains equal to zero. But if this is true, then by equation (3.9) no devaluation will take place.

For scenario 2 it is assumed that the fundamental variables suffer from a crisis situation, so that

$$\frac{e}{E_0} f(LB) - 1 > \phi. \tag{3.14}$$

In this case the threshold for capital flight is passed and for a devaluation CO equals Nk. But would a devaluation actually take place? As long as $CO = Nk < FER$ it would not take place since the authorities would be able to defend the peg even with large capital outflows. However, if $CO = Nk > FER$ then a devaluation is possible but not inevitable. As long as every investor expects exchange rate stability, that is, $D = 0$, the value of k will be zero and

Figure 3.1 Currency crises scenarios in the Sachs, Tornell and Velasco model

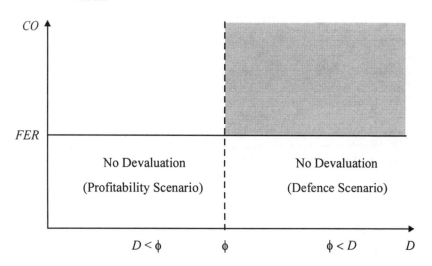

Source: Own compilation.

no devaluation is realized. If every investor expect a devaluation then in addition to $CO = Nk > FER$ the condition $D > \phi$ holds. Summarizing we can say that a balance of payments crisis and a consequent devaluation $(D > \phi)$ are only possible for $(e/E_0) f(LB) - 1 > \phi$ and at the same time $Nk > FER$.

The model predicts that a country with 'bad fundamentals' and a low level of international reserves is a prime target for speculative attacks. As depicted in Figure 3.1, three of the four identified regions are not candidates for an exchange rate collapse: either (southwest and northwest region) because the profitability of domestic assets exceeds any expected domestic currency devaluation, or because (southeast region) despite a profitability disadvantage, the monetary authorities are able to defend the prevailing exchange rate as their 'room to manoeuvre', that is, their foreign exchange reserves exceed the maximal potential capital outflow.

3.3   INTRODUCING CREDIT RATIONING AND LIMITED LIABILITY INTO THE SACHS, TORNELL AND VELASCO MODEL OF 1996

In his seminal paper of 1998, Paul Krugman has played with the idea of explaining financial crises along the lines of financial intermediaries subject to moral hazard problems; such effects are likely, if the liabilities of such institutions had, or at least were perceived as having, an implicit government guarantee *vis-à-vis* their liabilities (Krugman 1998a, p. 3).

> The core implication of moral hazard is that an adverse shock to profitability does not induce financial intermediaries to be more cautious in lending, and to follow financial strategies reducing the overall riskiness of their portfolios. Quite the opposite, in the face of negative circumstances the anticipation of a future bailout provides a strong incentive to take on even more risk – that is, as Krugman (1998[a]) writes to play a game of heads I win, tails the taxpayer loses. (Corsetti et al. 1998b, p. 23)

In our approach, we formulate the modelling of government guarantees with the help of the theory of limited liability, as presented by H.-W. Sinn (1982, 1997). This theory will be merged with the 'financial panic' model of Sachs et al. (1996a) presented above, which, for this purpose, will be enlarged and deepened. In the first place, however, we shall show that the credit rationing literature is capable of filling some of the 'black boxes' in all of the aforementioned papers with economic rationality.

A major weakness of the simple but ingenious approach chosen by Sachs et al. (1996a) lies in the following two facts. First, the variable 'LB' which appears on the left-hand side of equations (3.13) and (3.14) is not explained at all. It should be, and, when doing so, it should be explained along the lines of our earlier reasoning: a *lending boom* in this context means that the banking sector has exposed itself to the private sector of the domestic economy to a degree that its mere survival may be at stake: 'By mid-1998 large parts of the financial and corporate sectors in the most affected East Asian countries were insolvent or suffering severe financial distress' (World Bank 1998, p. 62). It is not sufficient to say that – before the crisis – the outstanding credits of the domestic banking sector *vis-à-vis* the private sector (likewise in relation to GDP) are high or are even growing at a high speed. Given the general presumption that banks are extending loans based on qualified information on borrowers, based on significant collateral and so on, a lending boom must be associated with something we may call *exaggerated optimism* (*EO*): 'at other times, excessive appetite for emerging markets' assets leads to an underestimation of risks' (Alba et al. 1998, p. 36). Excessive appetite or, in our own words, excessive optimism will go along with a relaxation of credit rationing on the domestic financial market. Therefore, in the following, we shall first review the main insights of the credit rationing literature.

The seminal paper of Stiglitz and Weiss (1981) shows, as is well known, that credit rationing, that is, a non-satisfaction of credit demand at the equilibrium interest rate $\tilde{r}$, arises because of the *adverse selection* and because of the *incentive effect* (see Stiglitz and Weiss 1981, pp. 395–401):

> The demand for loans is a decreasing function of the interest rate charged borrowers; this relation L^D is drawn in the upper right quadrant. The nonmonotonic relation between the interest charged borrowers, and the expected return to the bank per dollar loaned $\bar{\rho}$ is drawn in the lower right quadrant. In the lower left quadrant we depict the relation between $\bar{\rho}$ and the supply of loanable funds L^S. ... If banks are free to compete for depositors, then $\bar{\rho}$ will be the interest rate received by depositors. In the upper right quadrant, we plot L^S as a function of [r], through the impact of r on the return of each loan, and hence on the interest rate $\bar{\rho}$ banks can offer to attract loanable funds. (ibid., pp. 397–98)

A credit rationing equilibrium exists given the relations drawn in Figure 3.2; the demand for loanable funds at $\tilde{r}$ exceeds the supply of loanable funds at $\tilde{r}$ and any individual bank increasing its interest rate beyond $\tilde{r}$ would lower its return per dollar loaned (ibid., p. 398).

What is the impact of a relaxation (strengthening) of credit rationing on the (domestic) interest rate? According to the Stiglitz and Weiss model, the gap between the equilibrium interest rate $\tilde{r}$ and the market-clearing interest rate r_m may, but must not narrow. A relaxation of credit rationing will, however, in any case, lead to a higher equilibrium (most likely still not market clearing) interest rate! See for this result Figure 3.3, which corresponds to the fourth quadrant of Figure 3.2. From the banks' point of view, the new equilibrium interest rate $\tilde{r}'$ will be higher than the former, $\tilde{r}$ because the non-monotonic relation between the interest charged borrowers, and the expected return to the bank per dollar loaned $\bar{\rho}$ will be shifted upwards and to the right in the presence of 'exaggerated optimism' (*EO*) and this will occur for two, possibly alternative reasons:

1. one implication of 'exaggerated optimism' may be that all projects that are candidates for a bank's credit are weighted with a higher probability of success;
2. an alternative consequence could be that all projects are – at given probabilities of success or failure – assigned higher payoffs.

Notice also, that this has an important implication for equations (3.13) and (3.14): a relaxation of credit rationing is associated on the one hand with a higher credit supply ('lending boom'). On the other hand, an increased credit supply in the Stiglitz and Weiss model of credit rationing leads to a higher equilibrium interest rate. Hence, opposite to the results of the Sachs et al. model, the domestic interest rate and a lending boom are not independent from each other!

Figure 3.2   The basic model of credit rationing following Stiglitz and Weiss

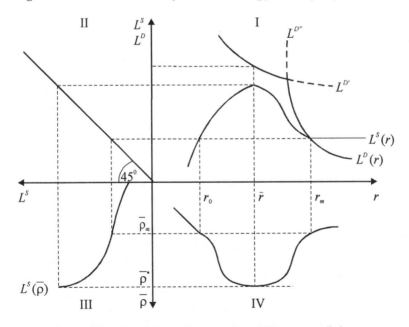

Sources: Sell (1993b, p. 78); Stiglitz and Weiss (1981, p. 397); own compilation.

Figure 3.3   Exaggerated optimism (EO) in the credit rationing model

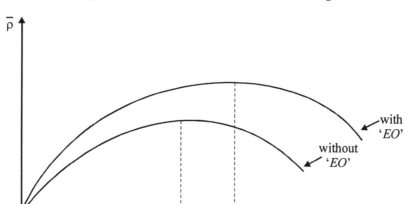

Sources: Stiglitz and Weiss (1981, p. 394); own compilation.

But here the next problem arises: what can motivate banks to relax the size of credit rationing? As the authors explain at a later stage of their paper, 'increasing collateral requirements will, under plausible conditions, lower the bank's return' (ibid., p. 403). In the same vein, we can argue that a limited liability of the banks' deposits encourages the banks to invest in more risky investment projects, *ceteris paribus*. This point will be elaborated in the following, carefully drawing on previous work by Sinn (1980, 1982, 1997) and basing our arguments on Figure 3.4: let us denominate the value of commercial banks' foreign(er) deposits as A and the sum of equity capital (EC), foreign and domestic (residents') deposits (that is, total capital) as K; for the sake of simplicity, we aggregate net equity capital and domestic deposits to gross equity capital. In the first period, total capital amounts to K_0 and the value of capital at the end of the new period 1 will be called K_1. Of course, K_1 is a random variable as long as period 1 has not expired.

In the first place, let us annualize an investment strategy of the representative bank in an emerging market country without any sort of limited liability/government guarantee for foreign deposits. Assume that the investment strategy is associated in period 1 with an expected total capital value of A, that is, an expected loss of the total of equity capital. As far as probabilities are concerned, we assume a symmetric distribution where the outcomes $\overline{K}$ and $\underline{K}$ both have a likelihood of ½. The expected utility stemming from a distribution of $\overline{K}$ and $\underline{K}$ can be drawn from the tendon which links the points A and B on the concave utility function of the investing agents. A safe capital of size $\underline{S}$ is – from the investors' point of view – equivalent to the uncertain outcome between $\overline{K}$ and $\underline{K}$ as the expected value of such a distribution is equal to $\underline{S}$. However, as $\underline{S}$ is well below A, capital owners and investors would never support such an investment strategy (Sinn 1997, pp. 143–44).

Figure 3.4   The role of limited liability for risky investment decisions

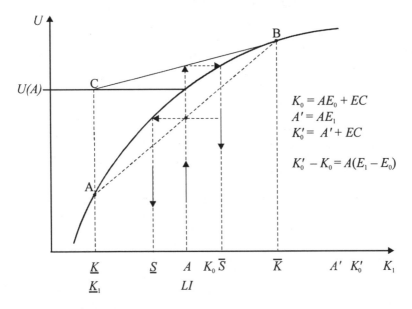

Sources: Sinn (1997, p. 144); own compilation.

In the second case, we introduce the possibility of a limited liability for the representative domestic bank which is organized by the government by giving an unconditional guarantee for all deposits to foreign creditors. Now, total capital K_1 can never fall below A, even if the investment project 'produces' a capital value in period 1 of $\underline{K}$. Note, this implies that to the left of A, the utility curve becomes horizontal, because the investor's utility cannot fall below the guaranteed minimum $U(A)$! Thereby, the overall concavity of the utility function is destroyed and we get a partially convex utility curve which signals risk-love. Hence, it is 'readily apparent that in evaluating a gross probability distribution, part of which covers the region to the left of [A], a decision maker might well behave as a risk-lover although, with respect to the corresponding net distribution, he is in fact a risk-averter' (Sinn 1982, p. 152). With this insight at hand, we have a key to explain the behaviour of domestic banks during a lending boom in emerging markets.

Assume that the expected value for the (invariant) investment strategy is still A; at the new kinked utility curve, the corresponding safe equivalent to A is now $\overline{S}$ instead of $\underline{S}$ which is higher than A! Obviously, investment now becomes a viable strategy as long as the initial capital value K_0 is below $\overline{S}$ and $\overline{S}$ is beyond $\underline{S}$ (see Sinn 1997, p. 144). And, given the probability distribution chosen – which may well differ from the one presented in our example – investors would not risk undertaking the investment unless the government enabled limited liability.

As a first result we may summarize that given the amount of foreign deposits, the willingness to undertake or better to finance risky projects rises with the importance of government guarantees as they are provided by deposit insurance schemes. Reality resembles our modelling, as the following statement tends to demonstrate:

> Typically, a government bailout consists in guaranteeing all bank deposits, including interbank cross-border liabilities – as was the case in Korea, Thailand and Indonesia. This implies that the government is assuming responsibility for the gap created by the bad loans on the asset side of the banks' balance sheet. In the case of an explicit bank re-capitalization, the government takes over the bad loans of the banking system in exchange for safe government bonds (loans for bond swap). The fiscal cost is the interest payment on these bonds. (Corsetti et al. 1998b, p. 14)

At the same time, it holds that at a given size of government guarantees, the readiness for risky financing correlates positively with the amount of foreign(ers') deposits. Assume – as in Figure 3.5 – that the initial endowment with foreign deposits is A^1 which is lower than A, further away from K_0 and corresponds to a safe equivalent of $\overline{S}^1$. In this initial situation the risky investment would not have been chosen. However, if foreign deposits reach the new level A with the corresponding safe equivalent $\overline{S}$, we are back at the scenario from above!

Finally, it can easily be shown in Figure 3.6 that a systematic undervaluation of risks – or an overestimation of chances along the lines of Paul Krugman's 'Panglossian values' – leads in an analogy to the above to similar risky investment strategies as with existing deposit insurance schemes. In Figure 3.6, we find that if the estimated distribution of possible capital value outcomes is no longer $\overline{K}$ and $\underline{K}$, but instead $\overline{K}$ and $\underline{K}$, then an investment strategy A^2 with the corresponding safe equivalent $\overline{S}$ seems to be viable. Investment would not be undertaken if the 'true' capital value bounds $\overline{K}$ and $\underline{K}$ were chosen.

In the following, we aim to explain the behaviour of foreign depositors immediately before and the 'credit crunch' after the exchange rate regime collapse during a financial market crisis along the lines of our basic model in

Figure 3.5   The relevance of foreign deposits for risky investment decisions

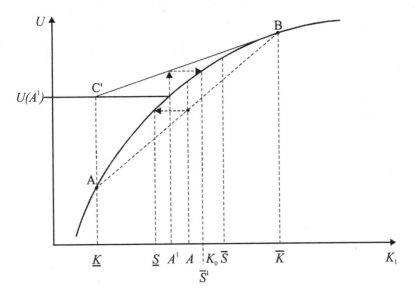

Source: Own compilation.

Figure 3.6   The analogy between risk underestimation and limited liability

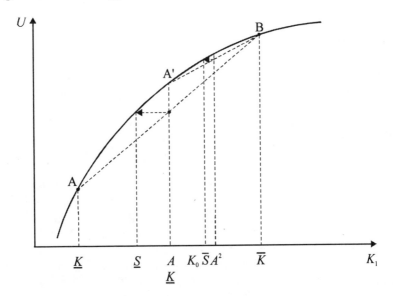

Source: Own compilation.

Figure 3.4. If we want to explain the motivation of foreign depositors and of domestic investing banks immediately before the crisis occurs, let us begin with the case where all foreign depositors anticipate a sharp devaluation of, say, 100 per cent of the domestic currency (with E_0 as the old and E_1 as the new exchange rate) and consider the threat to remain 'locked in' after the exchange rate shock has affected the country. At the new exchange rate, total capital value amounts to K_0' and the equivalent of foreign deposits correspondingly to A'. As we can easily detect (as $\overline{K}$ always falls short of both K_0' and A'), no investment could ever be so successful that it could avoid losses in excess of total initial capital value, that is, bankruptcy. As a result, a vast majority of foreign depositors will (at least intend to) withdraw their capital on the eve of the exchange rate crisis.

The observed 'credit crunch' after the collapse of the pegged exchange rate regime should be explained analogously, that is, taking the turnaround in the credit market as a strengthening of credit rationing. After investment has taken place and period 1 is over, K_1 is no longer a random variable. If the representative bank financed a 'bad project', it will find itself confronted with a sure total capital value of $\underline{K}_1$ at the end of period 1. If foreign investors, meanwhile, have withdrawn the total of their deposits (A), these funds may perhaps have been replaced by a central bank 'infusion' of the same size (LI). The gap between K_0 and $\underline{K}_1$ determines the size of gross bank losses. Either these are covered by fresh central bank funds or the bank has to close down (as happened with a large number of finance companies in Thailand during 1997).

Most likely, the surviving institutions will react in the following way: they will correct their payoff expectations downwards with regard to future investment projects ($\underline{K}$ and $\overline{K}$ move leftwards along the $\underline{K}_1$ axis). Their utility curve will behave strictly according to a risk-averse attitude (the horizontal part disappears), given that the government can no longer give guarantees on foreign deposits (the country as a whole will be rationed on the international capital market). As a consequence, new projects will either not be financed – depending on the size of the new value of total capital – or, if they are, they will have a much lower expected return and, hence, the equilibrium interest rate, $\tilde{r}$ (see above), declines.

A second shortcoming in the original model of Sachs et al. lies in the heroic assumption to take ϕ on the right-hand side of (3.14) as given; if, as most papers argue, the currency crisis goes hand in hand with a domestic financial crisis, the domestic interest rate is a *systemic* variable of the model. The explanation of the domestic interest development can – in principle – follow (at least) two different lines of reasoning (see the introduction of this paper for a typology of approaches). First, one could (again) argue with the Stiglitz and Weiss model of 1981 in which adverse selection and incentive effects explain why loan rates rise with the riskiness of the projects and the hazardous behaviour of investors. In this context, a rising share of most likely bad loans is accompanied by higher interest rates, which in turn raises ϕ, *ceteris paribus*! A second possibility lies in the explanation of a stock price index bubble in the same vein as Blanchard (1979); here, there is also a strong link between domestic interest rates and the stock prices index development. Depending on the approach chosen (either way), the domestic interest rate will be affected, and so will ϕ. We prefer to proceed with the approach chosen here, which is based on credit rationing and limited liability theory.

3.4 A REFORMULATION OF THE SACHS, TORNELL AND VELASCO MODEL

Now, we have to rethink the content of equations (3.13) and (3.14) and of Figure 3.1 (the basics of the Sachs et al. model) against the background of our achieved results. In order to motivate exaggerated optimism (*EO*) in the domestic banking sector, limited liability and the incentives associated (see above) have to be accompanied by huge capital inflows (*CI*) from abroad: 'at the core of the Asian crisis were large-scale foreign capital inflows into financial systems that became vulnerable to panic' (Radelet and Sachs 1998b, p. 2). Moreover, there is a link between financial market (including the capital account) liberalization, capital inflows from abroad and moral hazard: 'in the presence of distortions related to moral hazard, a process of financial liberalization is a key factor magnifying the adverse implication of moral hazard on macroeconomic stability' (Corsetti et al. 1998b, p. 16). As long as the fixed exchange rate is considered credible, only the difference in interest rates determines the behaviour of foreign capital investors:

$$CI = \alpha_0(r - r^*). \qquad (3.15)$$

EO is most likely proportional to the size of external capital inflows,[1] but also positively dependent on the share of guaranteed private debt in total private debt, G:

$$EO = \alpha_1 CI + \alpha_2 G = \alpha_0 \alpha_1 (r - r^*) + \alpha_2 G \qquad (3.16)$$

with

$$\alpha_1 = \frac{\partial EO}{\partial CI} > 0 \ \text{ and } \ \alpha_2 = \frac{\partial EO}{\partial G} > 0. \qquad (3.17)$$

'With financial and industrial policy enmeshed within a widespread business sector network of personal and political favoritism, and with governments that appeared willing to intervene in favor of troubled firms, markets operated under the impression that the return on investment was somewhat "insured" against adverse shocks' (Corsetti et al. 1998b, p. 21).

The relaxation of credit rationing (*CRR*), on the other hand, is positively dependent on the degree of exaggerated optimism:

$$CRR = \alpha_3 \left[\alpha_0 \alpha_1 (r - r^*) + \alpha_2 G \right]; \quad \alpha_3 = \frac{dCRR}{dEO} > 0. \tag{3.18}$$

The lending boom (*LB*) itself is taken to be positively related to the credit rationing relaxation:

$$LB = \alpha_3 \alpha_4 \left[\alpha_0 \alpha_1 (r - r^*) + \alpha_2 G \right]; \quad \alpha_4 = \frac{dLB}{dCRR} > 0. \tag{3.19}$$

Finally, the domestic interest rate, as we demonstrated above, is a positive function of the lending boom:[2]

$$r = \alpha_3 \alpha_4 \alpha_5 \left[\alpha_0 \alpha_1 (r - r^*) + \alpha_2 G \right] = \alpha_6 (r - r^*) + \alpha_7 G; \quad \alpha_5 = \frac{dr}{dLB} > 0 \tag{3.20}$$

and with

$$\alpha_5 = \frac{dr}{dLB} > 0$$

$$\alpha_6 = \alpha_0 \alpha_1 \alpha_3 \alpha_4 \alpha_5 = \frac{dr}{d(r - r^*)} > 0 \tag{3.21}$$

$$\alpha_7 = \alpha_2 \alpha_3 \alpha_4 \alpha_5 = \frac{dr}{dG} > 0.$$

Solving for *r* gives:

$$r = \frac{\alpha_7}{1 - \alpha_6} G - \frac{\alpha_6}{1 - \alpha_6} r^*. \tag{3.22}$$

This gives us a reduced form for the lending boom:

$$LB = \frac{\alpha_6}{\alpha_5}(r - r^*) + \frac{\alpha_7}{\alpha_5}G = \frac{\alpha_6}{\alpha_5}\left(\frac{\alpha_7}{1-\alpha_6}G - \frac{1}{1-\alpha_6}r^*\right) + \frac{\alpha_7}{\alpha_5}G. \quad (3.23)$$

Collecting terms, we achieve:

$$LB = \frac{\alpha_7}{\alpha_5(1-\alpha_6)}G - \frac{\alpha_6}{\alpha_5(1-\alpha_6)}r^*. \quad (3.24)$$

Making use of (3.24), the expression for D now becomes:

$$D = \begin{cases} 0 & \text{if} \quad CO \leq FER \\ \dfrac{e}{E_0}f\left[\dfrac{\alpha_7}{\alpha_5(1-\alpha_6)}G - \dfrac{\alpha_6}{\alpha_5(1-\alpha_6)}r^*\right] - 1 & \text{if} \quad CO > FER \end{cases} \quad (3.25)$$

with

$$\phi = r - r^* = \frac{\alpha_7}{1-\alpha_6}G - \frac{\alpha_6}{1-\alpha_6}r^* - r^* = \frac{\alpha_7}{1-\alpha_6}G - \frac{1}{1-\alpha_6}r^*. \quad (3.26)$$

Let us reconsider scenarios 1 and 2 from above, where from a profitability point of view, foreign investors should not get rid off, but should 'hold'[3] domestic assets in the case of (3.27),

$$\frac{e}{E_0}f(G,r^*) - 1 \leq \phi(G,r^*) \quad (3.27)$$

but should 'escape' from the country or likewise 'sell'[4] their assets whenever:

$$\frac{e}{E_0}f(G,r^*) - 1 > \phi(G,r^*). \quad (3.28)$$

The question now arises, whether a rise (drop) in the foreign interest rate decreases (increases) the right (left)-hand side of (3.27) more than the left (right)-hand side; for the right-hand side we find that

$$\phi_{r^*} = \frac{\partial \phi(G,r^*)}{\partial r^*} = -\frac{1}{1-\alpha_6} < 0 \quad (3.29)$$

while

$$f_{r^*} = \frac{\partial f(G,r^*)}{\partial r^*} = \left(-\frac{1}{1-\alpha_6}\right)\frac{\alpha_6}{\alpha_5} < 0; \quad \frac{\alpha_6}{\alpha_5} = \alpha_0\alpha_1\alpha_3\alpha_4. \qquad (3.30)$$

In both cases, we assume α_6 to be less than one; this is plausible though not necessary. If, on the other hand, $\alpha_6 < 1$, and $\alpha_6/\alpha_5 > 1$, then it must hold that $\alpha_5 < \alpha_6 < 1$! When comparing (3.29) and (3.30), everything depends on the size of the coefficient α_6/α_5; if it is greater (smaller) than one, a drop in the foreign interest rate may turn (3.27) ((3.28)) into (3.28) ((3.27)), that is, make it rational to pull the money out of (leave one's assets in) the country. Remember that α_5 is some sort of elasticity of the domestic interest rate with regard to the lending boom and α_6 is a compound of various coefficients. The decision to be taken by foreign investors also depends on the coefficients 'embodied' in (3.31) and (3.32); how much does an exogenous increase in the share of guaranteed private debt in total private debt, that is, a higher degree of limited liability, affect the left- and the right-hand side of (3.27) or (3.28)?

$$\phi_G = \frac{\partial\phi(G,r^*)}{\partial G} = \frac{\alpha_7}{1-\alpha_6} > 0 \qquad (3.31)$$

$$f_G = \frac{\partial f(G,r^*)}{\partial G} = \frac{\alpha_7}{\alpha_5(1-\alpha_6)} > 0. \qquad (3.32)$$

Again, everything depends on the size of one coefficient (α_5); if α_5 is greater (smaller) than one, the partial derivative of (3.16) exceeds (falls short of) the corresponding partial derivative of (3.32)!

In view of this enlargement of the original Sachs, Tornell and Velasco model, we can proceed to modify Figure 3.1; in Figure 3.7, the upper graph reproduces the earlier graphical analysis. In the middle part, we have depicted the case of a relaxation of credit rationing during the 'lending boom', motivated by a drop in the foreign interest rate and/or by a higher share of guaranteed private debt in relation to total private debt. Note that in the graph we have assumed the interest rate differential to increase. In the bottom part, we show the situation after the exchange rate collapse and the floating of the domestic currency.

There is more to ask in relation to 'lending booms' in emerging markets; rethinking the above story, one may as well say that the proportion of non-performing loans (*BL*) in total loans outstanding (*TLO*) is some sort of function of the extent of the lending boom:

Figure 3.7   Currency crises in the enlarged Sachs, Tornell and Velasco
model

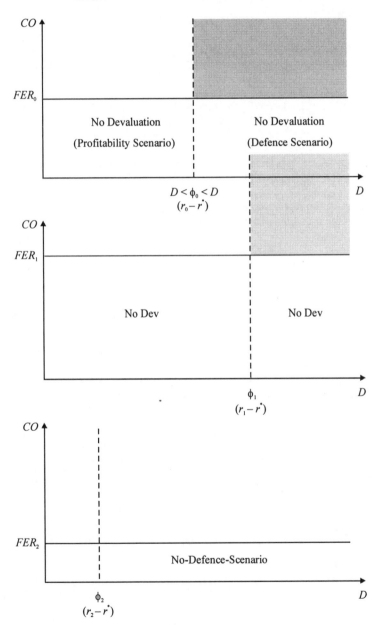

Source: Own compilation.

$$\frac{BL}{TLO} = \alpha_9 LB \qquad (3.33)$$

so that (3.33) holds. Making use of (3.24), we achieve:

$$\frac{BL}{TLO} = \frac{\alpha_7 \alpha_9}{\alpha_5 (1-\alpha_6)} G - \frac{\alpha_6 \alpha_9}{\alpha_5 (1-\alpha_6)} r^*. \qquad (3.34)$$

With regard to the share of good loans (*GL*), we may *mutatis mutandis* also say that

$$\frac{GL}{TLO} = 1 - \frac{\alpha_7 \alpha_9}{\alpha_5 (1-\alpha_6)} G + \frac{\alpha_6 \alpha_9}{\alpha_5 (1-\alpha_6)} r^*. \qquad (3.35)$$

It is also useful to differentiate between non-performing loans, that is, bad loans (*BL*) on the tradables and on the non-tradables sector:

$$BL = aBL_{NT} + (1-a)BL_T \qquad (3.36)$$

where $a \geq \frac{1}{2}$. The reason for this distinction is that the market for claims on the non-tradables sector is less liquid than the market for claims on the tradables sector. Hence, non-performing loans to the non-tradables sector trade with a bigger discount, especially since they cannot contribute to the solution of the transfer problem after the crisis. Moreover, things have to be put into a broader, that is, into an international trade theory perspective: as a matter of definition, in the sector of non-tradables, the arbitrage process functions less well; for traded goods, there is a Schumpeterian process which eliminates monopoly rents/extraordinary rates of return in the short to medium run through imitating international competition. The search for extraordinary rates of return – remember – is in turn a major impetus for the amount and speed of international financial flows in a global economy. The less non-tradables are good substitutes for tradables, the more their rates of return (that is, the rates of return which accrue when producing and selling them) are set apart from the sector of tradables. As investors anticipate in the market for non-tradable goods a less dynamic erosion of profits in comparison to markets for international tradable goods, they have one good reason for investing/lending more (in)to such sectors for speculative reasons, *ceteris paribus*.

Here at last comes the important link to the 'emerging markets': given their low to medium level of technological knowledge, they are not good candidates for becoming Schumpeterian innovators – at least in the final goods' sector of tradables. This explains why the non-tradables sector – if at all – is capable of pulling in large capital flows from the world market. And if it wants to, it has to promise extraordinary rates of return!

Also, it has been observed in Thailand (Alba et al. 1998, p. 37) that a shift in investment towards the non-tradables sector was associated with 'lower overall productivity'. The case of Thailand is a lesson for another important aspect of financial crises in emerging markets: the asset price inflation and the subsequent bubble burst observed there happened in the housing and real estate sector which is a major part of the non-tradables sector. Hence, it is by no means a matter of chance to assume the parameter a in (3.36) to exceed ½! Taking (3.36) into account, we get:

$$\frac{aBL_{NT} + (1-a)BL_T}{TLO} = \frac{\alpha_7\alpha_9}{\alpha_5(1-\alpha_6)}G - \frac{\alpha_6\alpha_9}{\alpha_5(1-\alpha_6)}r^*. \tag{3.37}$$

Moreover, it is important to realize that capital inflows lead to a real appreciation of the exchange rate, and to an expansion of non-tradables sectors at the expense of tradeables sectors (see Radelet and Sachs 1998b, p. 9). Also, the inflow of huge foreign capital 'amplifies the fluctuations in the price of non-tradable inputs, which in turn, increases the volatility in firms cash-flows and therefore aggregate output' (Aghion et al. 1999, p. 21). In our framework, it suffices to state that the degree of overvaluation, e/E_0, is itself a function of the amount of capital inflows:

$$\frac{e}{E_0} = g(CI) = g\left[\alpha_0\left(\frac{\alpha_7}{1-\alpha_6}G - \frac{1}{1-\alpha_6}r^*\right)\right] \tag{3.38}$$

with

$$g_{r^*} = \frac{\partial g(G,r^*)}{\partial r^*} = -\frac{\alpha_0}{1-\alpha_6} < 0 \tag{3.39}$$

$$g_G = \frac{\partial g(G,r^*)}{\partial G} = \frac{\alpha_0\alpha_7}{1-\alpha_6} > 0. \tag{3.40}$$

Now (3.25) is transformed into:

$$D = \begin{cases} 0 & \text{if } CO \leq FER \\ g(...)f(...)-1 & \text{if } CO > FER \end{cases} \tag{3.41}$$

with

$$g(...) \equiv g\left[\alpha_0\left(\frac{\alpha_7}{1-\alpha_6}G - \frac{1}{1-\alpha_6}r^*\right)\right] \tag{3.42}$$

$$f(...) \equiv f\left[\frac{\alpha_7}{\alpha_5(1-\alpha_6)}G - \frac{\alpha_6}{\alpha_5(1-\alpha_6)}r^*\right]. \tag{3.43}$$

We can rewrite (3.41) to become

$$D = h\left[g(G,r^*), f(G,r^*)\right] \tag{3.44}$$

and the partial derivatives are:

$$\frac{\partial D}{\partial G} = \frac{\partial g}{\partial G}f(G,r^*) + \frac{\partial f}{\partial G}g(G,r^*) \tag{3.45}$$

$$\frac{\partial D}{\partial r^*} = \frac{\partial g}{\partial r^*}f(G,r^*) + \frac{\partial f}{\partial r^*}g(G,r^*). \tag{3.46}$$

Under these auspices, it is clear that any increase (drop) in the ratio of publicly guaranteed private debt (foreign interest rate) increases the likelihood that the expected devaluation exceeds the interest rate differential!

3.5   SELECTIVE EMPIRICAL EVIDENCE

In the following, we want to make the case for a selective empirical evaluation of the models presented above; there are three good reasons for doing so:

1.   The variables/parameters should be tested against the facts of some of the most prominent financial market crises of the recent past. Otherwise, our exercise would be pure academic.
2.   The cases to be studied should include not only 'traditional' emerging markets – that is, advanced developing countries – but also advanced transition economies. Only then can we claim to investigate financial market crises in 'emerging markets'.
3.   Recent research (Furman and Stiglitz 1998) has revealed that most papers which intended to provide cross-sectional econometric analysis based on a broad empirical data sample almost unanimously failed to predict *ex post* any of the important recent financial market crises. The literature on early warning indicators is still at its very beginnings (see

Sell 2000) notwithstanding the self-confidence of some of their advocates.

The following (single or compound) variables have been observed for Mexico (December 1994), Thailand (July 1997) and the Czech Republic (May 1997) ten months before and ten months after their respective currency and banking crises. All of these crises are considered as cases of 'first infection', thus there was no contagion at work. More importantly, this fact enables us to treat the financial market crises involved as independent events which may, hence, be considered and analysed simultaneously.

According to equations (3.1) to (3.4), net foreign exchange reserves and the stock of latent finance capital outflows held by foreigners are key variables for our model. As in Sell (1998, p. 294), and following Sachs et al. (1996a), we take the broad money aggregate M2 as a proxy for the deposits held by foreigners in the domestic financial system. This is motivated by the fact that in times of crisis not only the high-powered monetary base but total money supply M2 becomes the liability of the central bank (ibid., p. 189). In this context, the sterilization attempts of the Central Bank of Mexico as a reaction to capital outflows after the assassination of Colosio played an important role. With fixed or quasi-fixed exchange rates, continued capital outflows are reflected in a one-to-one reduction of the money supply. The effect was compensated through an expansive discounting policy to commercial banks. Importantly, this funding helped the banks in Mexico to survive the withdrawal of deposits by foreign investors (ibid., pp. 150–51). At the same time, chances for a devaluation rise with a lower relation of foreign exchange reserves to M2 (Sell 1998, p. 295).

In Figure 3.8 we can observe that both in Mexico and in Thailand the ratio between net foreign reserves and M2 was declining significantly before the collapse. This does not hold entirely for the Czech Republic, where the downwards movement by and large stopped four months before the crisis and showed a modest upward trend in the last two months. In Figure 3.9, we have computed the percentage change of the ratio depicted in Figure 3.8. It turns out that in all three countries positive growth rates dominate after the exchange rate collapse.

The next crucial variable according to equations (3.5) to (3.7) is the extent of overvaluation of the respective exchange rate in relation to its long-term equilibrium value. Figure 3.10 plots the percentage deviation of the respective real exchange rates from their purchasing power parities (PPPs): again the pictures for Mexico and Thailand are quite similar. There is a significant amount of overvaluation which decreases slightly as the crisis approaches. After the collapse of the exchange rate regime the large nominal depreciations lead to a real depreciation as well. In the case of the Czech

Republic there is a mild rising trend of overvaluation in the last seven months preceding the exchange rate collapse. But, surprisingly, things do not change much on the days, weeks and months afterwards!

Figure 3.8 Net foreign exchange reserves in relation to M2

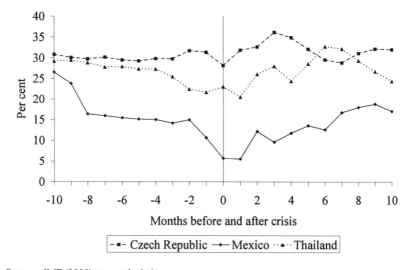

Sources: IMF (2000); own calculations.

Figure 3.9 Changes in net foreign exchange reserves in relation to M2

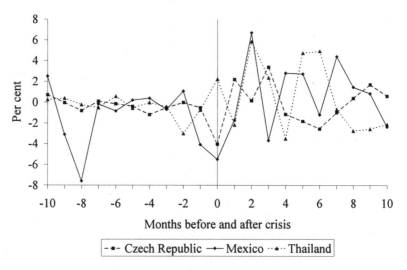

Sources: IMF (2000); own calculations.

Figure 3.10 Deviation of the real exchange from purchasing power parity

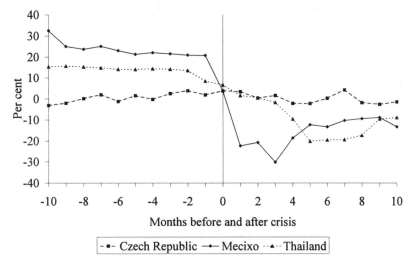

Sources: IMF (2000); own calculations.

Figure 3.11 Change in total claims of private banks in relation to GDP

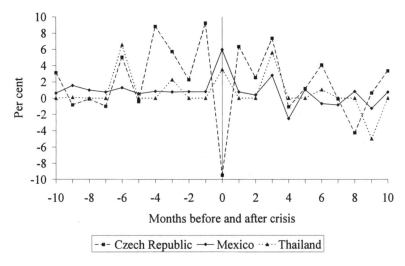

Sources: IMF (2000); own calculations.

Equations (3.8) and (3.9) paid special attention to the so-called 'lending boom'. In Figure 3.11, a lending boom was proxied by the growth rate of the ratio between the claims of the domestic banking system and the respective

GDP. Now all countries seemed to have played the same game with expansionary forces at work before and contractionary forces at work after the exchange rate collapse.

Equations (3.11) to (3.14) stress the importance of an interest rate differential of the respective domestic economies *vis-à-vis* the rest of world. This interest rate differential is shown in Figure 3.12: it was clearly there before the crisis erupted and it shot up endogenously in the aftermath of the exchange rate collapse due to the ensuing pressure on the domestic money market.

Figure 3.12 Interest rate differential vis-à-vis *the world interest rate*

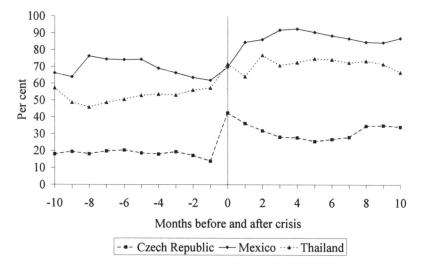

Sources: IMF (2000); own calculations.

It is a difficult task to assess empirically the amount/degree of limited liability/government guarantees and all the possible changes therein over time. The statistics screened by the IMF contain time series on private, but officially guaranteed external debt as a percentage of total external debt (Figure 3.13): in all of the three countries the available data show this ratio in the neighbourhood of 10 per cent before the crisis. While the ratio declines for Mexico after the exchange rate collapse, the opposite is true for Thailand and the Czech Republic. The case of Thailand is a very special one, however. Due to the 'crisis of confidence among depositors and creditors in the financial institution system', the Financial Institution Development Fund (FIDF) set out regulations concerning insurance for depositors and creditors in Act B.E. 2485 by virtue of the Bank of Thailand on 8 August 1997. This explains why the above ratio – almost by definition – rose to levels of 80 per cent about two months after the peak of the crisis. Quantitative information is not available, though many authors refer to this as an important phenomenon, on implicit government guarantees given to the majority of the Thai finance companies for a long time before the exchange rate collapse and the twin banking crisis erupted. Moreover, it is argued that Thai banks and finance companies even speculated on the formalization of government guarantees in the wave of a financial market crisis.

Figure 3.13 Private external debt guaranteed by the government in relation to total external debt

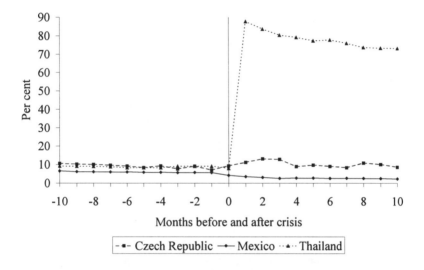

Sources: IMF (2000); own calculations.

In the case of the Czech Republic, there were also considerable amounts of implicit 'bailout clauses' present before the occurrence of the financial market crisis. The upward move in the above discussed ratio after May 1997 in Figure 3.13 merely stands for the partial conversion of former implicit into explicit government guarantees.

Capital inflows play an important role in our modelling. In Figure 3.14 we have concentrated our interest on the ratio between short-term capital inflows and domestic GDP. It can be argued that financial panic reactions will be reflected mostly in the short-term figures. Contrary to some of the relevant literature, we find that this ratio – for all three countries/case studies – has clearly declined about nine months and to become negative or at least zero about four months before the eruption of the crisis. This matches quite well the insights of our basic model (Figure 3.4) which explains the pull-out movement of foreign depositors under the impact of exchange rate expectations.

Figure 3.14 The relation of short-term external capital inflows to GDP

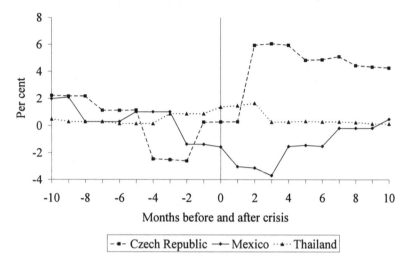

Sources: IMF (2000); own calculations.

3.6 CONCLUSIONS

In recent years, the economics profession has contributed a 'portfolio' of different approaches to explain financial crises in emerging markets, where each of them highlights specific aspects. In this chapter, we stress the impor-tance of the turnaround in attitudes and expectations on the eve of financial crises. What has been called a 'lending boom' in emerging markets is put into the framework of the theory of credit rationing (Stiglitz and Weiss 1981) and of the decision theory under the circumstances of limited liability (Sinn 1980, 1982, 1997). Based on these theoretical foundations, we reformulate a model presented by Sachs et al. in 1996; the model is able to identify the relevant coefficients/elasticities responsible for foreign investors revising their earlier decision to invest huge amounts in the emerging market economy and to provoke, when withdrawing their assets, not only a currency, but also a financial market crisis.

Selective empirical analyses for Mexico (1994), the Czech Republic (1997) and Thailand (1997) tend to back up the earlier theoretical insights.

Furthermore, the likelihood of the onset of a crisis is enhanced by the degree of exchange rate overvaluation, the lack of coverage of M2 by net foreign reserves, the size of the 'lending boom' at work in the domestic economy, significant differences between domestic and foreign interest rates (to the detriment of the latter) – which are an incentive to large capital inflows as long as the fixed exchange rate regime looks credible – and a pronounced propensity among domestic authorities to guarantee large parts of private foreign deposits in the domestic banking system. All of these variables have already figured prominently in our theoretical approach.

NOTES

1.   As McKinnon and Pill put it, it may be that, in the first place, there were reforms on the domestic financial market which preceded huge external capital inflows: 'Such reforms generate enormous excitement and optimism, encouraging people to expect that their national output and household incomes would be much higher in the future' (1998a, p. 6). At the same time, the euphoria about the expected success of the reforms is fuelled by the 'overly optimistic implicit signal ... contained in loose credit conditions' (ibid., p. 14). This statement translates into the terms of our own model by saying that 'exaggerated optimism' leads to a relaxation of credit rationing, which, in turn pushes the lending boom!
2.   Quite analogously, in the 'overborrowing syndrome' model of McKinnon and Pill (1998a) banks raise the interest rate in the 'rational beliefs equilibrium' as compared to the 'first best financial equilibrium' in the domestic liberalized economy (pp. 11–12).
3.   See Figure 2.3.
4.   Ibid.

4. 'Contagion': What is it and Who is Susceptible to it?

4.1 INTRODUCTION

Centuries ago, a young or perhaps not even yet existing scientific discipline, which we nowadays denote 'economics', became a student of natural sciences, of medicine in general and of blood circulation in particular in order to learn more about circulation and 'laws' in the economy: that was the high time of the physiocrats. Much later, modern macroeconomics for small open economies of the late 1970s and the early 1980s operated successfully with the notion of 'disease'; the famous 'Dutch disease' (see Corden and Neary 1982; Enders 1983; Sell 1988a) figures prominently among the possible examples. There was, however, no general consensus about the correct use of the term 'disease'. As a matter of fact, some of the professionals in economics still maintain that 'Dutch disease' can be better described as the 'economics of a lucky country'!

A similar problem was present as economists drew on concepts of epidemiology when they started to research processes of diffusion of technical knowledge and progress (see, for example, Mansfield 1968; Davies 1979; Silverberg et al. 1988; and Lücke 1992, 1993) making analogies to the epidemic spread of diseases. As technical progress is a key variable for the explanation of economic growth, the diffusion of technical progress can be taken as a prerequisite for the catch-up process of poorer countries, and hence for convergence, in the world economy. One can, therefore, hardly think of a more healthy 'epidemic' disease.

Inspired by the convergence–divergence debate, international trade has attracted new interest through the observation that 'trade generates cross country knowledge spill-overs, which have a positive impact on the technological progress in the trading countries' (Xie 1999, p. 165). Models in this area of research maintain that it takes contact through personal interaction before a technological gap between advanced and less-advanced countries can be closed. Knowledge must be transferred through personal contact, that is, active teaching and learning (ibid., pp. 166–67). However, as we shall demonstrate below, it is totally misleading to define such positive cross-country spill-overs as 'contagion'.

Mathematical social sciences (see Osei and Thompson 1977; Dunstan 1982; Sudbury 1985; Goswamy and Cumar 1990; Tuteja and Gupta 1992; and Lefevre and Picard 1994) and/or sociology (Minnitti 1998) have been perhaps more cautious when drawing on the epidemic model: their focus, for example, is the explanation for the spread of *rumours* or the social contagion effects related to the geographical concentration of crime in some communities and not in others.

In recent years, the economics profession has resumed its interest in the terminology and in the semantics of epidemiology: related to the ERM crisis of 1992–93 (Gerlach and Smets 1995) and, later on, to the spread of the Mexican crisis of 1994–95 to other Latin American countries (the so-called 'Tequila effect', see Agénor 1997) and of the Thai crisis to other Southeast Asian countries (the 'Asian Flu') in the late summer and autumn of 1997 (see Alba et al. 1998), the notion of 'contagion' has become a popular term. Moreover, 'contagion effects' were 'identified' on the occasion of the rouble crisis in August–September 1998 although the most affected economy, that of Brazil, was neither in the regional neighbourhood of Russia nor did its trade or financial linkages to Russia exhibit any type of remarkable significance.

As these very few examples tend to demonstrate and as we shall show in the next section, there is a huge variety of meanings/contents associated with the term 'contagion'. It is a term one can rarely find in the index of an epidemiological monograph; yet, it symbolizes what everybody who is not a medicial doctor, but perhaps an economist, presumes to 'understand' intuitively and to apply to economic diseases.[1] As Drazen has observed, 'carefully-reasoned explanations of the causes of contagion, or even what constitutes contagion, are as rare as discussions of the phenomenon are common' (1999, p. 4).

Sometimes the term is only a synonym for 'spill-over effects' (Frankel and Schmukler 1998, p. 232).[2] Some authors at least differentiate – when they talk about 'contagion' – between less and 'more durable forms of spill-over effects, over and beyond those that typically arise in moments of crises' (Calvo and Reinhart 1996, p. 10). As we have successfully made use of the spill-over concept for many years in (macro)economics, one may ask: why should there be a substitute? Masson prefers to draw a distinction between 'spill-over' and 'contagion' and claims that the latter should only be associated 'where a crisis in one country may conceivably trigger a crisis elsewhere for reasons unexplained by macroeconomic fundamentals' (1998, p. 4). According to this concept, contagion can apply only to speculative attacks which 'shift' from one country to another country and are not founded in weak fundamentals of the other country.

Other authors simply state that 'some crises become contagious and spread' (Glick and Rose 1998, p. 6). Some are looking for more sophisticated interpretations, like Masson, who argues that there is a 'jump between equilibria triggered by a crisis elsewhere' (1998, p. 13). As a consequence, it comes as no surprise that there is no generally accepted, let alone consistent, economic interpretation of 'contagion' to be found in the economic literature so far (for a similar view, see Frankel and Schmukler 1998, p. 235). An overview of the most prominent economic interpretations given to contagion is presented in Section 2. But, if – by and large – the meaning of contagion is and should be somehow related to the linguistic roots of the Latin expression *'contagiare'*, our story must be concerned with *the spreading of a* (still to be defined) *disease*. Therefore, it should be worthwhile to explore in detail (Section 3) what modern epidemiology has contributed to the systematic explanation of contagious processes. This will serve to reinterpret the economic implications of contagion in Section 4. Section 5 will then discuss how economic policy can possibly contribute to stopping the negative repercussions of contagious economic crises or perhaps even find means of 'immunization' and/or 'prevention' against 'infection'. In Section 6 we give a short summary and draw some conclusions.

4.2   CONTAGION IN RECENT ECONOMIC LITERATURE

4.2.1 Herding

'Herding' has for some time already been an issue of great relevance in the literature dealing with financial markets; it is an interesting topic because it helps us to understand why 'with sequential actions, the earliest decisions can have a disproportionate effect' and how, when 'all agents follow the lead of the market, completely ignoring their private information', we may achieve a so-called 'informational cascade' (Avery and Zemsky 1998, p. 724).

So-called 'herding effects' in capital markets are frequently given as an example for the prevalence and working of 'contagion'; as a matter of fact, 'herding' seems to be closest to the epidemic interpretation that modern, stochastic sociology has assigned to the spread of *rumours* phenomenon (see, for a similar view, Calvo and Mendoza 1997; Calvo 1999; Choueiri 1999). Therefore, with good reason, Frankel and Schmukler tend to define 'herding behavior contagion' as 'true contagion' (1998, p. 235). But, as we shall see later, this applies only when investor and herding behaviour act as an *intermediary* between bad events (fundamental crisis) or news (non-fundamental crisis) in the 'first-victim' country and in 'non-first-victim' countries!

Calvo and Mendoza draw *expressis verbis* on the notion of 'rumour' in their attempt to explain the events after the Mexican, the Thai, and the Russian crises in 1995, 1997 and 1998, respectively (1999, p. 8), where 'investors seemed to follow the "market" rather than take the time and expense to make their own assessment of each country's fundamentals' (ibid., p. 1). They define contagion as a situation 'in which utility maximising investors choose not to pay for information that would be relevant for their portfolio decision – thereby making them susceptible to react to country-specific rumors – or in which investors optimally choose to mimic arbitrary "market" portfolios' (ibid., p. 2).

At the heart of the herding hypothesis is the distinction between informed and more or less uninformed foreign investors. The latter are assumed to have a twofold information problem: on the one hand, they are (if at all) only poorly informed about the emerging market economy(ies) in general and about its (their) financial assets in particular. Such a status of weak information is not irrational, however. There is a trade-off for investors between the gains from diversification and the costs of information gathering. Consequently, the more diversified a portfolio[3] is, the less a representative investor will collect and process information on an individual asset.

On the other hand, poorly informed investors have, as Calvo (1999, p. 3) calls it, a 'signal extraction problem': from what they observe as (dis)investment behaviour among the informed investors, they cannot qualify whether, when this group pulls out of a country, it is because there are problems with the fundamentals of this country in particular or with the fundamentals of all emerging markets in general. In extending E.S. Phelps's (1999) famous categories of confusion, we are dealing here with a *general–particular–confusion* among rational, but uninformed investors.[4] The 'tragedy' of this mechanism and its implied multiplier effects lies in the fact that 'emerging markets could be innocent victims of shocks that lie completely outside their realm and control' (Calvo 1999, p. 5). Why? As far as the well-informed investors are concerned, even 'small' negative news will provoke a radical reaction, that is, a 'fire-sale' of the assets. Informed investors are most likely highly leveraged. 'A margin call in one market would therefore require that these investors liquidate various positions to satisfy the margin call' (Schinasi and Smith 1999, p. 5). This first effect is magnified by the tendency of uninformed investors to mimic the behaviour of the informed investors, so that sales by individual investors will quickly translate into a stampede of sales giving rise to speculative attacks (Griffith-Jones 1996, p. 3).

It is also said that *globalization* and its increasing possibilities for diversification has contributed to creating more opportunities for herding:

> When investors have a set of investment alternatives they have less incentive to obtain costly information regarding individual countries. Investment in each particular country becomes more sensitive when investment opportunities increase. Investors are able to switch to other countries when they receive bad news about one nation. Therefore, diversification leads to more ignorance and herding behavior on the part of international investors. (Frankel and Schmukler 1998, p. 236)

As Calvo and Mendoza (1997, p. 27) put it, globalization of securities markets reduces the incentives for information gathering, and hence produces high volatility in capital flows as a result of optimal herd behaviour. 'This occurs because (a) globalization generally reduces the gains derived from paying fixed costs for country-specific information, and (b) in the presence of reputational effects, globalization widens the range of portfolios inside of which investors find it optimal to mimic market portfolios' (ibid.).

What do these herding approaches to contagious economic crises have in common? In the case of herding, countries simultaneously become patients because they are victims of the (by and large) undifferentiated *disinvestment decisions* of (a majority of) poorly informed foreign investors. Obviously, there is no *direct* contagion whatsoever among the countries themselves. If anything, rumour spread like epidemia among the (un)informed investors. We may later call this form of contagion 'indirect'. This classification is plausible, but not totally convincing, though: if we are essentially looking for the spreading and transmission of *diseases*, herding behaviour in capital markets cannot account for the fact that those investors do not become ill if they reallocate their portfolios and steer a large part of their portfolios into 'safe havens'! Moreover, their reallocation decisions may rather be taken as measures of prevention to protect their own health. Also, what we observe among countries may be a sort of *simultaneous infection*, the 'virus' consisting in the removal of a highly needed resource for emerging markets to survive in the world economy: capital. And yet, the picture of an *infection* is, in a way, still misleading: neither macro- nor microparasites are known for taking conscious decisions as human though uninformed investors do! Also, any infection is, in the first place, to be understood as the inflow of a virus into a living organism and must not lead directly to the occurrence of the disease!

4.2.2 Rational Investors' Behaviour

A more 'fundamentalist' explanation of the informed rational investors' behaviour argues with 'large' negative news, in the sense that events in one country 'may have led market participants to revise their model of development broadly, and thus have affected asset prices in a larger group of countries' (Alba et al. 1998, p. 53).[5] As Fratzscher puts it, investors detect weak fundamentals in one country and if the country finds itself locked in a crisis, they tend to become more sensitive to the risks in other countries with similar fundamentals, reduce their exposure to these countries and, thereby, contribute to spread the crisis across economies (1998, pp. 667–8).

Agénor and Aizenman define the above-mentioned 'Tequila effect' or 'Tequilazo' as 'an ensuing sharp swing in investor's sentiment toward emerging markets' (1998, p. 208) triggered by a currency and banking crisis in another emerging market. As Calvo puts it for the events of 1998, 'upon seeing Russia default, investors thought that other emerging-market countries would follow suit, tried to pull out their funds and drove those economies into a crisis equilibrium' (1999, p. 2).

Agénor has made an effort to 'measure' this kind of spreading more accurately; he comes up with the view that a non-first-victim country is affected by a Tequilazo on account of a 'temporary increase in the autonomous component of the risk premium that domestic borrowers must pay (above the "safe" lending rate) on world capital markets' (1997, p. 26). Although exogenous to the country in question, the Tequila effect is triggered by 'a loss of confidence of investors in the country's economic prospects' (ibid., p. 7), and, in the particular case in the aftermath of the Mexican crisis, 'the perception that the exchange rate regime was about to suffer the same fate as Mexico's' (ibid.).

Another rational investor-related explanation for the spill-over of a crisis from one country to others highlights *the role of illiquidity* (Goldfajn and Valdés 1997): crises 'can spread contagiously to other countries when international investors encountering liquidity difficulties as a result of the banking crisis in one country respond by liquidating their positions in other national markets' (Eichengreen et al. 1996, p. 470).

Diversification is and always has been one of the main ingredients of portfolio theory; in the same vein, Schinasi and Smith argue that contagion can be explained by basic portfolio theory: 'a loss on a specific position ... may be sufficient to cause a leveraged investor to reduce risky positions in all markets'[6] (1999, p. 3) and in doing so he is just rebalancing an optimal portfolio following a portfolio management rule. What one can observe then, is defined by Schinasi and Smith as 'contagious selling': a withdrawal 'by an investor from many risky assets when an adverse shock occurs to only one of them' (ibid., p. 5).

Kodres and Pritsker (1999) attribute a great deal of responsibility for the occurrence of contagion to the *cross-market hedging activities* of value investors: consider three countries 1, 2 and 3, where 1 and 3 have no risk factors in common.

> Specifically, in response to a negative information shock in country 1, informed value investors sell country 1's assets, reducing their portfolio exposure to risk factor 1. They hedge the change in exposure by buying the assets of country 2, increasing their exposure to risk factor 2. They then hedge this by selling the assets in country 3, completing the chain of contagion from country 1 to country 3 through country 2 [which serves as a conduit]. (ibid., pp. 17–18)

Prices in countries 1 and 3 will drop significantly, but prices in country 2 will remain essentially unchanged.

We have seen above that herding behaviour among more or less uninformed investors contributes to the explanation of the turmoil which affects emerging, but non-first-victim markets. The same economic consequences hit the emerging markets concerned, by and large, if the acting agents are well-informed, rational investors. Hence, it is not important for the resulting contagious effects that rational investors' behaviour is established quite differently from herding.

4.2.3 Contagion through Integrated Capital Markets

In the case of highly integrated capital markets of two or more economies, shocks 'to the larger country are quickly transmitted to the smaller one through trade in assets' (Calvo and Reinhart 1995, p. 3). This argument does not necessarily hinge upon the distinction between a small and a large country, it also works for two or more economies of equal size and represents a *pecuniary negative externality*. The differentiation between large and small, however, aggravates (reduces) the spill-over problem for the small (large) economy: when capital markets are less (well) developed and 'thin' ('broad'), the likelihood for strong price effects in the small (large) economy rises (declines), *ceteris paribus*.

When it comes to detecting 'contagion' statistically through integrated capital markets, however, one may doubt whether some of the proposed empirical procedures, such as investigating whether the 'degree of co-movement' across equity and bond returns for emerging markets increased in the wake of a first-victim crisis (ibid., p. 16), are appropriate: the co-movement of body temperature of healthy people may just be higher in comparison with patients who suffer from the same disease (see below)!

4.2.4 Contagion through Institutional Practices

Frankel and Schmukler illustrate the problem which arises due to institutional innovations among the capital markets of industrialized countries in the last 10 to 15 years: 'for example, a fund that invests in Latin American markets or in all emerging markets may be led by capital losses on its Mexico holdings to sell other holdings' (1998, p. 236) in order to keep its country shares in proper proportion, to balance portfolios and to optimize the overall risk/return ratio (Fratzscher 1998, p. 669), thereby 'depressing prices in other countries' stock markets. In the case of open-end funds, managers may also be forced to raise cash to meet redemptions whenever there is a price fall in one country' (Frankel and Schmukler 1998, p. 236).

Buckberg has found econometric evidence for the hypothesis that institutional investors follow a two-step portfolio allocation process – first determining what share of their portfolio to invest in developing countries, and then allocating those funds across the emerging markets. Developing countries' equity markets are treated as a separate asset class. If, for instance, institutional investors experienced a shift in sentiment away from Mexican securities in 1994–95, and Mexican securities served as a benchmark for other Latin American country securities, a widespread selling of developing country securities across the board in the immediate wake of the Mexican peso devaluation in December 1994 came as no surprise: institutional 'investors make investment decisions in developing country markets primarily by comparing the markets to each other, not by comparing each market to the world portfolio' (Buckberg 1996, p. 16).

4.2.5 Rational Speculators' Behaviour

Tornell's recent paper (1999) is very appealing as it goes back to some of the 'roots' of modern contagion literature, for instance, the seminal paper of Gerlach and Smets (1995), where the purpose was to explain contagious speculative attacks. Surprisingly, since then the vast majority of authors have not been interested in the agents who are responsible for the occurrence of speculative attacks: rational speculators. This gap is filled by Tornell's approach. He argues that

> [s]ince the short positions involved in a currency attack entail significant costs, an individual money manager will attack a country if he/she expects other money managers to attack the country, and anticipates that the country will respond with a sizeable depreciation. The eruption of a crisis in a certain country indicates to each investor that other investors will attack vulnerable countries in the future. Although investors do not communicate among themselves, they do not attack countries randomly. (Tornell 1999, pp. 2–3)

Rather, there exists a co-ordinating device or a signal and this signal is the occurrence of a crisis in a first-victim country itself; this event and its underlying causes point to the likelihood of further attacks on currencies that are expected to react with a sizeable depreciation in response to a capital outflow.

Now, when are countries strong candidates for a large depreciation, and which countries are they? As the Mexican and the Thai cases showed, this will be the more likely, the stronger the real appreciation of the currency in question, the lower the foreign exchange reserves of the country involved and the weaker – that is, the less it can afford high interest rates hiked by the government to defend the exchange rate parity – the domestic banking system.

4.2.6 Contagion through (Regional) Trade

One trade-related story goes more or less like this: once a country has suffered a speculative attack, its trading partners and competitors are disproportionately likely to be attacked themselves (Glick and Rose 1998, p. 4). And, 'since trade patterns are strongly negatively affected by distance, currency crises [and, hence, contagion] will tend to be regional' (ibid., p. 5). More precisely, a representative hypothesis maintains that 'in episodes in which the ground zero country [the first-victim country] depreciates, other countries will depreciate and/or lose reserves the more they compete in world markets with country 0' (ibid., p. 15). Depreciation of currency 0 will turn the trade balance of partner countries into a deficit requiring a devaluation to balance the trade account. This type of story is very much related to the 'first generation' models of currency crises (Krugman 1979), triggered by inconsistent macroeconomic fundamentals in the first-victim country.

A somewhat different story emphasizes the role of trade in transmitting currency crises induced by self-fulfilling expectations in the first-victim countries to regional trade partners (Loisel and Martin 1999, p. 3). Such approaches draw on the so-called 'second generation' models of speculative attacks.

4.2.7 Contagion as a Consequence of Co-operation/Co-ordination which Lacks Credibility

In the same vein, Loisel and Martin (1999) have recently introduced the issue of contagion into the international policy co-ordination framework. Here, only unexpected devaluations of one country can have real effects on the other country: devaluation, in equilibrium, can hence not improve competitiveness (ibid., p. 7) *vis-à-vis* the rest of world. But, 'out of equilibrium, when the devaluation is not expected, the gain and therefore the incentive to devalue is higher the more dependent on trade the country is' (ibid., p. 17).[7]

In such a setting, 'co-operation imposes solidarity on both governments. Since it may lead to outcomes which prove not unilaterally stable, because they are not Nash equilibria, it appears not necessarily credible for private agents' (ibid., p. 9). Moreover, even co-ordination which is a much weaker requirement than co-operation since governments commit themselves only to informing/consulting one another and can then move instantaneously to a specific Nash equilibrium, may become an incredible institutional arrangement for private agents.

Co-ordination, however, has ambivalent effects on the likelihood of contagion; on the one hand, co-ordination can convince governments to renounce on devaluations, as, in equilibrium, devaluation has no real effect. On the other hand, the temptation to devalue will nevertheless increase co-ordination if one of the countries is hit by a negative shock which weakens its fundamentals, such as rising nominal wages which induce more unemployment. In such a scenario, the co-ordinated announcement that none of the countries will devalue is no longer credible from the private sector's point of view. This, in turn, increases the 'probability of devaluation in both countries' (ibid., p. 24).

4.2.8 Contagion through the Balance of Payments/Money Demand

The crises in the ERM during 1992 and 1993 have inspired Gerlach and Smets to address the question why speculative attacks tend to spread, and, more precisely, 'whether the collapse of one parity can lead to a speculative attack on another parity that otherwise could not have occurred' (1995, p. 59). A precondition for such an event is that both countries are closely connected with each other by trade ties, so that parity changes via depreciations of one country have a strong impact on the competitiveness of the other country. In such a scenario, the exchange rate floating of the first currency after a successful speculative attack on its earlier peg, can trigger another speculative attack on the second currency, even if in the absence of the first speculative attack the pegged exchange rate regime of the second currency would have remained viable. The transmission channel for such an outcome is the balance of payments, domestic output and prices, and, ultimately, money demand.

The collapse of the first currency

leads to a real appreciation of the second currency, which depresses prices [via the composition of the price index effect] and income [with arbitrage between domestic and foreign goods, the appreciation of the second currency puts pressure on its own goods; at sticky wages this partly results in higher unemployment] in the second country. (Gerlach and Smets 1995, p. 47)

Both the price and the income effect in turn reduce money demand in the second country which – according to the monetary approach to the balance of payments – ultimately causes a loss of foreign exchange reserves. The latter is a signal for speculators that the credibility of defending the peg of the second currency has weakened and, hence, increases the likelihood of a speculative attack.

4.2.9 Political Contagion

This very recently presented approach (Drazen 1999) emphasizes that maintaining a fixed exchange rate regime – one which can be attacked – can be motivated by several *political reasons*; one reason may be for the politicians of one country to form or to stabilize political and economic integration with their neighbours. It may also well be that there are conflicting objectives for the policymakers. Speculators, now, will have to make a guess, that is, they have only incomplete information, about the importance that politicians assign to the integration objective and also the associated costs (above all, a high interest rate level and a minimum stock of reserves to defend the exchange rate) when they stick to the parity. The higher these estimated costs are, the stronger are the speculators' beliefs about the probability of a devaluation, *ceteris paribus*.

When attacking the currency of such a country this has at least two effects: not only will speculators be either successful or not, but also, in either case, they learn more about the 'true' preferences of the respective government with regard to the fixed parity; if it is revealed to be 'a weaker commitment than previously believed, [this] creates an externality in the form of a lower commitment of all other potential members. They will therefore be more vulnerable to attack' (Drazen 1999, p. 11).

Not only speculators learn from the effective devaluation by one country. Politicians of other countries realize that the devaluation is a signal which contains the information that this country is less likely to become a member, of, say, a monetary union. This lowers

> the value of membership to other potential members, making them more likely to devalue. ... An unanticipated devaluation by one potential member will reveal a lower commitment to fixed exchange rates than previously believed, not only to speculators, but also to other potential members. This raises the probability they assign to that country devaluing in the future, and thus lowers the probability they assign to her meeting the membership criterion when it becomes effective. (ibid., pp. 19–20).

Drazen has classified this specific form as 'membership contagion' (ibid., p. 24).

4.3   CONTAGION IN EPIDEMIOLOGY

4.3.1 Clarifying the Notions

The biology of infectious diseases (Anderson and May 1991, p. 13) divides the population which can become host to microparasites into the following classes of individuals: susceptible (uninfected), infected (latent, infectious) and recovered/immune. The latent period is defined as the average period of time from the point of infection to the point when an individual becomes infectious to others, the infectious period denotes the average period over which an infected person is infectious to others, and the period from the point of infection to the appearance of symptoms of disease is termed the incubation period (Anderson and Nokes 1997, p. 692). The duration of symptoms of disease, as depicted in Figure 4.1, is 'not necessarily synchronous with the period during which an infected host is infectious to susceptible individuals' (Anderson and May 1991, p. 14).

Figure 4.1   The development of an infectious disease

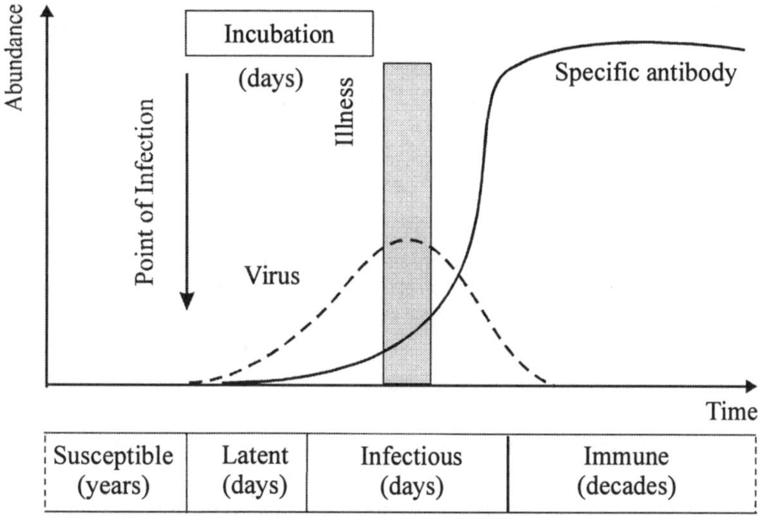

Source: Anderson and Nokes (1997, p. 692).

Surprisingly, 'contagion' is not a key term in epidemiology: instead, the equivalent notion is 'transmission'; the so-called 'transmission coefficient' determines the rate at which 'new infections arise as a consequence of mixing between the susceptible and infected individuals' (ibid.). The so-called 'force of infection' is the *probability that a given susceptible host will become infected* (ibid., p. 63).

Note also that indirect transmission exists; in this case, 'the parasite passes through one or more species of intermediate hosts in order to complete its life cycle' (ibid., p. 22). There is an average stay of the microparasites in the infected class who recover and survive the disease and there is also an average stay of the virus among the class of immune individuals. During recovery, viral abundance decays to zero/very low levels and antibodies specific to viral antigens rise to high levels. 'Recovered hosts are almost invariably fully immune to further infection in the case of viral parasites' (ibid., p. 31). However, the duration of human immunity is not lifelong in the majority of cases. This is why ex-immunes become by definition newly susceptible.

A major issue in the framework of spreading epidemic diseases is the effective reproductive rate of a parasite (F); a parasite must have a basic reproductive rate (F_0), that is, the average number of successful offspring it is capable of producing, of $F_0 > 1$. In a human environment, F_0 is more precisely defined as the 'average number of secondary infections produced when one infected individual is introduced into a host population where everyone is susceptible' (ibid., p. 17). In equilibrium, the effective rate will be just one and, in particular, this is known as the 'endemic equilibrium' (Anderson and Nokes 1996, p. 238):

$$F = F_0 s^* = 1 \qquad\qquad (4.1)$$

where s^* is the fraction of the host population that is susceptible in equilibrium (Anderson and May 1991, p. 17).[8] If the prevalence or incidence of infection is stable through time, the effective reproductive rate F must equal unity in value; this is a situation in which each primary case gives rise, on average, to a single secondary infectious individual (Anderson and Nokes 1997, p. 700). This result is important for the economic modelling of infection and contagion in economics as it points to the possibility of restriction he analysis to a two-country or two-investor perspective.

Let us explore this phenomenon in more detail. On invasion, the vast majority of hosts are susceptible, and hence provided $F_0 > 1$, the epidemic expands as illustrated in Figure 4.2.

However, as the epidemic progresses, more and more of the contacts made by an infected host are either immune or already infected. As the effective reproductive number declines, and eventually at equilibrium it settles to the value of unity where each infected person generates an average of one secondary infection. (Anderson 1998, p. 33)

Figure 4.2   The expansion process of an epidemic

Generation	1	2	3	4	5	6	7	8
Number infected	1	1	2	2	3	4	6	7
F_0		1	2	1	1.5	1.33	1.5	1.16

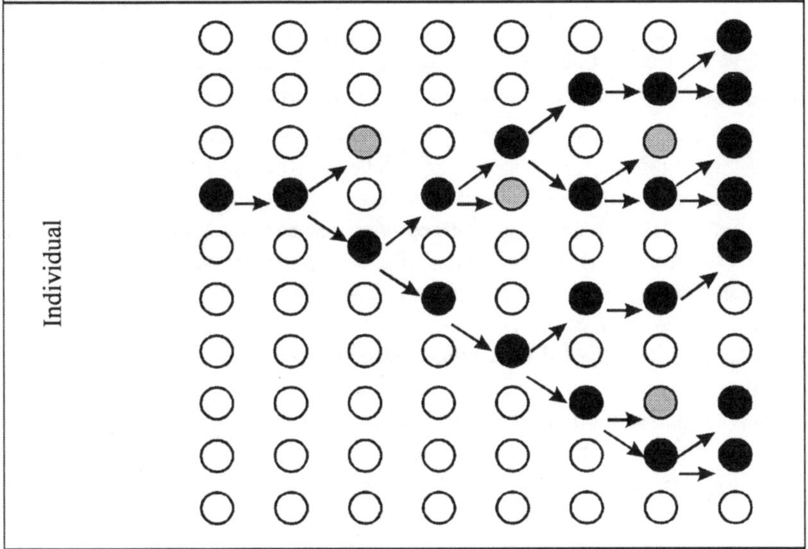

Source: Anderson (1998, p. 33).

Note that in periods 1 and 2 (4 and 5) the associated transmission from an individual 4 (6) to an individual 4 (7) is of the 'latent domino effect' nature; the same applies to individual 2 in periods 6 and 7. However, 'real domino effects' apply only when we find a chain: this is the case with individuals 6 (period 6 = start), 6, 5 (period 8 = end). 'Pure contagion', that is, situations where for each infected individual $F_0 > 1$, are better represented by all remaining cases of transmission depicted in Figure 4.2! Hence, we may conclude that domino effects are only a partial aspect of contagion! F_0 can be approximated by the following formula:

$$F_0 = \beta S T \tag{4.2}$$

that is the number of susceptibles present with which the primary case can come into contact (S), multiplied by the length of time that the primary case is infectious to others, T, multiplied by the transmission coefficient, β. Hence, we achieve:

$$F = \beta S T s^* = 1 \tag{4.3}$$

$$s^* = 1/\beta S T. \tag{4.4}$$

There is a critical level for S such that F_0 is set at one and the broad reproductive rate is lower than necessary for an epidemic expansion.

$$S_T = 1/\beta T. \tag{4.5}$$

In this case, if the density of susceptibles can be reduced to less than S_T in value, an eradication of the virus (by a mass vaccination for instance) becomes feasible (Anderson and Nokes 1997, pp. 700–701).

4.3.2 A Simple Model of Contagious Disease

Consider a stable population of size N which consists of:

$$N = M + S + H + Y + Z \tag{4.6}$$

where M is the number of infants with maternally derived immunity, S is the number of susceptibles, H is the number of infected, but not yet infectious individuals, Y is the number of infectious individuals and Z is the number of immunes. Figure 4.3 shows in a flow chart how these variables are related to one another.

It is assumed that the net birth rate is equal to the natural per capita mortality rate (μ) so that the number of births is μN; δ is the per capita rate of movement out of class M; β is the rate of transmission that defines the probability of contact and infection transfer between a susceptible and an infectious person, σ defines the per capita rate of leaving the latent class; γ is the per capita rate of leaving the infectious class and (not included in Figure 4.3) τ is the per capita disease-induced death rate (Anderson and May 1991, p. 58; Anderson and Nokes 1997, p. 693). With this notation, one may define the following system of differential equations:

$$dM/dt = \mu N - (\delta + \mu)M \tag{4.7}$$

$$dS/dt = \delta M - (\beta Y + \mu)S \tag{4.8}$$

$$dH/dt = \beta S Y - (\sigma + \mu)H \tag{4.9}$$

$$dY/dt = \sigma H - (\tau + \gamma + \mu)Y \qquad (4.10)$$

$$dZ/dt = \gamma Y - \mu Z. \qquad (4.11)$$

The net rate of infection βSY, is approximated by a relationship proportional (β) to the density of susceptibles (S) multiplied by the density of infectious individuals, Y (Anderson and Nokes 1997, p. 694). The equations (4.7) to (4.11) constitute a simple model of infection transmission; the equilibrium properties of this system ('endemic equilibrium') can be examined by setting the time derivatives equal to zero, 'that is such that there are assumed to be no further changes in the number of individuals within each infection class because the flows into and out of any one category are equal' (ibid., p. 695):

$$M^{*} = \frac{\mu}{\delta + \mu} N \qquad (4.12)$$

Figure 4.3   Different classes within a population affected by an infectious disease

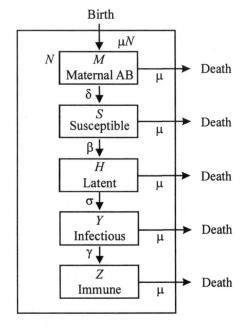

Source: Anderson and Nokes (1997, p. 604).

$$S^* = \frac{(\sigma + \mu)(\gamma + \tau + \mu)}{\beta\sigma} \qquad (4.13)$$

$$H^* = \frac{(\gamma + \alpha + \mu)}{\sigma} Y^* \qquad (4.14)$$

$$Y^* = \frac{(\delta M^* - \mu S^*)}{\beta S^*} \qquad (4.15)$$

$$Z^* = \frac{\gamma}{\mu} Y^*. \qquad (4.16)$$

The interpretation of the steady-state solutions is straightforward. From these ten equations, at least six, (4.8) and (4.13), (4.10) and (4.15), and (4.11) and (4.16) deserve our special interest, as we have to establish a link to 'contagion' in economics later on. Hence, in the following, we shall focus on a reduced set of equations which are able to show how an epidemic arises, but also when it may die out. If we disregard the infants with derived immunity, equation (4.8) simplifies to:

$$dS/dt = \mu N - (\beta Y + \mu)S. \qquad (4.17)$$

If we also neglect τ and the distinction between latent and infectious individuals, we achieve:

$$dY/dt = \beta SY - (\gamma + \mu)Y. \qquad (4.18)$$

Finally, the immunes are modelled as before:

$$dZ/dt = \gamma Y - \mu Z. \qquad (4.19)$$

Total population now consists of:

$$N = S + Y + Z. \qquad (4.20)$$

With this reduced set of equations we can now easily simulate three scenarios: (i) no epidemic, (ii) transitory epidemic and (iii) persistence (latent epidemic)! Consider in the first case (i) a population which is totally susceptible, but not affected by mortality (then μ is zero in all of the above equations) where we introduce a few infecteds. The epidemic will not occur if the basic reproductive rate is less than one ($F_0 = 0.005$) and the density of susceptibles does not reach the critical threshold value ($S_T = 10,000$). See Figure 4.4 for a simulation of this first case.

Figure 4.4 The no-epidemic case

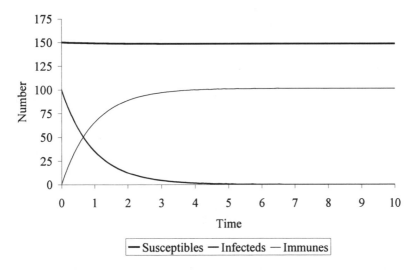

Notes: At time $t = 1$: $S = 150$, $Y = 100$, $Z = 0$, $\beta = 0.0001$, $\gamma = 1$, $F_0 = 0.015$, $S_T = 10,000$.

Sources: Anderson and Nokes (1997, p. 702); own calculations.

The epidemic will, however, occur (ii) if the basic reproductive rate is greater than or equal to one ($F_0 = 5$) and the density of susceptibles exceeds the threshold value ($S_T = 100$). But, even in the outbreak of an epidemic case, 'as time progresses, the density of susceptibles will decline, until the effective reproductive rate F is less than unity (that is, the number of susceptibles falls below the threshold ($S_T = 1/\beta T$) and the infection dies out' (Anderson and Nokes 1997, p. 701). For a simulation of this second case, see Figure 4.5.

For an epidemic to become persistent (latent epidemic), one of two things must happen. In the first example for (iii), we shall limit our scope to the case where[9] susceptibles are *continually introduced into the population by births* at a net rate of μN, where μ is the per capita birth rate and at the same time the rate of mortality, so that total population is maintained at a constant level. The infection will persist in the population, provided that $F_0 \geq 1$ (Anderson and Nokes 1997, pp. 701–2). Let us calculate the *endemic equilibrium* implied by looking at the steady-state values of equations (4.17), (4.18) and (4.19):

Contagion in Financial Markets

$$0 = \mu N - (\beta Y^* + \mu)S^*$$
$$\beta S^* Y^* = \mu(N - S^*)$$
$$\frac{S^* Y^*}{S_T} = \frac{\mu}{\gamma}(N - S^*).$$

$$(4.21)$$

In equilibrium (4.18) turns into

$$0 = \beta S^* Y^* - (\gamma + \mu)Y^*$$
$$(\gamma + \mu)Y^* = \beta S^* Y^*$$
$$\frac{(\gamma + \mu)}{\gamma} Y^* = \frac{S^* Y^*}{S_T}.$$

$$(4.22)$$

Introducing (4.21) gives:

$$Y^* = \frac{\mu}{(\mu + \gamma)}(N - S^*).$$

$$(4.23)$$

The steady-state solution for the immunes is straightforward:

Figure 4.5 The transitory epidemic case

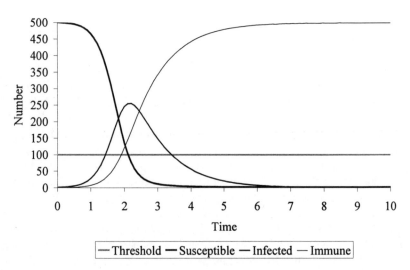

Notes: At time $t = 1$: $S = 500$, $Y = 1$, $Z = 0$, $\beta = 0.01$, $\gamma = 1$, $F_0 = 5$, $S_T = 100$.

Sources: Anderson and Nokes (1997, p. 702); own calculations.

$$Z^* = \frac{\gamma}{\mu} Y^*. \tag{4.24}$$

As in equilibrium $S^* = S_T$, (4.23) gives:

$$Y^* = \frac{\mu}{(\mu + \gamma)}(N - S_T). \tag{4.25}$$

The stationary solutions, S^*, Y^*, Z^* define the set of variables in the endemic equilibrium. A simulation of this first example for an infection which persists in a community (iii) is provided by Figure 4.6.

Figure 4.6 Persistence of an infection (renewal due to births)

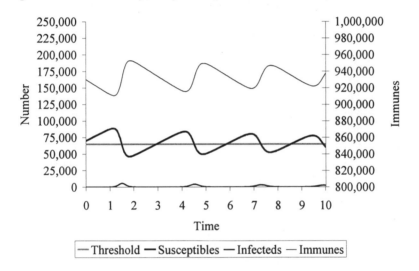

Notes: The conditions for the persistence of an infection in a community when renewal of susceptibles is due to births are at time $t = 1$: $S = 70,000$; $Y = 1$; $Z = 930,000$; $\beta = 0.0004$; $\gamma = 26$; $\mu = 0.02$; $\varepsilon = 0$; $F_0 = \beta N/(\mu + \gamma) \approx 15.37$; $S_T = 65,050$.

Sources: Anderson and Nokes (1997, p. 702); own calculations.

The second example for (iii) abstracts from new births and from mortality ($\mu = 0$), but rather concentrates on the possibility that immunity is of short duration with $1/\varepsilon$ as the average duration of immunity and hence ε as the rate at which immunes 'regain' susceptibility. The respective equations then change into:

$$dS/dt = -\beta YS + \varepsilon Z \tag{4.26}$$

$$dY/dt = \beta SY - \gamma Y \qquad (4.27)$$

$$dZ/dt = \gamma Y - \varepsilon Z. \qquad (4.28)$$

The endemic equilibrium values now are:

$$Y^* = \frac{\varepsilon}{(\varepsilon + \gamma)}(N - S_T) \qquad (4.29)$$

$$Z^* = \frac{\gamma}{\varepsilon} Y^*. \qquad (4.30)$$

A simulation of this second case of (iii) is found in Figure 4.7.

Figure 4.7   Persistence of an infection (renewal due to waning immunity)

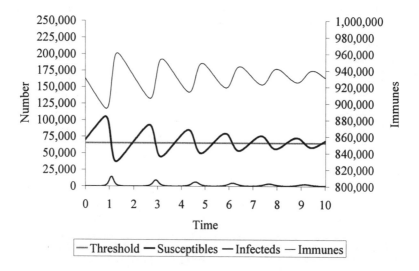

| —Threshold —Susceptibles —Infecteds —Immunes |

Notes: The conditions for the persistence of an infection in a community when renewal of susceptibles is due to waning immunity are at time $t = 1$: $S = 70,000$; $Y = 1$; $Z = 930,000$;
$\beta = 0.0004$; $\gamma = 26$; $\mu = 0.05$; $\varepsilon = 0.05$; $F_0 = \beta N/(\mu + \gamma) \approx 15.37$; $S_T = 65,050$.

Sources: Anderson and Nokes (1997, p. 702); own calculations.

4.3.3 Illness and Recovery in a Two-Agent-(Dis)Equilibrium Setting

A better understanding of contagion is provided when we concentrate on the
differences with regard to a composite *m* of main medical indicators –

temperature, blood pressure, pulse frequency and blood composition (density of red blood cells, number of infected cells, percentage of infected cells and so on, see Anderson 1994, p. 474) of, say, two hypothetical patients i, j. When two individuals of comparable characteristics (age, size and so on) are both healthy, key medical indicators for the functioning of their organisms tend to show little difference (*first equilibrium*):

$$m_i^* \cong m_j^* . \qquad (4.31)$$

If one of the two individuals suffers an infection, the difference in these indicators will shoot up quickly:

$$m_i(t) \neq m_j(t) . \qquad (4.32)$$

Contagion will have been effective if we observe a strong tendency of those indicators to pursue a similar though lagged pattern in the following, as depicted in Figure 4.8. After recovery of both individuals has begun, the indicators tend to normalize. In the hopefully new, *second equilibrium* the indicators of both individuals will resemble each other as they did at the time of the *first equilibrium*. Note that 'illness' is treated as a temporary all-time-high scenario for the respective indicators $m_i(t)$, $m_j(t)$.

Figure 4.8 Illness and recovery in a two-patient setting

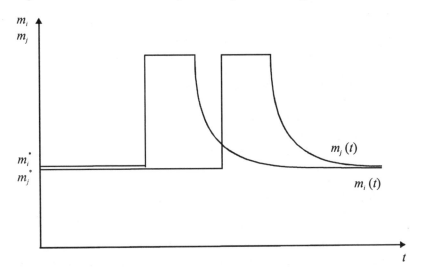

Source: Own compilation.

4.3.4 How to Deal with the Identification Problem?

With the help of the sequence depicted in Figure 4.9, which is nothing but a three-individual overlapping time profile of an infection, we may try to avoid the so-called 'identification problem' in epidemiology: 'when differential vulnerability to an unobserved common shock[10] reflects unobserved characteristics, we may get what looks like true contagion, since a crisis in one country will be followed by a crisis in another, with no apparent explanation than the original crisis itself' (Drazen 1999, p. 5).

Figure 4.9   The overlapping time profile of an infection (three individuals)

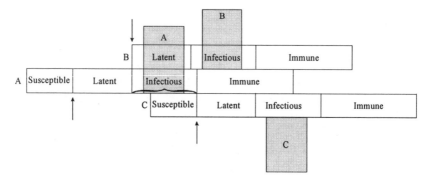

Source: Own compilation.

Individual A can – as the example was designed – at most transmit the disease to B and C; however, we cannot be sure a priori if individual C was infected by A or by B! When time-series data were available, we would have to apply Granger causality tests. Notice that when B (A) Granger causes the infection of C (only B), we have 'latent domino effects' (see above).

A problem with 'contagion' in economics, however, is that we have to identify the time durations within each of the identified classes in Figure 4.1 and 4.9! If we think about contagion among investors in the sense of herding (see above), for instance, it is most likely that we have to deal with much shorter time intervals.

4.3.5 What about Exogenous Immunization and other Means of Prevention?

So far so good; doctors of medicine *and* economists would be delighted if they could rely on the endogenous process of immunization described above. However, in many cases, severe infections require means of prevention and exogenous immunization. Note that exogenous immunization (either active or passive) is one of the possible prevention instruments. Other means of prevention against infection from microparasites among individuals are hygiene, quality controls of water and air, the removal and recycling of dust, and food hygiene.

A synonymous term for exogenous immunization is vaccination; to eradicate an infection by mass vaccination it is indispensable that the proportion of the population successfully immunised, v, exceeds a critical value v_C, where:

$$v_C = 1 - 1/S_0 \qquad (4.33)$$

so that too few susceptibles remain to perpetuate transmission, that is:

$$S < S_T. \qquad (4.34)$$

Therefore, the larger the value F_0, the higher the coverage (v_C) needed to eliminate infection, *ceteris paribus*!

4.4 A REINTERPRETATION OF 'CONTAGION' AS A TERM IN ECONOMICS

4.4.1 The Insights Gained from Epidemiology

A major lesson that contagion literature in economics can learn from epidemiology is first, to differentiate painstakingly between infections without epidemic (i), transitory epidemic (ii), and epidemic oscillations around an endemic equilibrium (iii). Second, it should be clear that the first case is not of much relevance for economics, whereas the second and the third are of considerable relevance. Third, it seems to me, however, that there is to the best of my knowledge not a single contribution in the contagion literature which distinguishes – as there should be – between cases (ii) and (iii)!

4.4.2 Towards a Useful Definition

First of all: what is (are) the disease(s) we are talking about? We are interested in economic crises triggered by financial market and exchange rate crises, the latter defined 'broadly to include not only devaluations but also successful defence of a peg that involves substantial increases in interest rates and losses of reserves' (Masson 1998, p. 4).

As our analysis has shown, 'contagion' is a term which has its own 'merits': contrary to the notions of 'spill-over effects', 'spreading' and so on, it clearly points at a *negative* (though in most cases pecuniary) *externality*. It makes no sense to link the notion of contagion to positive externalities, like, for example, Calvo and Reinhart (1995, p. 14) do, or to introduce a degree of unnecessary ambiguity like Eichengreen et al. (1996, p. 469) when they claim that 'contagion is selective: the shock to the center spills over negatively to some members of the periphery but positively to others'.

The statement that 'countries may have been affected by the occurrence of a similar external shock' (Alba et al. 1998, p. 53) or 'face common external shocks' (Fratzscher 1998, p. 667) to their economic fundamentals is a clear case of 'similarities in changes in underlying external conditions' for the countries in question, but *not* at all a case of contagion (see, for a similar judgement, Eichengreen et al. 1996, p. 474)![11] Also, it is unconvincing to state that 'contagion is ... [an] increased market co-movement which can not be explained' (Forbes and Rigobon 1999, p. 7) by channels which interlink the economic fundamentals of different countries. A change in investors' expectations, the correlation of bad memories or the interdependent political economy of central bankers' decisions may be signals for contagion but could well be just the cause of a common infection. Hence, one should emphasize that contagion is in essence a process where the markets/countries which are no-first-victim cases and are hit by developments outside their control have fundamentals unrelated (Calvo and Mendoza 1999, p. 3) to the sources of the disease.

A change in 'cross-market linkages' or a strengthening of 'international propagation mechanisms' (ibid., p. 8) during periods of market turmoil should not be confuse with contagion itself; they merely stand for the (increased) aggressiveness of the virus in question and/or for a more intensive contagion process. It may just be the case that diseases or bad news do spread more or 'better' than good news. If increased real or financial linkages between markets were identical to contagion, why not call globalisation contagion?[12] We realize that the term would then lose its bite.

If contagion should become a meaningful notion in the field of modern economics, it can be well understood only as the direct or indirect *spreading of asymmetric negative stochastic shocks throughout interrelated economies*. The type of interrelationship can be, but does not have to be, a direct one. It may, for example, be intermediated by foreign investors (funds). This is a far more precise wording than 'country specific shocks which affect the economic fundamentals of other countries' (Forbes and Rigobon 1999, p. 3). And, as Uribe (1996, p. 18) has correctly stated, *before* contagion, domestic economic fundamentals of the subsequently infected countries are completely unrelated to the original shock(s). The nature of these shocks is ambivalent *ex ante*: they may reflect *single events* (acting as catalyst) like an increase in unemployment (fundamental crisis), but may also well come as *new information* (non-fundamental crisis)[13] and/or as a *shift in the interpretation*[14] *given to existing information* (Masson 1998, p. 4).[15] Of course, as Drazen puts it, 'as a contagion story, one must make clear what *new* information that is *relevant* to the second currency [or country] is being provided by the collapse of the first currency' (1999, p. 7). It is clear in economics that 'facts' do not exert more pressure than 'news' and the concomitant 'revision of expectations' (Masson 1998, p. 13). We know from the time-inconsistency literature that a rise in inflationary expectations worsens instantaneously the possible welfare outcomes, for instance in a game between the central bank and the private sector (see Maaß and Sell 1998, pp. 525–31).

Thus, we may define, following Levy-Yeyati and Ubide: a *fundamental contagion* (or *direct* contagion as we said above) may occur whenever countries have fundamental links with other countries, while a *non-fundamental contagion* (or *indirect* contagion as we said above) is triggered by non-fundamental factors such as 'swings in the investment sentiment [of investors] towards emerging markets as a whole' (1998, p. 16). Putting together the sources of contagion and the possible routes it can take, gives Table 4.1.

Table 4.1   A systematic categorization of 'contagion'

Nature of original shocks	Fundamental contagion (direct)	Non-fundamental contagion (indirect)
Single event	Example 1	Example 2
New information	Example 3	Example 4
New interpretation of old information	Example 5	Example 6

Source: Own compilation.

Let us first inspect in example 1 the onset of a single event-induced crisis in one country A which later on spreads to other countries B, C and so on: why unemployment in one country may easily give rise to a speculative attack on its currency is reported by Drazen:

[H]igh unemployment leads market participants to anticipate a future loosening of monetary policy, inducing speculation against the currency. The costs of defending the currency rise, due in part to the induced upward pressure on interest rates,[16] so that a country may in fact devalue where they would not have in the absence of speculative pressure. Hence the expectation of monetary loosening becomes self-fulfilling. (Drazen 1999, p. 9)

In the case of direct contagion, trade and financial flows between the country of origin of the crisis and its partners are responsible for 'contagion': in a fixed exchange rate regime, partners are affected by at least two negative pecuniary externalities, even if we abstract from capital flows: their exchange rate appreciates in nominal and in real terms, while the recession in country A dampens their own exports. Both effects draw on the foreign exchange reserves of their respective central banks. The credibility of the authorities to defend the new parity instead of confronting country A with an own devaluation, will, in fact, not be very high.[17]

The mechanism put forward above by Drazen – political contagion – is a good case of example 2: the belief of speculators about the true preferences of politicians with regard to fixed parities and/or a forthcoming monetary union ('integration') will be shattered after country A's realignment and will enhance the probability of speculative attacks on the exchange rate regimes of countries B, C and so on.

New information about institutional weaknesses (think of the almost permanent struggle between Russia's former President Yeltzin and the Duma), on political turbulences (remember the Colosio assassination in 1994 in Mexico), or on changed preferences among politicians (as was the case in Argentina (and Brazil) with regard to their (semi-)currency board during 1998 and 1999) 'invites' speculators to test the vulnerability of the respective currency. This case illustrates the origin of the contagion processes represented by examples 3 and 4.

The Asian Flu is perhaps a good case for the type of processes which followed the collapse of the Thai baht in July 1997 and serve to illustrate the origins of examples 5 and 6: information on Thailand's stumbling economy was already available by mid-/end of 1996 and the issue was raised, among others, by the then IMF director, Michel Camdessus.[18] However, it took another five or six months before this information was taken more seriously and speculators put pressure on the baht. More generally: 'Although some of the problems, such as corruption, had long been recognized, the new emphasis could have led to the belief that they were significantly worse than had been previously realized' (Furman and Stiglitz 1998, p. 7).

4.4.3 Transmission Channels

What about the main *transmission channels* of 'contagion'? In principle, there are as many transmission channels as there exist 'windows' from one country to the world economy. The majority of these are items collected and categorized in the balance of payments: trade of goods and services, capital account transactions (foreign direct investment (FDI), portfolio investment, official and private bank credits and so on), and foreign exchange market interventions by the domestic central bank (including re- and devaluation).

There are two types of *trade links* with relevance for contagion: bilateral trade among other countries and the infected country or competition between other countries and the infected country in a common third market (Kaminsky and Reinhart 1998, p. 20). As Choueiri and Kaminsky argue, 'while trade links have not increased substantially over the last decade, financial connections have surged, with capital flows in the 1990s averaging about 10 percent of GDP for many countries in East Asia and Latin America' (1999, p. 5). As far as the *trade channel* is concerned, Diwan and Hoekman make a distinction between price and income effects: a devaluation of one trade partner affects consumer and producer prices of the other (1999, p. 6); while lower consumer prices are good for households, producers will suffer from lower product prices if the two countries produce and export similar goods. Negative income effects may stem from a recession in one country which lowers its import demand and hence the export scope of the other country. In an extensive econometric study on 20 industrial countries for the time span between 1959 and 1993, Eichengreen and Rose found that 'trade, rather than revisions of expectations based on macroeconomic factors, has been the dominant channel of transmission for contagious crises for the bulk of the sample period' (1997, p. 33). However, the trade channel is not convincing in explaining the Asian Flu: Thailand's bilateral trade relationships with the most affected countries were simply too small 'to generate such wide-ranging contagion' (Goldstein 1998, p. 18).

The *financial or investment channel* may have different forms (see above); one aspect is foreign direct investment: a recession/sharp devaluation in one (perhaps large) country tends to reduce FDI outflows into other countries; a small country, on the contrary may become more attractive for FDI after a strong devaluation for large countries while other small countries may be put under pressure to follow (Diwan and Hoekman 1999, pp. 6–7). Another aspect is the role of common lenders, 'in particular commercial banks' (Kaminsky and Reinhart 1998, p. 7): if a bank is confronted 'with a marked rise in non-performing loans in one country it is likely to be called upon to reduce the overall risk of its assets by pulling out of other high risk projects elsewhere' (ibid., p. 15). A third aspect – which we have discussed extensively above in Sections 4.2.2 and 4.2.3 – is portfolio investment.

A third channel results from the *competitive dynamics of devaluation*: as 'one country after another in a region undergoes a depreciation of its currency, the countries that have not devalued experience a deterioration in competitiveness, which in turn makes their currencies more susceptible to speculative attacks' (Goldstein 1998, p. 19).

4.5 IMMUNIZATION AND/OR PREVENTION AGAINST CONTAGION?

What is 'immunization' in the context of the spreading of financial market and exchange rate crises: are those countries 'immune' that 'will not suffer an attack during turbulent times' (Tornell 1999, p. 2)?

Karmann raises the issue of an economy which may become 'immune against financial contagion' (1999, p. 2) or likewise may be equipped with a 'timely immunisation strategy against international financial rumour' (ibid.); by this he means the capability of a country to be provided with buffers 'absorbing financial turbulences' (ibid.). As a matter of fact, he diagnoses that 'foreign [exchange] reserves seem to play a major role in an immunisation strategy' (ibid.). The *immunization* strategy is also related to exchange rate policy as he finds it possible to detect an 'immune' exchange rate path (ibid. p. 3).

However, immunization should not be confused with *prevention*: while there are cases where immunization is exogenous and serves as a part of the primary stage of prevention, in other cases it is an endogenous process and is not at all related to prevention. Lane defines prevention in economic terms as a means of avoiding 'the build-up of vulnerabilities' (1999, p. 5) to contagious economic crises. As examples of preventive measures he enumerates 'maintenance of sound economic policies ... improved financial supervision and regulation ... transparency ... and strengthened international surveillance with closer monitoring of the financial sector' (ibid., p. 5).

It is a much discussed matter whether *capital controls* of different degree can help to prevent the onset and/or the spreading of economic crises; as Levy-Yeyati and Ubide claim, there may be contradictory recommendations to first-victim countries and to non-first-victim countries: the first countries may be worse off if they restrict 'portfolio investment by preventing liquid international investors from operating in the local equity markets and exacerbate the impact of a financial crisis on asset values' (Levy-Yeyati and Ubide 1998, p. 4). The reason for this is that foreigners are less sensitive to disturbances in the home country than are less-diversified and hence overreacting local investors, with the consequence that they play a stabilizing role during crisis episodes (ibid., p. 51). The opposite is true for their role in making the crisis spread: if healthy economies 'happen to be in the same asset group as the crisis country' (ibid.), analogous behaviour among the investors 'would increase the probability and the extent of the contagion' (ibid.).

An often-cited means of prevention is 'that policymakers should try to ensure that they avoid a certain range of fundamentals, for instance, by reducing their exposure to short-maturity, foreign exchange debt, by avoiding a severe real appreciation of the currency and by fostering the domestic banking system' (Tornell 1999, p. 6). Also, it is said that the vulnerability to contagion 'is greater when there is a large (floating rate) debt, when reserves are low and when the trade balance is in deficit' (Masson 1998, p. 13). But strengthening macroeconomic policies and improving public debt *management* (Mussa et al, 1999, p. 2) is not enough. There is also need for *institutional* reforms.

Vulnerability may be reduced by strengthening financial regulation, improving the legal framework governing relations between creditors and debtors, enhancing data dissemination, doing away with implicit and explicit guarantees (ibid.) and so on. Encouraging more transparency and regulatory reforms in emerging markets can be promoted by the industrial countries 'by setting standards' (ibid.). These standards should include codes on 'accounting and auditing, the capital adequacy of banks, principles of bank and securities regulation, bankruptcy laws, and reporting of data by national governments' (ibid.).

If we disregard for a moment the capital controls issue (see above), we may say that open markets will force countries to choose between the extremes of a flexible exchange rate regime on the one hand and moving to a single currency in a monetary union on the other. As the majority of recent and less recent theoretical and empirical contributions have shown, anything between full flexibility of the exchange rate and totally fixed parities (as is the case with a monetary union) is prone to give rise to speculative attacks and, hence to 'contagion', under certain circumstances.

Contagious currency crises can be 'circumvented' (almost by definition) if the countries in question decide to build a monetary union; as De Grauwe pointed out years ago, a monetary union is the only credible fixed exchange rate arrangement (1992, pp. 53–5). However, the question remains if and how an asymmetric shock spreads within the common currency area. Unless it is an optimum currency area (see Mundell 1961), the likelihood of those countries leaving the monetary union if the common monetary policy is unable to cover their specific, possibly asymmetric economic problems or, on the contrary, to insulate one's own economy from the developments in different countries, remains positive, greater than zero.

One answer to the foregoing analysis could read: provided that countries of various regions decide to build a monetary union and the currency area in question meets the optimum currency area criteria, the participating regions are prepared to accommodate negative interregional shocks. Of course, this is no answer for the question of how to insulate from shocks coming from outside the monetary union. If the union as a whole maintains a flexible exchange rate *vis-à-vis* the rest of the world, then the incidence of speculative attacks against the union's currency is not an issue. But then we are brought back to an old, perhaps unsolved issue: how well and to what extent are flexible exchange rates capable of insulating economies from the turmoils in other parts of the world economy?

4.6 SUMMARY AND CONCLUSIONS

In this chapter, our primary aim was to impose some order and classification on to the fast-growing literature on the phenomenon of 'contagion' in economics. As we have shown, it is worthwhile learning from epidemiology basic terms and mechanisms of infection and the transmission of infectious diseases before applying these notions to problems in the field of international finance and monetary economics. This, however, is only a first step and there are a huge variety of possible 'adaptations', 'translations' and son on from epidemiology to economics. A prerequisite for doing so must be to forget about 'naive' and/or 'intuitive' applications of well-defined terms from epidemiology in the field of financial market and/or currency crises and their possible spread to other economies. Also, it should be taken into account that there are many different sources of 'contagion' in economics which go far beyond the occurrence of single events like new information or a new interpretation of old information. Besides direct or fundamental contagion, there are a number of indirect or non-fundamental channels of contagion such as the swing in the sentiments of (un)informed investors – both in the perception of risk and the willingness to bear it (Furman and Stiglitz 1998, p. 14) – or the uncertainty among domestic agents about when an expected event is going to happen effectively/which information from a non-first-victim country should be taken as relevant.

There is a long way to go, though. The economics profession should invest its skills in exploring much more carefully the nature of transitory crises *vis-à-vis* persistent/latent epidemic crises with an endemic equilibrium. This implies the need to identify the key variables for which there possibly exist 'threshold levels' along the lines defined in epidemiology. When these are exceeded, the likelihood that an epidemic crisis will start will be much higher than otherwise. In a way, this methodological procedure should replace early warning systems that were used and still are in use today.

NOTES

1. Ito, in a comment on Eichengreen and Rose, describes their paper as the 'detective work of two doctors fighting an epidemic of financial crises. Determining whether the disease (financial crisis) is contagious, caused by a virus, or non-contagious but caused by an environmental change like a heat wave is the problem' (Ito 1997, p. 51).
2. Calvo and Reinhart speak of 'spill-over or contagion effects' (1995, p. 1).
3. Though making use of a related terminology, these approaches are not 'pure' portfolio-based explanations, but rather models of market imperfections (Schinasi and Smith 1999, p. 5).
4. Maaß and Sell (1998) show in a time (in)consistency framework of central banks, why and when it may be 'rational' for a large proportion of investors, that is, the public, to remain by and large uninformed.
5. Krugman played with this hypothesis in 1997 when he blamed the Asian dragons for basing their 'economic miracle' more on 'transpiration than on inspiration', which can be translated into the economics language as a loss in the capacity to detect one's own comparative competitive advantage.
6. Leverage can be interpreted as debt 'financing of investment positions, including margined positions' (Schinasi and Smith 1999, p. 6).
7. It will be worthwhile, later on, to reconsider traditional criteria for optimum currency areas in the tradition of Bob Mundell's seminal paper of 1961, as to what degree they are related to the transmission channels of 'contagion'.
8. If, for instance, $R_0 = 5$, then, in equilibrium, $x^* = 0.2$.
9. The other option is to assume 'that immunity is of short duration such that individuals leave the immune class Z to re-enter the susceptible class at a per capita rate ε where $1/\varepsilon$ is the average duration of immunity' (Anderson and Nokes 1996, p. 238).
10. Eichengreen et al. call this phenomenon a 'disease conducive nature of the environment' (1996b, p. 482).
11. Masson has come up with the term 'monsoonal effects' to distinguish those phenomena strictly from contagion (1998).
12. Calvo and Mendoza are among the very few authors who make a clear distinction between globalization and contagion: 'globalization exacerbates contagion because the indeterminacy range widens as the market grows' (1999, p. 2).
13. For example, news about the creditworthiness of a sovereign borrower may affect the spreads charged to others (Calvo and Reinhart 1995, p. 6).
14. The so-called 'wake up call' (Goldstein 1998) among investors can serve as an example.
15. By including all of the mentioned varieties, our definition is much broader than the one given by Paul Masson who only accepts 'changes in expectations that are not related to changes in a country's macroeconomic fundamentals' to be 'pure contagion' (1998, p 5).
16. Note that interest rate pressure can motivate the authorities to give up even a currency board, which at first glance seems to be 'immune' to speculative attacks.
17. See the next chapter for a more thorough discussion of fundamental links and channels between economies vulnerable to speculative attacks.
18. 'Doubts about Thailand began to grow from 1996 – right up to the onset of the crisis, including the IMF, the World Bank, the financial rating agencies, and most independent economists' (Radelet 1998, p. 119).

5. A Simple Model of Contagious Financial Crises

5.1 INTRODUCTION

In the following our aim is to consider all the insights gained so far for the construction of a simple model albeit capable of reflecting some of the main economic transmission channels of contagion and at the same time consistent with the 'rules' of epidemiology. Many contributions in the relevant literature served as examples and background (Flood and Marion 2000; Gangopadhyay and Singh 2000; Jeanne and Masson 2000; Corsetti et al. 1999; Drazen 1999; Irvin and Vines 1999; Tornell 1999; Agénor and Masson 1999; Buiter et al. 1998; Chang and Velasco 1998a, 1998b; Edwards 1998; Yan 1998; Ozkan and Sutherland 1998; Bensaid and Jeanne 1997; Obstfeld 1996; Drazen and Masson 1994; Devarajan and Rodrik 1992; Girton and Roper 1977). But none of these excellent contributions had such an extraordinary influence on the design of this chapter as the papers of Sachs et al. (1996b) and Velasco (1996).

While we have identified in our earlier chapters the main factors responsible for the onset of a financial market crisis in an individual country – Mexico, Thailand and the Czech Republic served as reference cases here – the purpose is now to incorporate a 'key features' economy into a reduced model world where transmission of financial crises is possible and likely. For this purpose, remember that a financial crisis is a sort of a mix of an exchange rate (or likewise a balance of payments crisis), a foreign debt and a banking crisis. The theoretically most appealing but at the same time most challenging case for exemplifying 'contagion' is not the 'Tequilazo' the 'Asian Flu' or the 'Brazilian Samba' (see above). It is the 'Russian Virus' which spread to Latin American countries in general and to Brazil in particular in the late summer/autumn of 1998. As we have indicated above, this case is most proximate to what the economics profession nowadays generally calls 'pure contagion': the two countries are not in a common geographic or economic area, they have few economic ties with each other, and they are quite different in that Brazil is an advanced, newly industrializing economy while Russia is the most turbulent economy in transition one can find in the eastern hemisphere.

Basically the model to be presented below will draw on the application of game theory in the field of international macroeconomics in the tradition of Hamada (1974), Rogoff (1985), Canzoneri and Henderson (1991) and Currie and Levine (1993). Our analysis starts with the premise that it is either exchange rate pressure or the devaluation itself in one of the countries (player 1) which triggers the contagious effects on the other country (player 2). Both countries are small measured by their absolute and relative 'power' on the world's goods and financial markets. Also there is a third or 'foreign' (rather passive) player involved, which is the US economy (player *). Both countries (1, 2) have an exchange rate target (zone) *vis-à-vis* the US dollar and a large amount of both internal debt (which is denominated in local currency) and of foreign debt (which is denominated in US dollars).

Direct trade and financial linkages between the two players are weak. However, indirect linkages are strong: both compete on third markets with semi-finished and finished products, with the goods being invoiced in US dollars. This gives room to 'trade contagion effects'. At the same time, bonds, bank credits and/or shares in the respective stock markets of players 1, 2 are in the portfolios of international (*) investors (or funds of investors). For the sake of simplicity one may think of these investors as coming exclusively from the US. The international interest rate net of spreads and fees is given for both emerging economies. However, the emerging market spread on the one hand, and the country-specific spread on the other, are endogenous and change during a financial crisis. The idea of a spread element in the interest rate which accrues to emerging markets, but not to industrialized countries (with developing countries having a different, though in most cases even higher spread) goes explicitly beyond the Stiglitz–Weiss framework of signalling (adverse selection, incentive effects) in a world of asymmetric information. However, in the light of the experiences in the 1990s, this assumption fits well with the reality on international financial markets.

This allows for the present of 'financial contagion effects'. These can take different forms, such as 'wake-up calls' or portfolio reallocation, and they can also put an end to herding behaviour and so on. The domestic banking sector in the country from where the virus leaps (1, Russia) is in bad shape. The reasons for this can be traced back to our earlier explanations for the onset of a financial market crisis ('third generation models'). This, in turn, is not necessarily the case in the country affected by the spreading virus (2, Brazil). Both countries make use of interest and foreign exchange reserve policy to defend their currencies against speculative attacks, as assumed in our model for the onset of financial market crises and is also obvious in our selective empirical findings.

While we have shown above that contagion basically consists in the transmission of shocks (new events, new information, new interpretation of old information) this statement does not imply that the onset and the spreading of financial crises comes as an unforeseen 'catastrophe' to policymakers. On the contrary, as the studies of the rouble and the real crises have revealed, it is well established that the decision-making process before, during and after a financial market crisis follows optimizing (mainly non-cooperative) strategies by the governments involved. This supposition is consistent with the logic of the so-called 'second generation models' (Obstfeld 1996; Velasco 1996), where multiple equilibria and self-fulfilling expectations figure prominently. Note, therefore, that third generation-type models serve to identify the mechanism for the onset of financial market crises, but second generation-type reasoning also contributes to the explanation of 'contagion'.

Epidemiology has worked out a nice 'catalogue' for contagious diseases. There can be either (i) no epidemic, (ii) transitory epidemic or (iii) persistence or latent epidemic with an endemic equilibrium. Some of these important distinctions should be captured by the model. As we have seen above, for each of these scenarios there are key variables. One is the *force of infection*, another is the *basic reproductive rate*, and a crucial one is the existence of *threshold values* for the number of susceptibles in a given population. These notions, of course, cannot be translated 'one to one' into the language of economic modelling. It remains to be seen how we can integrate their content into a framework of contagious economic diseases. However, the insight from epidemiology, that in equilibrium the effective rate of reproduction is just one (see Chapter 4), helps to defend the working hypothesis that modelling 'contagion' implies no more than a two-country case! Also, the notion of being 'susceptible' to a financial market crisis is obviously linked to the factors examined in Chapter 3 as there were, for example, an overvalued exchange rate, an ongoing lending boom, implicit bailout clauses in favour of the domestic banking system and so on.

The structure of this chapter is the following. In the next section we shall introduce first the stylized facts in the sequencing of contagious financial crises of the Russia–Brazil type. This will help us to determine the number of periods necessary in the modelling part in order to capture the main features of contagion. It should also help us to identify the character of the game the respective governments are playing during a contagion process. After that, the first-victim country will be modelled in detail. We go beyond the 'onset of the financial market crisis' put forward in Chapter 3 and introduce a second phase (in a two-period decision problem) which ultimately leads to the collapse of the exchange rate regime. The rationality of contagion towards the second-victim country will be analysed in depth in Section 5.4. The exposition ends with a welfare analysis of the policy alternatives discussed and with concluding remarks.

5.2   THE CONTAGIOUS SETUP

If we recapitulate for a moment the chronicle of events in Russia and Brazil between July 1998 and January 1999 (see above), as far as the exchange rate policy is concerned, there is a clear three-step development of regime(s) changes:

1.   A narrow exchange rate band with a *fixed* central parity towards the US dollar is defended by means of foreign exchange intervention(s) of the central bank and by soaring short-term interest rates on the domestic money market. This regime will be designated *f*.
2.   A discretionary widening of the target zone corresponding to a devaluation of well above 10 per cent. Interventions on the foreign exchange market continue if necessary and short-term interest rates remain high. This regime will be designated *df*.
3.   Strong exchange rate pressure leads to the abandonment of the target zone. Interventions on the foreign exchange market cease, the domestic currency is *floated* and the central bank aims at reducing interest rates on the domestic money market. The domestic currency suffers severe losses on the foreign exchange market *vis-à-vis* the US dollar. This regime will be designated *dfl*.

The difference between phases (2) and (3) with regard to the currency depreciation is only gradual: the discretionary widening of the exchange rate band may result in a similar size of devaluation of the domestic currency as its possible subsequent floating. Before entering into the discussion of the contagion process itself, we shall first address the incentive structure for the policymakers in the country in which the 'first infection' or the onset of a financial market crisis, occurs. Given the sequencing of possible regime changes from above, we have to deal with a two-period decision problem in a three-period framework where period zero serves as the base line. We depart from the following assumptions:

1.   A government which has floated its currency in period t will always maintain the float in period $t+1$ unless it establishes a currency board. The latter possibility, however, will only be considered in the final part

of this chapter. Hence, in the first place, we follow here Ozkan and Sutherland, assuming 'that once a country has switched to a floating rate regime it cannot ... switch back into the fixed rate regime' (1998, p. 343).

2. A government which has widened its target zone around the central parity in period t and remains with the new band in period $t+1$ is considered as 'fixing' the exchange rate again in period $t+1$. If the government has widened the band once, the public will, however, possibly be reluctant to believe in a new fixing of the exchange rate.

3. A crawling exchange rate band regime, that is, a well-defined band with a regularly devaluing central parity, can increase its rates of devaluation, but can never return to a sustainable fixed rate.

4. As in Drazen and Masson (1994), it can be taken that exchange rate pressure will increase in period $t+1$, if exchange rate pressure was already prevalent in period t and if the government continues to refuse to devalue/float in period t without changing its monetary and fiscal policy.

5. A devaluation in the sense of significantly broadening a target zone can be applied only once. If it occurs in period t and there is need for a further devaluation in period $t+1$, the depreciation is then to be realized by letting the exchange rate float.

All in all there is a set of six effectively possible objective functions (from a total of nine) from which a government – facing strong exchange rate pressure – has to choose the one which minimises the expected value (E) of total welfare losses over the two relevant periods, given the above assumptions. It is understood that in the base period (0), the prevailing exchange rate regime is a narrow target zone which is designated a 'fixed regime' (f). Note that at this step we disregard a discount factor.

$$E(L_2^f + L_1^f) \tag{5.1}$$

$$E(L_2^{df} + L_1^f) \tag{5.2}$$

$$E(L_2^{dfl} + L_1^f) \tag{5.3}$$

$$E(L_2^{dfl} + L_1^{df}) \tag{5.4}$$

$$E(L_2^f + L_1^{df}) \tag{5.5}$$

$$E(L_2^{dfl} + L_1^{dfl}). \tag{5.6}$$

In our context cases (5.2), (5.3), (5.4) and (5.6) signal a severe financial crisis (in ascending order), whereas cases (5.1) and (5.5) stand for a government that withstands the exchange rate pressure. Contagion will be effective whenever strategies (5.2), (5.3), (5.4) or (5.6) dominate strategies (5.1) and (5.5) in the infected country (I) on the condition that the first-victim country (J) has chosen strategy (5.2), (5.3), (5.4) or (5.6). More precisely, strategy (5.4) was in fact the course taken by exchange rate policy first in Russia and, later on, also in Brazil.

The *observed* 'contagion' in our setting implies then that Brazil (country I) chooses strategy (5.4) *on the condition* that Russia (country J) does so (which implies that strategy (5.4) is the optimal strategy for Russia out of four *unconditional* strategies) and provided that this conditional strategy is optimal (minimizing the expected value of the sum of welfare losses) for Brazil in comparison to the *conditional strategies* (5.2), (5.3) and (5.6).

$$E^I(L_2^{dfl} + L_1^{df}) \big| E^J(L_2^{dfl} + L_1^{df}) < \begin{cases} E^I(L_2^{df} + L_1^{f}) \big| E^J(L_2^{dfl} + L_1^{df}) \\ E^I(L_2^{dfl} + L_1^{dfl}) \big| E^I(L_2^{dfl} + L_1^{df}) \\ E^I(L_2^{dfl} + L_1^{f}) \big| E^J(L_2^{dfl} + L_1^{df}). \end{cases} \quad (5.7)$$

Note, however, that the conditional strategy as stated in (1.7) is only one, albeit the most stringent case for 'contagion'. A thorough analysis of the contagion phenomenon within the framework of the time (in)consistency theory, will reveal more and also 'diversified' policy approaches.

5.3   THE FIRST-VICTIM COUNTRY

The government of the first-victim country will be assumed not to default on its liabilities, domestic or external. This assumption does not contradict the Russian moratorium of summer 1998 as this was active only temporarily. Also, it is assumed that the domestic public sector can borrow and lend on the international financial market at the market rate (Corsetti et al. 1998b, p. 7). For the base-line period zero we can presuppose either a balanced budget or a manageable fiscal deficit, with an exchange rate peg organized as a target zone. Part of the relevant literature for our subject claims that the main ingredients of the first generation models, as, for instance, the important role assigned to *fiscal deficits* and to *public debt*, are almost totally irrelevant for the explanation of recent financial crises. This argument, however, misses the point. Against the background of a policy of implicit government guarantees (see Chapter 3) towards the banking sector, fiscal deficits before a crisis may be low or even zero, but the bailouts represent a serious burden on the future fiscal balances. This insight is backed by the Chilean experiences (see Chapter 2 above), where the recorded public sector budget deficit was rather small for several years throughout 1981. *Ex post* it turned out that the public sector had been accumulating contingent liabilities towards foreign as well as domestic deposit holders (ibid., p. 13). Hence limited liability creates a sort of hidden public debt which has to be served effectively once the domestic banking crisis becomes obvious.

Monetary policy has to be consistent as well with the prevailing exchange rate regime in the base-line period. Raising inflation tax instead of ordinary taxes is inconsistent with a fixed exchange rate regime in the strict sense. A fixed exchange rate regime in the base-line period zero can hence be taken as an empty target zone (see Chapter 2). This is so because under a fixed exchange rate regime the rate of monetary growth must be zero, and hence inflation tax revenues, if the world's monetary growth rate is normalized at zero.

The timing of the financial market crisis in the first-victim country is as follows: as explained in Chapter 3, foreign depositors will 'sell' their holdings in the domestic banking sector once the expected rate of devaluation exceeds the relevant interest differential. The government will react according to a constrained loss minimization problem with a defence of the central parity or with a devaluation made effective by a broadening of the target zone. As in our model for the onset of a financial market crisis (Chapter 3), foreign exchange reserves play a crucial role. There is a threshold level for these: 'as soon as reserves hit the threshold that triggers a financial crisis, the government needs to mobilize resources to finance its bailout plans' (ibid., p. 18). That is, foreign creditors will only accept the refinancing of domestic firms/banks against public guarantees in so far as the stock of official reserves remains about some minimum threshold. The overall loss function associates devaluations with welfare losses (see Sachs et al. 1996b). This is the first stage or, in other words, the 'onset' of the financial market crisis in the first-victim country where financial panic by *foreign investors* triggers a banking and a foreign exchange/exchange rate crisis. At this time foreign creditors are either unwilling to provide further credit to the domestic financial sector or they will provide it only under the condition of an expected total bailout of the government. Hence, large parts of the domestic financial sector are on the brink of bankruptcy unless the government 'intervenes by absorbing the difference between foreign private liabilities and domestic capital'[1] (Corsetti et al. 1998b, p. 7).

As shown above, the domestic financial sector is then left with a large amount of bad debts and an enormous shortage of liquidity. This makes it necessary for the government to instigate rescue actions. Once the reserves hit the critical threshold level, the government has to think about mobilizing resources for the rescue of the domestic financial sector. However, the government's transfer payments for such a rescue have to respect the public finance constraint of the government. This gives rise to the second stage of the financial market crisis.

The currency side of this second part of the financial crisis can now be understood as a consequence of the anticipated fiscal costs of financial restructuring, which generate expectations of a partial monetization of future fiscal deficits and a fall in economic activity induced by the required structural adjustment among *domestic agents* (ibid., pp. 3–4). These agents rationally expect that if the first part of a financial crisis materializes (see above), the government chooses to intervene and to validate agents' expectations of a bailout. These transfers to the domestic financial sector either cause or enlarge an existing fiscal deficit (ibid., pp. 8–9). Hence, in a multi-period setting, fiscal imbalances and the associated ways of financing them by ordinary taxes or by the inflation tax have to be modelled explicitly. In what concerns the overall loss function (see below), it is assumed that a low ordinary tax regime is *ceteris paribus* preferred to a high tax regime by the government. In this second phase of the financial crisis, the target zone for the exchange rate will definitely be violated and a sharp devaluation will occur once the currency is floated. Now, the defence of the central parity is no longer feasible because exchange rate pressure exceeds foreign exchange reserves beyond any threshold level.

The only means of avoiding this self-fulfilling expectations crisis would be if the government is able to set up a credible, permanent fiscal reform such that perspective tax revenues are sufficiently high and there is no need for seigniorage financing (ibid., p. 15).

5.3.1 The One-period Problem

In what follows, we make use of the excellent modelling work put forward by Velasco (1996) and Sachs et al. (1996b) which will be extended and modified considerably. At first we consider the problem in a one (base-line period) plus one (crisis period) framework. This crisis period is the period in which the target exchange rate collapses (see below).

The government faces the following budget constraint:

$$Rb_t + \theta(\pi_t^e - \pi_t) = x_t; \theta > 0 \qquad (5.8)$$

where R is the world real gross rate of interest which emerging markets have to afford. Note that this interest rate is not identical with the real interest rate which industrialized countries have to bear. For the moment we take R as exogenous to our emerging market economy and we assume any country-specific spread away. The variable *b* stands for the inherited stock of net foreign liabilities of the consolidated government (including the central bank). The actual rate of devaluation, π, will be identical with the actual rate of inflation, thus purchasing power parity prevails. Hence, the world inflation rate is assumed to be zero and, as stated above, an empty target zone is only sustainable at zero inflation in the domestic economy. Expected inflation corresponds to expected devaluation, π_t^e. The government can raise tax revenues amounting to *x*. The term $\theta(\pi_t - \pi_t^e)$ can be interpreted as inflation tax revenues (Velasco 1996, p. 1025). The government's objective or loss function which is to be minimized reflects the fact that governments in emerging markets dislike both devaluing (or, likewise inflating) and raising taxes. Devaluing means destroying the credibility of the exchange rate regime while raising taxes jeopardizes the re-election of the incumbent. Presidential campaigns in Russia as well as in Brazil during the 1990s tend to confirm this view quite impressively.

$$L = \frac{1}{2}(\alpha \pi_t^2 + x_t^2); \ \alpha > 0. \tag{5.9}$$

When taking the expectations of the public (domestic and foreign) as given, the government minimizes (5.9) subject to (5.8) and gets the discretionary, time-consistent solution for the control variables π and *x*:

$$\pi_t = \frac{\theta}{\alpha + \theta^2}(Rb_t + \theta \pi_t^e); \ \theta > 0 \tag{5.10}$$

$$x_t = \frac{\alpha}{\alpha + \theta^2}(Rb_t + \theta \pi_t^e). \tag{5.11}$$

The corresponding loss of devaluing and cheating (see superscript *c*) for the policymakers (introducing (5.10) and (5.11) into (5.9)) is:

$$L^c(b_t) = \frac{1}{2}\left(\frac{\alpha}{\alpha + \theta^2}\right)(Rb_t + \theta \pi_t^e)^2. \tag{5.12}$$

Using

$$0 < \lambda \equiv \frac{\alpha}{\alpha + \theta^2} < 1 \tag{5.13}$$

we can rewrite (5.10), (5.11) and (5.12) to get

$$\pi_t^c = \pi_t = \frac{(1-\lambda)}{\theta}(Rb_t + \theta\pi_t^e) \tag{5.14}$$

$$x_t^c = x_t = \lambda(Rb_t + \theta\pi_t^e) \tag{5.15}$$

$$L^c(b_t) = \frac{1}{2}\lambda(Rb_t + \theta\pi_t^e)^2. \tag{5.16}$$

If the public has rational expectations $(E(\pi_t) = \pi_t^e)$, we take the expectations of (5.14) to achieve the 'taking the medicine' solution (see Maaß and Sell 1998, p. 530) for the government:

$$\pi_t^e = \frac{(1-\lambda)}{\theta}(Rb_t + \theta\pi_t^e) = \frac{(1-\lambda)}{\theta\lambda}Rb_t \tag{5.17}$$

and hence with superscript *t* for the taking the medicine solution

$$\pi_t^t = \pi_t = \frac{(1-\lambda)}{\theta\lambda}Rb_t. \tag{5.18}$$

Because of the budget constraint and $\pi_t^t = \pi_t^e$, taxes now are:

$$x_t^t = Rb_t. \tag{5.19}$$

The corresponding loss for the government equals:

$$L^t = \frac{1}{2\lambda}(Rb_t)^2. \tag{5.20}$$

If the government instead sticks to its pre-commitment to maintain the target exchange rate (see superscript *f* for 'fixing'), we get the time-inconsistent 'rule' solution:

$$\pi_t^f = \pi_t = 0 \tag{5.21}$$

which, because of the budget constraint implies:

$$x_t^f = x_t = Rb_t + \theta\pi_t^e. \tag{5.22}$$

The corresponding loss of not devaluing is then:

$$L^f(b_t) = \frac{1}{2}(Rb_t + \theta\pi_t^e)^2.\tag{5.23}$$

Assume the government has cheated already on the exchange rate target and wants to regain its reputation (see superscript r). Hence it follows that

$$\pi_t^r = \pi_t = 0\tag{5.24}$$

$$x_t^r = x_t = Rb_t + \theta\pi_t^e.\tag{5.25}$$

and the final loss for the government is

$$L^r(b_t) = \frac{1}{2\lambda^2}(Rb_t)^2.\tag{5.26}$$

As in the famous seminal paper of Barro and Gordon (1983), it holds that if and only if $\lambda < 1$:[2]

$$L^r > L^t > L^f > L^c.\tag{5.27}$$

Hence it is obvious when disregarding trigger mechanisms that the government is tempted to devalue in period t provided it can count on no-devaluation expectations among the public ($\pi_t^e = 0$). If it cannot, then (5.27) shows that it would be better staying with the fixed regime. In Table 5.1 we have systematized the different pay-offs in matrix form.

Table 5.1   Pay-off matrix of different regimes in the one-period approach

Public	Government	
	$\pi_t = 0$	$\pi_t = \dfrac{(1-\lambda)}{\theta\lambda} Rb_t$
$\pi_t^e = 0$	$L^f(b_t) = \dfrac{1}{2}(Rb_t)^2$	$L^c(b_t) = \dfrac{1}{2}\lambda(Rb_t)^2$
$\pi_t^e = \dfrac{(1-\lambda)}{\theta\lambda} Rb_t$	$L^r(b_t) = \dfrac{1}{2\lambda^2}(Rb_t)^2$	$L^t(b_t) = \dfrac{1}{2\lambda}(Rb_t)^2$

Source: Own compilation.

As in Velasco (1996) and Sachs et al. (1996b) one may argue with the associated costs which accrue after 'engineering' a surprise devaluation. Let us call these costs C. Cheating, that is, devaluation, then is only profitable as long as:

$$L^c(b_t, \pi_t^e) + C < L^f(b_t, \pi_t^e). \tag{5.28}$$

Hence, the following inequality must be satisfied:

$$\frac{1}{2\lambda}(Rb_t + \theta\pi_t^e)^2 + C < \frac{1}{2}(Rb_t + \theta\pi_t^e)^2. \tag{5.29}$$

After some manipulation we achieve:

$$Rb_t + \theta\pi_t^e > \kappa, \text{ where } \kappa \equiv \frac{\sqrt{2C}}{\sqrt{1-\lambda}} > 0. \tag{5.30}$$

'Hence, a devaluation will occur in equilibrium whenever inherited debt or expectations of devaluation are sufficiently high' (Sachs et al. 1996b, p. 270). This statement can, however, be qualified further so that the existence of multiple equilibria in the tradition of Obstfeld (1986, 1996) emerges. Remember (see (5.17)) that it is rational to build expectations according to:

$$\theta\pi_t^e = \begin{cases} 0 & \text{if } Rb_t \leq \kappa \\ \dfrac{(1-\lambda)}{\lambda} Rb_t & \text{if } Rb_t > \kappa. \end{cases} \tag{5.31}$$

The lower term in the brace can now be introduced into condition (5.30):

$$Rb_t + \frac{(1-\lambda)}{\lambda} Rb_t > \kappa. \tag{5.32}$$

The respective expectations will be fulfilled (only) if: $Rb_t > \lambda\kappa$. In contrast, as long as $Rb_t \leq \lambda\kappa$ the devaluation expectations of the public will never be validated by the government. Hence it is not rational for the public to expect devaluation when the exchange rate regime is fully credible. For levels of debt larger than $\lambda\kappa$ but no larger than κ (here a devaluation will inevitably take place) a devaluation will (not) become effective if the agents (do not) expect a devaluation according to (5.18)!

The costs associated with devaluation now are:

$$L'(b_t) = \frac{1}{2\lambda}(Rb_t)^2 + C. \tag{5.33}$$

If an equilibrium with no devaluation materializes, the costs remain:

$$L^f(b_t) = \frac{1}{2}(Rb_t)^2. \tag{5.34}$$

When comparing (5.34) with (5.33), we realise that within a one-period decision problem, a fixing strategy strictly dominates a 'taking the medicine' strategy.

5.3.2 The Two-period Problem

We shall now proceed to a two-period framework, so that the subsequent aspects of a typical financial market crisis in an emerging market (see above) can be traced appropriately. Our former present period t will now be called the second period while the previous or first period will be $t-1$. During this period – as we said above – the government observes the occurrence of financial panic among foreign investors as well as a liquidity squeeze in the domestic financial sector. This forces the government to a flow of forced fiscal spending due to contingent liabilities. The corresponding variable, z_t, is stochastic *ex ante*, that is, before the government realizes the extent of the rescue actions to be taken. It is assumed that z is distributed with mean $\bar{z}$ and variance σ^2. $\bar{z}$ can be thought of as an exogenous government income (profits from state banks and other public financial intermediaries) which the government extracts only when confronted with a turmoil in the financial sector and the need to finance rescue actions. Hence $\bar{z}$ is not relevant in the second period t. The random variable $z_{t-1} - \bar{z}$ has mean zero (Velasco 1996, p. 1025). The budget constraint for the previous period will be linked to the present period in the following way:

$$Rb_{t-1} + (z_{t-1} - \bar{z}) + \theta(\pi_{t-1}^e - \pi_{t-1}) - x_{t-1} = b_t. \tag{5.35}$$

This implies that new debt b_t must be incurred in the second period, whenever:

$$Rb_{t-1} + (z_{t-1} - \bar{z}) + \theta(\pi_{t-1}^e - \pi_{t-1}) - x_{t-1} > 0 \tag{5.36}$$

which implies that:

$$\theta(\pi_{t-1} - \pi_{t-1}^e) < Rb_{t-1} + (z_{t-1} - \bar{z}) - x_{t-1}. \tag{5.37}$$

The new objective function of the government now reads:

$$\frac{1}{2}\sum_{s=t-1}^{t}\frac{\alpha\pi_t^2 + x_t^2}{R^{(s-t+1)}}, \quad \alpha > 0. \tag{5.38}$$

We assume in the first case that the policymaker decides to devalue (or likewise to broaden the target zone) in period $t-1$; agents with rational expectations will then also expect a devaluation for the following period t. The corresponding expected devaluation rate is given by (5.17) and the associated loss by (5.20) if the policymaker decides *to take the medicine* in period t. A policymaker is then confronted in period $t-1$ to minimize (5.39) subject to (5.35):

$$L^t(b_{t-1}) = \min\left\{\frac{1}{2}(\alpha\pi_{t-1}^2 + x_{t-1}^2) + \frac{1}{2R\lambda}(Rb_t)^2 + C\right\}. \tag{5.39}$$

The first-order conditions are:

$$x_{t-1}^t = x_{t-1} = \frac{R}{\lambda}b_t \tag{5.40}$$

$$\pi_{t-1}^t = \pi_{t-1} = \frac{\alpha}{\theta}\frac{R}{\lambda}b_t. \tag{5.41}$$

Introducing (5.40) and (5.41) into (5.35) determines the optimal size of debt in the second period:

$$b_t^t = b_t = \frac{\lambda^2}{(\lambda^2 + R)}w_{t-1} \tag{5.42}$$

where

$$w_{t-1} \equiv Rb_{t-1} + z_{t-1} - \bar{z} + \theta\pi_{t-1}^e. \tag{5.43}$$

The term w_{t-1}, can be identified as 'the total amount of commitments the government faces at time $t-1$' (Sachs et al. 1996b, p. 274). This term is hence the larger,

1. the higher the relevant interest rate on inherited foreign debt;
2. the higher the contingent payments of the government due to a crisis in the domestic financial sector in the previous period;

3. the lower the exogenous flow of government income; and
4. the higher the devaluation expectations of the public in the previous period.

Using (5.42) we can rewrite (5.40) and (5.41) to become

$$x_{t-1}^t = \frac{\lambda R}{(\lambda^2 + R)} w_{t-1} \tag{5.44}$$

$$\pi_{t-1}^t = \frac{\alpha}{\theta} \frac{\lambda R}{(\lambda^2 + R)} w_{t-1}. \tag{5.45}$$

After introducing (5.40), (5.41) and (5.42) into (5.39), the corresponding loss now amounts to:

$$L^t(w_{t-1}) = \frac{1}{2} \frac{\lambda R}{(\lambda^2 + R)} w_{t-1}^2 + C. \tag{5.46}$$

We recognize that the losses associated with this strategy are the higher, the greater, *ceteris paribus*, the size of forced government spending on rescue actions in the domestic financial market, z_{t-1}, the more pronounced the prevailing exchange rate expectations, π_{t-1}^e and, last but not least, the higher the inherited debt, b_{t-1}, at a given real interest rate, R. These are, however, not all the choices for a government in period t which has devalued in period $t-1$: the government may decide on the rather costly strategy of *regaining its reputation* in period t, being aware of the fact that it has lost its standing and its credibility when devaluing in $t-1$:

$$L^r(b_{t-1}) = \min\left\{ \frac{1}{2}(\alpha\pi_{t-1}^2 + x_{t-1}^2) + \frac{1}{2R\lambda^2}(Rb_t)^2 + C \right\}. \tag{5.47}$$

Minimizing (5.47) subject to (5.35) gives the first-order conditions:

$$x_{t-1}^r = x_{t-1} = \frac{R}{\lambda^2} b_t \tag{5.48}$$

$$\pi_{t-1}^r = \pi_{t-1} = \frac{\alpha}{\theta} \frac{R}{\lambda^2} b_t. \tag{5.49}$$

Introducing (5.48) and (5.49) into (5.35) gives the now modified size of the 'optimal debt' in period t:

$$b_t^r = b_t = \frac{\lambda^3}{(\lambda^3 + R)} w_{t-1}.$$ (5.50)

Using (5.50) we can rewrite (5.48) and (5.49) to become

$$x_{t-1}^r = \frac{\lambda R}{(\lambda^3 + R)} w_{t-1}$$ (5.51)

$$\pi_{t-1}^r = \frac{\alpha}{\theta} \frac{\lambda R}{(\lambda^3 + R)} w_{t-1}.$$ (5.52)

Introducing (5.50), (5.51) and (5.52) into (5.47), we can compute the corresponding minimized loss function of the 'regaining reputation' strategy

$$L^r(w_{t-1}) = \frac{1}{2} \frac{\lambda R}{(\lambda^3 + R)} w_{t-1}^2 + C.$$ (5.53)

Let us now compare both strategies. First, we find that a strategy of regaining reputation in period t is associated with a lower 'optimal debt' in contrast to taking the medicine strategy; this can be verified easily by comparing (5.42) and (5.50):

$$b_t^r = \frac{\lambda^3}{(\lambda^3 + R)} w_{t-1} < \frac{\lambda^2}{(\lambda^2 + R)} w_{t-1} = b_t^t.$$ (5.54)

After some manipulation of (5.54) we can show that the inequality condition is met for and only for $\lambda < 1$. This always holds because of (5.13)!

Second, we see that the optimal tax as well as the optimal rate of devaluation in period $t-1$ is higher in a regaining reputation than in a taking the medicine strategy, if condition $\lambda < 1$ is fulfilled:

$$x_{t-1}^r = \frac{\lambda R}{(\lambda^3 + R)} w_{t-1} > \frac{\lambda R}{(\lambda^2 + R)} w_{t-1} = x_{t-1}^t$$ (5.55)

$$\pi_{t-1}^r = \frac{\alpha}{\theta} \frac{\lambda R}{(\lambda^3 + R)} w_{t-1} > \frac{\alpha}{\theta} \frac{\lambda R}{(\lambda^2 + R)} w_{t-1} = \pi_{t-1}^t.$$ (5.56)

Economically, it is interesting and at the same time reasonable that a government which devalues in the first period and then returns to a fixed rate in the second period in order to regain reputation, devalues its exchange rate and raises tax revenues in the first period more than a government which 'takes the medicine' and continues devaluing in the second period after the first devaluation in the first period. Why? Because if you give away again your instrument of devaluation in the second period, you are then deprived of inflation tax revenues, but you are still bound to respect the budget constraint in the second period, too.

However, everything remains ambiguous or at least incomplete as long as we do not compare the total two-period loss of the regaining reputation strategy with the total two-period loss of the taking the medicine strategy:

$$L^r(w_{t-1}) = \frac{1}{2}\frac{\lambda R}{(\lambda^3 + R)}w_{t-1}^2 + C > \frac{1}{2}\frac{\lambda R}{(\lambda^2 + R)}w_{t-1}^2 + C = L^t(w_{t-1}). \quad (5.57)$$

This again applies for and only for $\lambda < 1$, a fact we know from (5.13).

Moreover, the government faces two more options – which at the end of this section will be evaluated against the regaining reputation but also against the taking the medicine strategy: these options consist in fixing the exchange rate in period $t-1$ and then either to continue fixing the exchange rate ('following a non-discretionary rule') or then to devalue ('cheat after following a non-discretionary rule'). How credible the first of these options will be depends, among other things, on the size of the inherited debt.

We begin with the strategy of fixing the exchange rate in period $t-1$ and continuing to do so in period t; the associated loss function which has to be minimized is:

$$L^f(b_{t-1}) = \min\left\{\frac{1}{2}x_{t-1}^2 + \frac{1}{2R}(Rb_t)^2\right\}. \quad (5.58)$$

The first-order condition yields:

$$x_{t-1}^f = x_{t-1} = Rb_t. \quad (5.59)$$

Introducing $\pi_{t-1} = 0$ and (5.59) in (5.35) the 'optimal' debt in period t is:

$$b_t^f = b_t = \frac{1}{1+R}w_{t-1}, \quad (5.60)$$

hence

$$x_{t-1}^f = \frac{R}{1+R}w_{t-1}. \quad (5.61)$$

When considering (5.60) and (5.61) total losses amount to:

$$L^f(w_{t-1}) = \frac{1}{2}\frac{R}{(1+R)}w_{t-1}^2.$$

(5.62)

If the government, instead, decides to cheat, hence to devalue in the actual period t, the problem to be solved becomes:

$$L^c(b_{t-1}) = \min\left\{\frac{1}{2}x_{t-1}^2 + \frac{\lambda}{2R}(Rb_t)^2 + C\right\}.$$

(5.63)

The corresponding first-order condition now reads:

$$x_{t-1}^c = x_{t-1} = \lambda Rb_t.$$

(5.64)

Therefore, the corresponding debt in period t is:

$$b_t^c = b_t = \frac{1}{1+\lambda R}w_{t-1},$$

(5.65)

hence

$$x_{t-1}^c = \frac{\lambda R}{1+\lambda R}w_{t-1}.$$

(5.66)

The corresponding two-period loss is now equivalent to:

$$L^c(w_{t-1}) = \frac{1}{2}\frac{\lambda R}{(1+\lambda R)}w_{t-1}^2 + C.$$

(5.67)

Let us now compare both strategies with each other. What about the size of the optimal debt of the respective strategies? For this, we have to evaluate (5.60) against (5.65):

$$b_t^f = \frac{1}{1+R}w_{t-1} < \frac{1}{1+\lambda R}w_{t-1} = b_t^c.$$

(5.68)

Again, this condition is met, provided $\lambda < 1$. The optimal rate of devaluation in a fixing strategy is obviously zero and hence lower than under a cheating strategy. What about optimal tax collection? We evaluate (5.61) against (5.66):

$$x^f_{t-1} = \frac{R}{1+R}w_{t-1} > \frac{\lambda R}{1+\lambda R}w_{t-1} = x^c_{t-1}. \qquad (5.69)$$

We see that the optimal tax as well as the optimal rate of devaluation in period $t-1$ is higher in a 'fixing' than under a 'cheating' strategy, if condition $\lambda < 1$ is fulfilled.

Finally, we again compare the total two-period losses of the alternative strategies, that is (5.62) with (5.67):

$$L^f = (w_{t-1}) = \frac{1}{2}\frac{R}{(1+R)}w^2_{t-1} > \frac{1}{2}\frac{\lambda R}{(1+\lambda R)}w^2_{t-1} + C = L^f(w_{t-1}). \qquad (5.70)$$

This inequality holds, provided that

$$C < \frac{1}{2}\frac{R(1-\lambda)}{(1+\lambda R)(1+R)}w^2_{t-1}. \qquad (5.71)$$

Let us collect the results for the individual strategies achieved in the two-period approach in analogy to Table 5.1, in Table 5.2.

Table 5.2   Pay-off matrix of different regimes in the two-period approach

Public	**Government**	
	$\pi_t = 0$	$\pi_t = \dfrac{(1-\lambda)}{\theta\lambda}Rb_t$
$\pi^e_t = 0$	$L^f(w_{t-1}) = \dfrac{1}{2}\dfrac{R}{(1+R)}w^2_{t-1}$	$L^c(w_{t-1}) = \dfrac{1}{2}\dfrac{\lambda R}{(1+\lambda R)}w^2_{t-1} + C$
$\pi^e_t = \dfrac{(1-\lambda)}{\theta\lambda}Rb_t$	$L^r(w_{t-1}) = \dfrac{1}{2}\dfrac{\lambda R}{(\lambda^3 + R)}w^2_{t-1} + C$	$L^l(w_{t-1}) = \dfrac{1}{2}\dfrac{\lambda R}{(\lambda^2 + R)}w^2_{t-1} + C$

Source: Own compilation.

In order to analyse the courses of action available to the policymakers in period $t-1$, it makes sense to consider – in addition to the 'pure' strategies assembled in Table 5.2 – 'compound' strategies. A first alternative emerges for the case that the government does not devalue in period $t-1$. Then, there are two options for the subsequent period. The government may continue with a fixing of the exchange rate policy and the public will give some credibility to this option. However, the government also has a second option, which is to devalue the currency in the subsequent period.

According to Sachs et al. (1996b, p. 275) the second option is associated with no credibility among the public, hence (see (5.17)):

$$\pi_t^e = \frac{(1-\lambda)}{\theta \lambda} Rb_t.$$ (5.72)

This option materializes with probability q $(0 \le q \le 1)$. In contrast, credibility leads to:

$$\pi_t^e = 0$$ (5.73)

and materializes with probability $1 - q$. In a compound approach put forward by these authors, both options are assigned a certain (in principle unknown) probability of occurring. So the government which upholds its promise to fix the exchange rate in $t - 1$ expects a loss in the next period, or more precisely a two-period loss, which is a weighted average (the weights being q and $1 - q$) of the two possible outcomes, that is, options:

$$L^{for\,ac}(b_{t-1},q) = \min\left\{\frac{1}{2}x_{t-1}^2 + \frac{(1-q)}{R}\left[\frac{1}{2}(Rb_t)^2\right] + \frac{q}{R}\left[\frac{1}{2\lambda}(Rb_t)^2 + C\right]\right\}.$$ (5.74)

In (5.74), we designate this compound strategy *for ac*. This phrasing deserves a comment. If the government decides to devalue in period t this is seen by the public as a broken promise, as fixing was the maintained strategy for the period $t - 1$ and this strategy was also announced for period t. However, in a country which has been shaken by deep crises in the past, this sort of 'intended cheating' does not come as a surprise: when the government switches from a fixing strategy to a devaluation, the latter will be expected. Therefore, it makes sense to call the outcome *ac*, that is, 'anticipated cheating'.

As the government upholds its promise in period $t - 1$ we look only for a positive x_{t-1}, because $\pi_{t-1} = 0$. The losses in period t are taken from Table 5.1, but note that the solution for 'anticipated cheating' is enlarged by C. As π_{t-1} is now zero by assumption or according to the two options to be discussed, the first-order condition of (5.74) is:

$$x_{t-1}^{for\,ac} = x_{t-1} = \frac{\eta}{\lambda} Rb_t$$ (5.75)

where

$$0 < \eta \equiv \lambda + (1-\lambda)q < 1. \tag{5.76}$$

Using (5.35) yields:

$$b_t^{f \, or \, ac} = b_t = \frac{\lambda}{(\lambda + \eta R)} w_{t-1}. \tag{5.77}$$

Introducing (5.77) into (5.76) gives:

$$x_{t-1}^{f \, or \, ac} = \frac{\eta R}{(\lambda + \eta R)} w_{t-1}. \tag{5.78}$$

The two-period loss faced by the government that fixes the exchange rate in $t-1$ is calculated by introducing (5.77) and (5.78) into (5.74), which yields:

$$L^{f \, or \, ac}(w_{t-1}, q) = \frac{1}{2} \frac{\eta R}{(\lambda + \eta R)} w_{t-1}^2 + \frac{q}{R} C. \tag{5.79}$$

The problem with (5.79) and, hence a comparison between (5.79) on the one hand and (5.46) and/or (5.62) on the other, is that the loss computed in (5.79) is an *expected* loss from two different strategies, each of these weighted by an unknown probability q and $1-q$, respectively.

This is the only feasible compound strategy in the Sachs–Tornell–Velasco world, so to speak. This applies, because the authors deny the possibility of a choice between a taking the medicine strategy and a regaining reputation strategy in period t. This strategy, in principle, would receive the superscripts t or ar. Once the government has opted for devaluation in period $t-1$, so the 'agents will expect a devaluation with probability one' (Sachs et al. 1996b, p. 274). We do not share this view. Instead, we assign a positive probability q to a realization of the taking the medicine strategy and a positive probability $1-q$ to the realization of the anticipated regaining reputation strategy. Why citizens may give credibility to a policy shift can have several reasons. One is experience made with such shifts in the rest of the world: whenever countries achieved a 'true fixing' of their exchange rate, the former financial turmoil soon ended. Another explanation – in the vein of Argentina's President Carlos Menem's record in his country during the 1990s – relates the successful change of expectations among the public to the specific credibility of the (new) policymakers.

$$L^{t\,or\,ar}(b_{t-1},q) = \min \left\{ \begin{array}{l} \dfrac{1}{2}(\alpha\pi_{t-1}^2 + x_{t-1}^2) \\ + \dfrac{(1-q)}{R}\left[\dfrac{1}{2\lambda}(Rb_t)^2 + C\right] + \dfrac{q}{R}\left[\dfrac{1}{2}(Rb_t)^2\right] \end{array} \right\}. \quad (5.80)$$

The first-order conditions now are:

$$x_{t-1}^{t\,or\,ar} = x_{t-1} = \frac{\iota}{\lambda}Rb_t \qquad (5.81)$$

$$\pi_{t-1}^{t\,or\,ar} = \pi_{t-1} = \frac{\theta}{\alpha}\frac{\iota}{\lambda^2}b_t \qquad (5.82)$$

where

$$0 < \iota \equiv 1 + (\lambda - 1)q < 1. \qquad (5.83)$$

Using (5.35) yields:

$$b_t^{t\,or\,ar} = b_t = \frac{\lambda^2}{(\lambda^2 + \iota R)}w_{t-1}. \qquad (5.84)$$

Introducing (5.84) into (5.81) and (5.82) gives:

$$x_{t-1}^{t\,or\,ar} = \frac{\lambda\iota R}{(\lambda^2 + \iota R)}w_{t-1} \qquad (5.85)$$

$$\pi_{t-1}^{t\,or\,ar} = \pi_{t-1} = \frac{\theta}{\alpha}\frac{\lambda\iota R}{(\lambda^2 + \iota R)}w_{t-1}. \qquad (5.86)$$

Plugging equations (5.84) to (5.86) into (5.80) gives the two-period loss faced by a government that devalues at $t-1$ and has the choice either to take the medicine or to anticipate regaining reputation in period t:

$$L^{t\,or\,ar}(w_{t-1},q) = \frac{1}{2}\frac{\lambda\iota R}{(\lambda^2 + \iota R)}w_{t-1}^2 + \frac{(1-q)}{R}C. \qquad (5.87)$$

Consequently, we do not just follow the ingenious approach of Sachs et al. (1996b, pp. 276–9). Rather than proceed to compare the loss equivalent to their compound strategy of (5.74) with the associated losses of the 'pure strategies' (Table 5.2), we propose to identify first additional compound strategies which can be deduced from Table 5.2 and which fit nicely into the Barro–Gordon world.

If the country has experienced a less turbulent past, it is more likely that the devaluation works as a cheating device *vis-à-vis* the public, which then retains its trust towards the government. The corresponding compound strategy of the government now reads:

$$L^{forc}(b_{t-1}, p) = \min\left\{\frac{1}{2}x_{t-1}^2 + \frac{1}{2}\frac{(1-p)}{R}(Rb_t)^2 + \frac{p}{R}\left[\frac{1}{2}\lambda(Rb_t)^2 + C\right]\right\}. \quad (5.88)$$

Note that the alternative probabilities are now p and $1-p$ in order to clearly distinguish (5.88) from (5.74). As the government upholds its promise in period $t-1$ we only consider x_{t-1}, because $\pi_{t-1} = 0$. The losses in period t are taken from Table 5.1, but note that the solution for cheating is enlarged by C.

As π_{t-1} is now zero by assumption or according to the two options to be discussed, the first-order condition of (5.88) is:

$$x_{t-1}^{forc} = x_{t-1} = vRb_t \quad (5.89)$$

where

$$0 < v \equiv 1 + (\lambda - 1)p < 1. \quad (5.90)$$

Using (5.35) yields:

$$b_t^{forc} = b_t = \frac{1}{(1+vR)}w_{t-1}. \quad (5.91)$$

Introducing (5.91) into (5.89) gives:

$$x_{t-1}^{forc} = \frac{vR}{(1+vR)}w_{t-1}. \quad (5.92)$$

The two-period loss faced by a government which fixes the exchange rate in $t-1$ is calculated by introducing (5.91) and (5.92) into (5.88), which yields:

$$L^{forc}(w_{t-1}, p) = \frac{1}{2}\frac{vR}{(1+vR)}w_{t-1}^2 + \frac{p}{R}C. \quad (5.93)$$

Obviously, it remains to define a second 'compound' strategy which we may call $L^{t\,or\,r}$ and which by analogy to $L^{f\,or\,c}$ would encompass for period t a weighted average of the strategies L^t and L^r. The corresponding loss function to minimize reads:

$$L^{t\,or\,r}(b_{t-1},p) = \min\left\{\begin{array}{l} \dfrac{1}{2}(\alpha\pi_{t-1}^2 + x_{t-1}^2) \\[2mm] + \dfrac{(1-p)}{R}\left[\dfrac{1}{2\lambda}(Rb_t)^2 + C\right] + \dfrac{p}{R}\left[\dfrac{1}{2\lambda^2}(Rb_t)^2 + C\right] \end{array}\right\}. \quad (5.94)$$

The first-order conditions now are:

$$x_{t-1}^{t\,or\,r} = x_{t-1} = \frac{\chi}{\lambda^2}Rb_t \quad (5.95)$$

$$\pi_{t-1}^{t\,or\,r} = \pi_{t-1} = \frac{\theta}{\alpha}\frac{\chi}{\lambda^2}Rb_t \quad (5.96)$$

where

$$0 < \chi \equiv \lambda + (1-\lambda)p < 1. \quad (5.97)$$

Using (5.35) yields:

$$b_t^{t\,or\,r} = b_t = \frac{\lambda^3}{(\lambda^3 + \chi R)}w_{t-1}. \quad (5.98)$$

Introducing (5.98) into (5.95) and (5.96) gives:

$$x_{t-1}^{t\,or\,c} = \frac{\lambda\chi R}{(\lambda^3 + \chi R)}w_{t-1} \quad (5.99)$$

$$\pi_{t-1}^{t\,or\,r} = \pi_{t-1} = \frac{\theta}{\alpha}\frac{\lambda\chi R}{(\lambda^3 + \chi R)}w_{t-1}. \quad (5.100)$$

Plugging equations (5.98) to (5.100) into (5.94) gives the two-period loss faced by a government that devalues at $t-1$ and has the choice either to take the medicine or to regain reputation in period t:

$$L^{t\,or\,r}(w_{t-1},p) = \frac{1}{2}\frac{\lambda\chi R}{(\lambda^3 + \chi R)}w_{t-1}^2 + \frac{1}{R}C. \quad (5.101)$$

In Figure 5.1 we have depicted the logical structure of the sample of strategies available to the government. If the authorities decide to fix (devalue) the exchange rate in period $t-1$, then only the left (right) branch of the chart is relevant. In each case, four alternatives emerge for period t. Let us inspect first the left branch of the chart. Note that the L^f and the L^c strategies are accompanied by official 'announcements' that the government will stick to 'fixing' in this period. In one case, the promise is held, in the other it is broken. In contrast, the $L^{f\,or\,c}$ and the $L^{f\,or\,ac}$ strategies stand, respectively, for authorities which do not commit themselves to a goal in exchange rate policy, but rather leave it to their discretionary choice when deciding upon the course of exchange rate policy at the end of period $t-1$. With regard to the right twig of the chart, we realize that 'no announcements' are associated with the strategies $L^{t\,or\,r}$ and $L^{t\,or\,ar}$. The same applies to the L^t option. Not so in the case of L^r, where an official announcement as well as a strong commitment to regain reputation in exchange rate policy, is needed more than ever.

Figure 5.1 Choices and strategies in a two-period decision problem

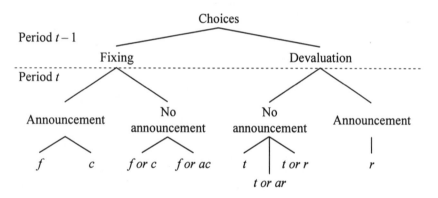

Source: Own compilation.

Before we begin with the discussion of contagion, it is useful to look at the graphs of all of the strategies presented in Figure 5.1. How do we proceed with the a priori unknown probabilities p and q (and $1-p$ and $1-q$, respectively)? From an economic point of view, p and q should not be confused as they assign probabilities to quite different strategies (see above). For the simulation exercise, however, unless there is some prior information, these weights should be 0.5 *each* and thereby we should follow the 'principle of insufficient reason' (Sinn 1980). This is exactly how we have simulated the compound strategies in Figures 5.2 and 5.3: in the first of the two graphs we have depicted the four strategies associated with the left branch of Figure 5.1, in the second those associated with the right one. The chosen values of the parameters correspond to the assumptions and/or the conditions found in the modelling part of this chapter. The interest rate, R, is assumed to be 0.1.

For reasonable parameter values, the fixing strategy L^f dominates before reaching a lower critical level of w_{t-1}. At this level, there is an intersection point with the L^c strategy. In other words: depending on the size of the 'commitments of the past', an unanticipated devaluation is welfare improving beyond that critical level. Suppose now, we have a government which no longer – at least in the foreseeable future – has the option to play L^c. The reason may be that the associated medium- and long-term loss of confidence among the public and among foreign investors outweighs the short-term welfare gains. In such a situation, a comparison between the L^f and the $L^{f\,or\,c}$ strategies now becomes relevant. As we can see in Figure 5.2, there is a second, higher critical level for w_{t-1}, beyond which it becomes lucrative for the government not to announce any exchange rate goal, but to decide on a discretionary basis what to do in period t. The danger embedded in this policy sequence comes from the possibility that on the day of the decision, $L^{f\,or\,c}$, the seemingly attractive strategy, is no longer available. Because of a shift in expectations, the authorities may rather be confronted with $L^{f\,or\,ac}$ and the much higher associated welfare costs (see above).

Figure 5.2   Possible strategies in period t *after fixing in period* t – 1

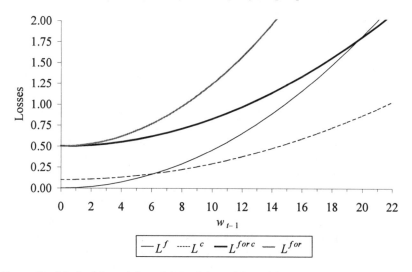

Notes: $R = 0.1; C = 0.1; q = 0.5; p = 0.5; \lambda = 0.4; \eta = 0.7; \nu = 0.7.$

Sources: Sachs et al. (1996b, p. 277); own calculations.

Figure 5.3   Possible strategies in period t *after a devaluation in period* t − 1

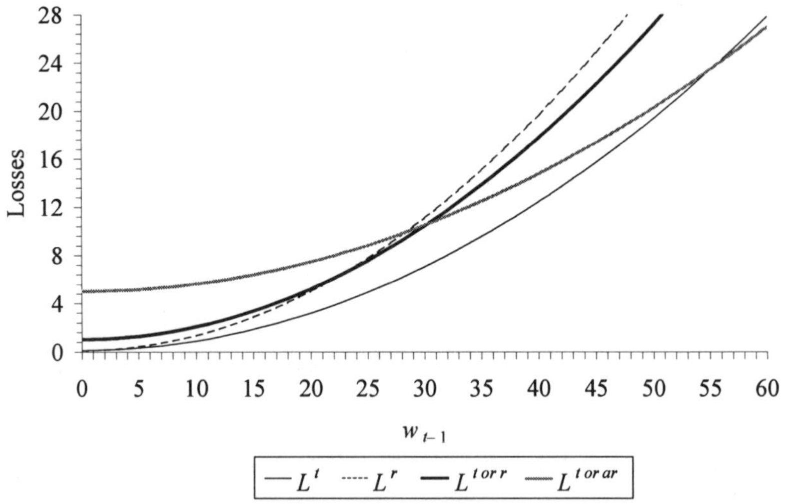

Notes: $R = 0.1$; $C = 0.1$; $q = 0.5$; $p = 0.5$; $\lambda = 0.4$; $\iota = 0.7$; $\chi = 0.7$.

Sources: Sachs et al. (1996b, p. 277); own calculations.

In Figure 5.3, we can evaluate the options available to the government after a devaluation in the previous period $t - 1$ has been decided. This time, there is an apparently dominating strategy (L^t) for a wide range of the possible levels of w_{t-1}. Again, there may be reasons why the government refuses to pursue this 'optimal' strategy. Allowing the domestic currency to depreciate in accordance with the devaluation expectations may give rise to a vicious circle – if we extend the time horizon to more periods – unless the authorities are able to establish a stable anchor for their currency by means of an inflation target. Even advanced emerging market economies, however, are often unable to quickly adapt and adjust their central banks to the requirements of this sophisticated monetary policy rule. An alternative lies in the establishment of a nominal anchor by means of a 'fixing' exchange rate policy. Currency boards are, for example, a possible outlet for the countries in question. A return to a fixing policy – as can be seen from Figure 5.3 – is quite costly. Over a wide range of values for w_{t-1}, the announced commitment to regain reputation in the field of exchange rate policy is comparatively the most expensive alternative. Beyond a critical level of w_{t-1}, the two compound strategies come into play. In the best case, the authorities may hope that the possibility of a discretionary introduction of a fixed exchange rate regime, albeit unanticipated, is associated with a positive shift of exchange rate expectations so that they would be confronted with $L^{t \, or \, ar}$ instead of $L^{t \, or \, r}$! Such an outcome may arise when there is widespread knowledge about the benefits of the fixing strategy and it is believed that the government is grasping its last chance.

5.4 CONTAGION: THE TWO-COUNTRY–TWO-PERIOD PROBLEM

Unfortunately, all of the analytical efforts made so far still do not deal with our main subject, 'contagion'. In the following, we shall introduce a second country which is symmetric to the first one with the exception that it does not face a domestic financial market shock in period $t-1$. We could implement this assumption by setting $(z_{t-1} - \bar{z})$ zero for the respective country. How do we inter-link both economies? In principle, there should be two major channels between them: one is that both countries compete with their finished and semi-finished goods on third markets with homogeneous goods and with intensive price competition. All of these goods are invoiced in US dollars. A devaluation of country 1's currency *vis-à-vis* the US dollar hence lowers country 2's competitiveness on the external goods markets and vice versa. In a similar vein, Corsetti et al. (1998a) have stressed that competitive devaluation pressures may arise even if two countries do not directly trade with each other. Such pressures may be present if the two countries are competing in a common third market. A lower external competitiveness will then depress net exports of the country in question and hence its domestic demand.

A second channel which may inter-link both emerging economies is the rate of interest, R. Until now, the single economy had to face an exogenous real interest rate in our model. This will no longer be the case. Instead, we assume that there is an emerging markets' specific rate of interest which is variable and affected in each period by the *exchange rate risk* as well as by the *default risk* associated with a large emerging market economy 'equipped' with a high external debt and some sort of pegging exchange rate regime. There may also exist country-specific spreads/fees in the eyes of international investors. These will not be taken into account in what follows. A higher real interest rate depresses, *ceteris paribus*, the respective domestic demand. Given the complex solutions already achieved in the one-country problem, we should try to keep things tractable. Therefore, we limit ourselves in the following to the real interest rate channel to inter-link both economies.

We assume that the world has – besides industrialized and developing countries – just two large emerging economies. The real interest rate these two countries have to face on international financial markets has two components. One is the real interest rate charged to industrialized countries,

R. The second component is a weighted average of country-specific risk premium (υ_t^I, υ_t^J) both being a function of the exchange rate risk, $E_{t-1}(\pi_t^{i,e})$ and the default risk (b_t^i). The reason for putting together these two risk premia and building a weighted average lies in the insight gained above (see Chapter 4) that emerging markets are treated by many fund managers as belonging to one portfolio (see above). Hence, we achieve:

$$R_t^{I,J} = R_t + l\upsilon_t^I\left[b_t^I, E_{t-1}(\pi_t^{I,e})\right] + (1-l)\upsilon_t^J\left[b_t^J, E_{t-1}(\pi_t^{J,e})\right] \qquad (5.102)$$

with

$$\upsilon_t^i > 0 \text{ and } \frac{\partial \upsilon_t^i}{\partial b_t^i}, \frac{\partial \upsilon_t^i}{\partial E_{t-1}(\pi_t^{i,e})} > 0; \; i = I, J \qquad (5.103)$$

where $R_t^{I,J}$ is the real interest rate relevant for both emerging economies. The weights l and $1-l$, of course, have to add to one. Economically, they are proxies for the relative weight each country is given by the international financial markets in the portfolio 'emerging markets'.

In Table 5.3, we have put together – from the point of view of the first-victim country – all possible levels of optimal debt (b_t) according to the eight strategies discussed above. These are matched by the four scenarios (three in Table 5.3 plus one hypothetical option, see (5.110)) one can think of with regard to the expectations of a devaluation. All the fields marked by a cross

Table 5.3   *Expected rate of devaluation and optimal debt under different strategies*

	b_t^l	b_t^r	b_t^f	b_t^c	$b_t^{f\,or\,ac}$	$b_t^{l\,or\,ar}$	$b_t^{f\,or\,c}$	$b_t^{l\,or\,r}$
$E_{t-1}(\pi_t^e) = 0$			×	×			×	
$E_{t-1}(\pi_t^e) = \dfrac{\theta}{\alpha}Rb_t$	×	×						×
$E_{t-1}(\pi_t^e) = q\dfrac{\theta}{\alpha}Rb_t$					×	×		

Source: Own compilation.

symbolize alternative situations for the first-victim country, characterized by the respective optimal debt sizes and the associated exchange rate expectations. If the first-victim country switches from one situation/strategy to another one which is characterized by a higher optimal debt and/or an increased expectation of a devaluation, then, according to (5.102) this should elevate the relevant interest rate not only for the first-victim country, but for all emerging market economies and hence lead to contagion.

The alternative exchange rate expectations are the following. If the government devalues at time $t-1$, then the expectation formed at time $t-1$ for period t is:

$$E_{t-1}(\pi_t^e) = \frac{\theta}{\alpha} Rb_t = \frac{\theta}{\alpha} \frac{\lambda^2 R}{(\lambda^2 + R)} w_{t-1}. \qquad (5.104)$$

If the government does fix the exchange rate in $t-1$ and continues to fix it in t, is able to cheat in t after fixing in period $t-1$ or decides on a discretionary basis upon (unanticipated) cheating in period t, the respective exchange rate expectation is:

$$E_{t-1}(\pi_t^e) = 0. \qquad (5.105)$$

What about rational exchange rate expectations if the government fixes the exchange rate in period $t-1$ and has the choice of either devaluing or fix the exchange rate in period t? If it devalues in t, then, in the eyes of the public, expected devaluation should be a weighted average of the two possible outcomes given by (5.106):

$$E_{t-1}(\pi_t^e) = \begin{cases} 0 \\ \dfrac{\theta}{\alpha} Rb_t. \end{cases} \qquad (5.106)$$

Hence,

$$E_{t-1}(\pi_t^e) = q \frac{\theta}{\alpha} \frac{\lambda R}{(\lambda + \eta R)} w_{t-1}. \qquad (5.107)$$

Note that expected devaluation in either case depends on three things (Sachs et al. 1996b, p. 277):

1. the accumulated stock of liabilities Rb_t;
2. the magnitude of the devaluation as a multiple of Rb_t, $\pi_t = (\theta/\alpha) Rb_t$; and
3. the probability that a devaluation will take place $(1-q$ versus $q)$.

It can be shown that for all allowable values of q it holds that the expected rate of devaluation (5.104) exceeds the rational exchange rate expectations (5.107):

$$\frac{\theta}{\alpha} \frac{\lambda^2 R}{(\lambda^2 + R)} w_{t-1} > q \frac{\theta}{\alpha} \frac{\lambda R}{(\lambda + \eta R)} w_{t-1}. \tag{5.108}$$

With $\eta \equiv \lambda + (1 - \lambda)q$, it follows that

$$\frac{\lambda + \lambda R}{(\lambda^3 + R)} > q. \tag{5.109}$$

This implies that the accumulated stock of liabilities (assets) is always higher (lower) at t if the government devalues at $t - 1$ (ibid.). Hence, the size of the expected devaluation will be decisive for the probability that devaluation will take place.

Finally, the last possible alternative is:

$$E_{t-1}(\pi_t^e) = p \frac{\theta}{\alpha} \frac{R}{(1 + vR)} w_{t-1} \tag{5.110}$$

which, however, does not enter as a real possibility in Table 5.3!

We suggest three hypothetical scenarios for a spreading crisis, that is contagion. The first case arises when a banking crisis occurs in the first-victim country during the period $t - 1$. This crisis is reflected in a higher value of $(z_{t-1} - \bar{z})$ and, hence according to (5.35), in a larger size of new debt, b_t, at *any optimizing strategy*. This first case represents an *exogenous* increase in b_t and the virus spreads to the second-victim country to the extent:

$$\frac{\partial R_t^{I,J}}{\partial b_t^I} = l \frac{\partial \rho_t^I}{\partial b_t^I}. \tag{5.111}$$

Hence, the impact of the interest rate spread depends on the elasticity of the risk premium specific to the first-victim country with regard to a higher external debt of this first country, weighted by the share of this risk premium for the overall emerging market economies' risk premium. Note that according to (5.104), (5.107) and (5.110), this may also have an impact on exchange rate expectations in the first-victim country. Whether it does or not ultimately depends on the credibility of the exchange rate policy among the public. If there is a likelihood that the government will lose its credibility, then (5.111) turns into

$$\frac{\partial R_t^{I,J}}{\partial b_t^I} = l\left[\frac{\partial v_t^I}{\partial b_t^I} + \frac{\partial v_t^I}{\partial E_{t-1}(\pi_t^{I,e})}\right]. \tag{5.112}$$

But, this is not the end of the story. Because exchange rate expectations (if positive) on their part depend on the interest rate (see above), additional interest rate increases will be fuelled unless the authorities regain credibility for their exchange rate policy. In the following, we shall abstract from this aspect which albeit complicates things further.

The second and the third cases consider the situation of the first-victim country according to the categories explained in Figure 5.1. Suppose for the second case that the government decided to fix the exchange rate in period $t-1$ and opts for a no-announcement strategy *vis-à-vis* the exchange rate in period t. This may be due to a comparison between the losses of the $L^{f\ or\ c}$ and the L^f strategies, respectively. As we said above, the stronger the commitments of the past (w_{t-1}), the more likely it is that the authorities will refrain from making further announcements of a fixing policy. In the worst case, the government will have to face the losses according to $L^{f\ or\ ac}$ which implies the loss of credibility among the public with probability q. Positive exchange rate expectations as given by (5.107) are sufficient for:

$$\frac{\partial R_t^{I,J}}{\partial E_{t-1}(\pi_t^{I,e})} = l\frac{\partial v_t^I}{\partial E_{t-1}(\pi_t^{I,e})}. \tag{5.113}$$

However, as we can infer from an inspection of Table 5.3, the size of the optimal debt is lower under a $L^{f\ or\ ac}$ than under a $L^{f\ or\ c}$ strategy. A comparison between (5.77) and (5.91) reveals that

$$b_t^{f\ or\ ac} = \frac{\lambda}{(\lambda+\pi R)}w_{t-1} < \frac{1}{(1+vR)}w_{t-1} = b_t^{f\ or\ c} \tag{5.114}$$

provided that $\lambda < 1$ and $p = q$. To be sure about induced interest rate increases, we hence must postulate that

$$\frac{\partial R_t^{I,J}}{\partial E_{t-1}(\pi_t^{I,e})} + \frac{\partial R_t^{I,J}}{\partial b_t^I} = l\left[\frac{\partial v_t^I}{\partial E_{t-1}(\pi_t^{I,e})} + \frac{\partial v_t^I}{\partial b_t^I}\right] > 0. \tag{5.115}$$

We may now inspect the consequences for the second-victim country in very simple terms. In order to do so, we assume the second country to follow a strict policy of announcing a fixed exchange rate regime as in the left branch in Figure 5.1. In the base-line scenario, the interest rate, R, is at 0.1.

As long as the 'commitments of the past' in this second country are at reasonable levels, the fixing strategy L^f inclines towards the temptation to cheat, that is, to realize an unanticipated devaluation (L^c).

However, according to Table 5.3, a shift from an L^f strategy towards an L^c strategy is associated with a lower optimal debt for the second country (see above). For the total effect on the interest rate we therefore have to take into account whether:

$$\frac{\partial R_t^{I,J}}{\partial E_{t-1}(\pi_t^{I,e})} + \frac{\partial R_t^{I,J}}{\partial b_t^I} + \frac{\partial R_t^{I,J}}{\partial b_t^J} = I\left[\frac{\partial \upsilon_t^I}{\partial E_{t-1}(\pi_t^{I,e})} + \frac{\partial \upsilon_t^I}{\partial b_t^I}\right] + (1-I)\frac{\partial \upsilon_t^J}{\partial b_t^J} > 0. \ (5.116)$$

In Figures 5.4–6 we simulate a stepwise increase in the interest rate from a level of 0.10 (Figure 5.4) to an intermediary level of 0.15 (Figure 5.5), and to a final level of 0.20 (Figure 5.6). The values of C and λ are constant (0.1 and 0.4, respectively).

It is rather obvious that the intersection point between the L^f strategy and the L^c strategy moves downwards to the left as a function of an increasing interest rate. In other words: given the commitments of the past (w_{t-1}), it becomes more and more likely that the second country does not stick to its commitment in exchange rate policy, but rather prefers to 'cheat'. As the literature on contagion stresses, this makes a remarkable difference to the first-victim country which – as we said above – cannot even think about the cheating option.

Figure 5.4   Fixing and cheating strategies at an interest rate of R = 0.1

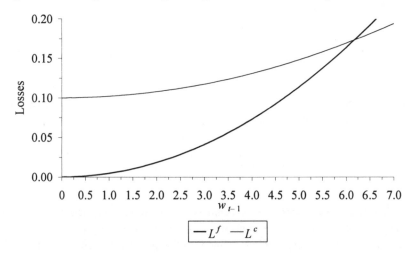

Source: Own calculations.

Figure 5.5 Fixing and cheating strategies at an interest rate of R = 0.15

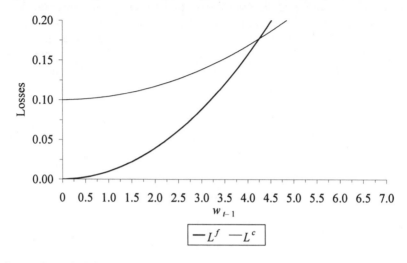

Source: Own calculations.

Figure 5.6 Fixing and cheating strategies at an interest rate of R = 0.2

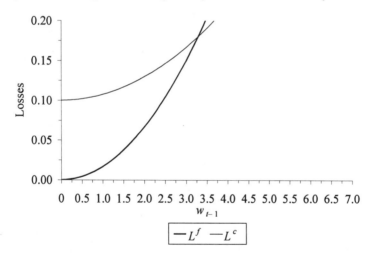

Source: Own calculations.

The third case assumes for reasons of simplicity the same parameter values as in Figure 5.6; suppose the first-victim country is one which is located on the right branch of Figure 5.1. The authorities decided to devalue in period $t-1$ and are now confronted with several alternatives for period t.

Contagion in Financial Markets

At first sight at Figure 5.7, the L^t option seems most promising. However, there is a level of the commitments of the past (w_{t-1}) beyond which the $L^{t \, or \, ar}$ alternative deserves attention because it is associated with a lower level of welfare losses. According to Table 5.3, the corresponding optimal debt is higher under the $L^{t \, or \, ar}$ strategy as long as $\iota < 1$. At the same time, however, exchange rate expectations are lower (see Table 5.3). If the 'debt effect' dominates the 'expectations effect', a spreading increase (contagion) in the emerging market economies' interest rate is to be expected, provided that condition (5.116) holds. If, however, the positive shift in expectations does not occur, then the authorities of the first-victim country would be confronted with the consequences of the much more costly $L^{t \, or \, r}$ strategy. Here, on the one hand, there is no positive shift in exchange rate expectations whatsoever. On the other hand, the optimal debt is lower under the $L^{t \, or \, r}$ strategy in comparison with the L^t option. Hence, we may get the curious result that

$$\frac{\partial R_t^{I,J}}{\partial b_t^I} + \frac{\partial R_t^{I,J}}{\partial b_t^J} = I\left[\frac{\partial \upsilon_t^I}{\partial E_{t-1}(\pi_t^{I,e})} + \frac{\partial \upsilon_t^I}{\partial b_t^I}\right] + (1-I)\frac{\partial \upsilon_t^J}{\partial b_t^J} < 0. \qquad (5.117)$$

This is a case where the hypothetical second-victim country can profit from a shift of the first-victim country in favour of a compound strategy which encompasses the possibility of regaining reputation.

Figure 5.7 Possible strategies in period t *after a devaluation in period* t – 1

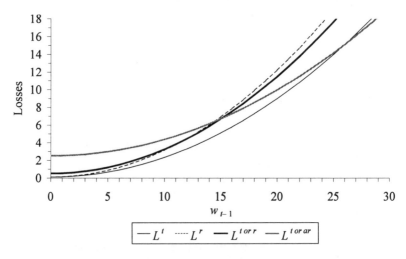

Notes: $R = 0.2$; $C = 0.1$; $q = 0.5$; $p = 0.5$; $\lambda = 0.4$; $\iota = 0.7$; $\chi = 0.7$.

Source: Own calculations.

5.5   EMPIRICAL EVIDENCE

On 13 October 1998, G.A. Calvo wrote:

> [A] large bailout package for Brazil should bring calm and confidence. The package has to be large enough, though. Otherwise, it could speed up exit and end up in a replay of the Russian crisis (in which this package was spent almost instantaneously, leaving behind a large stock of yet unpaid short-term debt). (Calvo 1998a, p. 11)

In the following, our main aim is to document that 'replay'. Therefore, we shall concentrate in this empirical section on the case of Russia and Brazil. At the end of this chapter we shall come back briefly to the Asian experience. As a matter of fact, both stories are seemingly independent from each other: but, as Komulainen correctly states, 'the Asian crisis helped trigger the Russian crisis. After the Asian crisis, investors monitored country fundamentals more carefully' (Komulainen 1999, p. 32).

There were also contagion effects of the Russian financial crises which affected Central and Eastern Europe: the exchange rates of these countries temporarily depreciated rapidly in the aftermath of the suspension of the short-term government bonds (GKO) market (see above) in Russia (Krzak 1998, p. 26). Also, the Russian crisis hit stock markets in Poland, Hungary, the Czech Republic and Slovakia in much the same way that the Thai crisis had rippled around the ASEAN countries in 1997. 'The Budapest stock market was the most severely affected of the respective stock exchanges because of the strong participation of foreigners' (ibid.). But also in Warsaw, estimates say that about 30 per cent of the capital listed on the stock exchange was owned by foreigners in 1998. From the different possible channels of contagion, the trade channel figured prominently during the Russian crisis and its impact on Central and Eastern European countries. Poland, for example, accounted for an export exposure to Russia of 8.4 per cent of its total exports in 1997 and the Russian crisis led to a contraction of exports to Russia.

All in all, the adverse impact of the Russian financial turmoil on the economy of Central and Eastern European countries was limited, however. In contrast to Brazil and Chile (see below), these countries did not raise interest rates to defend their currencies. Only a few countries were forced to make interventions on the foreign exchange markets and in none of these cases did exchange rate pressure result in an exchange rate regime collapse. The relative 'immunity' of the countries in question was attributed to several factors such as moderate current account positions, high foreign exchange reserves and low short-term debt exposure.

But, of course, the most interesting aspect of the Russian crisis was its spreading to the Brazilian economy. It is fair to say that Brazil had made considerable efforts to become 'susceptible': at the end of 1997, real interest rates reached levels of 40 per cent; consequently, over the first quarter of 1998, $20 billion (mainly short-term and exchange rate unhedged debt) entered the country. This amount was equivalent to the inflows for the whole year of 1997 and nearly twice the amount of Brazilian exports of that quarter (Palma 1998, p. 802). Furthermore, major Brazilian fundamentals were in bad shape: the deficit in the public account was more than 4 per cent of GDP, the deficit in the current account was the same and the real rate of exchange towards the US dollar was experiencing a strong appreciation.

In Figure 5.8, we have depicted in one diagram the daily exchange rate development of both the real and the rouble over the relevant time span. It is quite astonishing to see that the movement made by the rouble in relation to the real bears a remarkable resemblance to the content of Figure 4.8 ('Illness and recovery in a two-patient setting'). The fact that the precipitous daily devaluations of the real started in Brazil about four months after the collapse of the rouble exchange rate regime does not imply that infection did not occur earlier. This is documented impressively in Figures 5.9 and 5.10.

Figure 5.8   Daily exchange rate development in Russia and Brazil,
*   13 January 1998 to 30 December 1999*

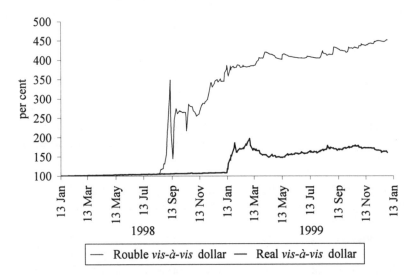

Notes: National currency *vis-à-vis* US dollar; 13 January 1998 = 100.

Sources: Federal Reserve Board (2000) and Central Bank of the Russian Federation (2000a).

In Figure 5.9, we have contrasted the short-term interest rate volatility of Russia with the respective volatility in Brazil between January 1998 and December 1999. Though at different absolute levels (see the different scaling on both vertical axes), we observe a common peak in late August/early September of 1998, that is, long before the real fell on at the foreign exchange market (see above), but precisely when the rouble had to be floated. In the case of Russia, short-term interest rates have come down almost steadily since then. Note also that Russian interest rates recorded 'local peaks' in November 1998, January and March/April 1999. These were periods when the Brazilian short-term interest rates experienced analogous, albeit much more pronounced peaks. The volatility of short-term Russian interest rates has remained high since September 1998, at much lower absolute levels, however. By contrast, Brazilian interest rates experienced a second strong peak in March/April of 1999. Since then, short-term interest rates have declined considerably and their volatility has been modest in comparison to Russia.

Figure 5.9   Daily short-term development of interest rates in Russia and Brazil, 13 January 1998 to 30 December 1999

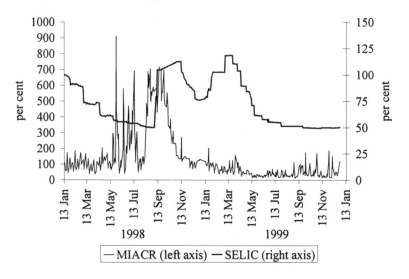

Note: 13 January 1998 = 100.

Sources: Lunar Finance (2000) and Central Bank of the Russian Federation (2000b).

Figure 5.10 is even more impressive in terms of 'contagion'. Before the summer of 1998, the correlation between the two stock market-related time series of Russia on the one hand and of Brazil on the other is detectable, but not overwhelming. Since the deep rouble crisis in late August/early September of 1998, both time series for the respective stock market indices show an increasing tendency for co-movement. This co-movement is only briefly interrupted by a period of three months (May to September 1999) when the two series do not seem to be interrelated.

These stock market data from Brazil and Russia are a good test for the assumptions made in the theoretical model; if shares from both of these countries are truly part of an emerging market portfolio, then an increasing correlation of the stock market indices during and in the aftermath of an exchange rate crisis of one of the countries should not come as a surprise.

Figure 5.10 Daily stock market development in Russia and Brazil,
13 January 1998 to 30 December 1999

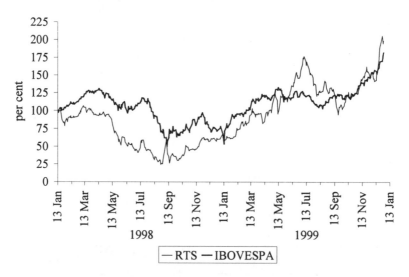

Notes: Prices in national currencies; 13 January 1998 = 100.

Sources: Bovespa (2000) and Russian Trading System (2000).

In Figure 5.11,[3] we get an impressive view of the course of action in Latin American foreign exchange markets during the turmoil years 1997–99. As the data reveal, the collapse of the real in January 1999 did not affect exchange rates in other major Latin American countries significantly. This can be explained: either the countries in question were not 'big enough' to be part of a Brazil plus Russia plus X portfolio, or their exchange rate regime was not susceptible to a speculative attack.

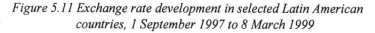

Figure 5.11 Exchange rate development in selected Latin American countries, 1 September 1997 to 8 March 1999

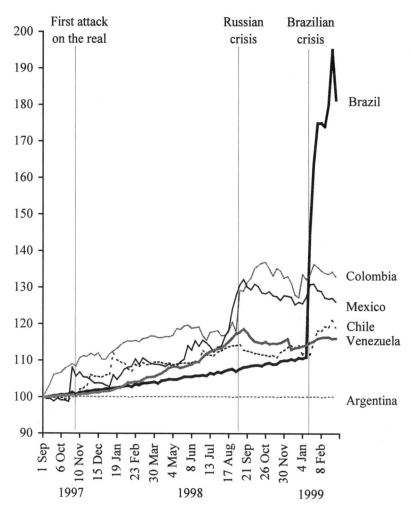

Notes: National currency *vis-à-vis* US dollar; 1 September 1997 = 100; in per cent.

Source: Nunnenkamp (1999, p. 12).

Then, it is less of a surprise that 'the rise in Brazilian interest rates since January 1999 has not induced rising interest rates in these other Latin American countries' (Nunnenkamp 1999, p. 13). In Figure 5.12 we have the details.

Figure 5.12 Short-term interest rates in selected Latin American countries,
27 August 1997 to 8 March 1999

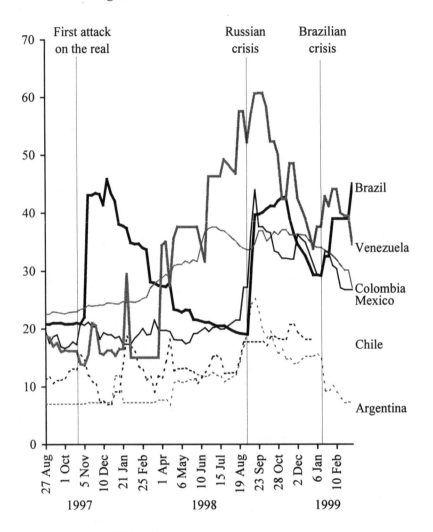

Source: Nunnenkamp (1999, p. 14).

   The lack of financial contagion as measured by the co-movement of short-term interest rates in an area with intensive trade ties, geographic proximity and common culture is a strong argument against the hypotheses of 'regional contagion' at least in the strong and exclusive sense put forward by some authors (see chapters above).

In contrast to exchange rates and short-term interest rates, market prices on the stock exchange in Brazil and on the respective markets in other Latin American countries do show a strong correlation until January 1999 (see Figure 5.13)

Figure 5.13 Stock market developments in selected Latin American countries, 1 September 1997 to 8 March 1999

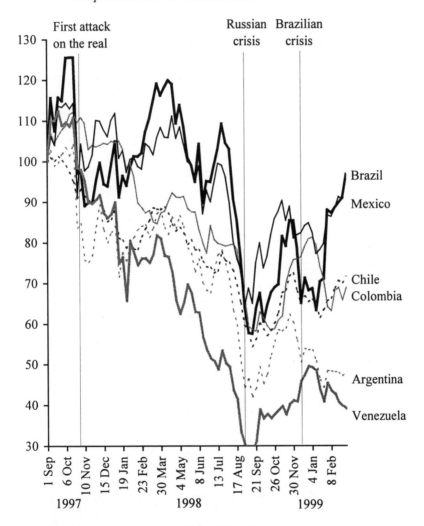

Notes: Prices in national currency; 1 September 1997 = 100; in per cent.

Source: Nunnenkamp (1999, p. 15).

Thereafter, the floating of the real brought relief to Brazil's stock market, while at the stock markets of its neighbours there were divergent developments: 'share prices increased in Chile and Mexico, but declined in Colombia, Venezuela and – though only marginally – in Argentina' (ibid., p. 13). These findings are in sharp contrast to the observations made above with respect to Russia and Brazil. In their cases, correlation was weak/semi-strong before the rouble crisis and has become stronger ever since then. The strong correlation of stock market indices among Latin American countries until January 1999 reflects the interrelated business cycles of the countries in question more than any substantial financial contagion from Brazil. This is a much more differentiated view than the one put forward by Fratzscher (1999, p. 14), who attempted to measure *financial* interdependence by measuring continuously the correlation of weekly stock market returns. As we have seen, the clue lies in *when* we observe an increase in correlation and whether this increase is related to a foreign exchange crisis in a first-victim country.

At first glance, these results for Brazil and its Latin-American partners seem to fit well with the events experienced during the Asian Flu: here, it was observed that correlations between the stock markets were greater than the currency markets (Baig and Goldfajn 1999, p. 178). Correlations among stock price data observed during the Asian financial crisis are at the centre of Tan's empirical research (1998). From increased co-movement among stock returns, Tan infers the occurrence of contagion. What remains unclear in Tan's analysis – as in many other papers – is whether he really captures contagious effects of the Thai crisis on the other ASEAN countries or rather the negative consequences on the respective economies as measured by the deep recessions in the aftermath of the Thai financial crisis. The critical sub-period chosen (2 July 1997 to 27 March 1998), which is then compared to the 'base-line' sub-period (1 June 1995 to 1 July 1997), is much too long to avoid such a confusion.

When citing Tan, we note that he has not the slightest understanding of the nature of contagious processes (see Chapter 4):

> Apparently, there has been an increase in the degree of contagion during the crisis since the ratios of the mean absolute deviations for the crisis period to those of the pre-crisis period are more than one. Also, there is an observed increase in the degree of contagion as the crisis deepened. (Tan 1998, p. 11)

This passage proves that Tan fell victim to a confusion between contagion on the one hand and international business cycles on the other. But the Asian Flu tends to demonstrate that in this case also, the portfolio from the international investors' point of view did comprise the ASEAN countries as correlations between short-term interest rates and sovereign spreads of the affected countries increased (in comparison to tranquil periods) 'significantly and substantially in the crisis phase' (Baig and Goldfajn 1999, p. 181). Thus, there may have been contagion, even if economists sometimes missed the correct variables to detect it.

The extensive econometric research work (pooled cross-country time series analysis for 61 countries during 1991 and 1998) done by Caramazza et al. (2000) confirms our view that the first-victim country and the major susceptible country should be in the same portfolio of investment funds or of banks' assets: 'the indicators of vulnerability to international financial spill-over and of financial fragility (reserve adequacy) are highly significant. In particular, a strong financial linkage with the major creditor of the first country (common creditor) appears to substantially raise the probability of a crisis' (Caramazza et al. 2000, p. 35). Through its loan portfolio

> a bank may be exposed to a country that has a financial crisis. If the crisis occurs, it impacts the bank's balance sheet; the bank is faced with the need to re-balance its portfolio. ... Other countries which were borrowing from the affected bank will be vulnerable to a cutback in their lines of credit. (Kaminsky and Reinhart 1999, pp. 5–6)

Complementary to these findings, Ahluwalia could confirm in his empirical results (for three episodes and 19 emerging economies) that 'investors sort "weak" countries from "strong" ones' (2000, p. 3) and, for them 'the first crisis serves as a "wake-up call" to investors who then focus their attention on that country's macroeconomic weaknesses ... in order to decide which ones are vulnerable' (ibid., p. 4).

Some authors give rise to possible misunderstandings of contagion simply by using the wrong semantics; for instance, when Lowell et al. argue with 'possible episodes of cross-border financial contagion' (1998, p. 11). As we have seen above, this notion would not apply to the cases of Russia and Brazil; if anything, cross-ocean financial contagion would be the more accurate description here. The same authors, however, are quite right when they approach the contagion phenomenon by letting the baht/US dollar bilateral exchange rate be the financial variable which triggered both stock and currency market turbulences in the other ASEAN countries in the summer of 1997 (ibid., p. 24).

Moreno and Trehan correctly warn those economists who are so enthusiastic about the new notion of 'contagion' that 'common shocks can explain between sixty to eighty percent of the variation in the total number of currency crises over the post-Bretton Woods period, depending upon the group of countries one is looking at' (2000, p. 2). For example, a shock to a single small country ends up affecting everyone because it affects international capital flows. In that case, 'contagion' can seem like a common shock to capital flows (ibid., p. 25). The bunching of currency crises in time

is not a sufficient condition for the occurrence of 'contagion'. This is –
among other things – why in this book we have preferred to argue on a
country-by-country basis, at least in this empirical part.

In the case of the ASEAN countries it has frequently been argued in the
literature that their real exchange rates were only mildly overvalued *vis-à-vis*
the US dollar, if at all. True or not, one could observe real appreciations
relative to non-dollar currencies in the 18-month run-up to the currency crisis
of July 1997. These were noteworthy because they presumably contributed to
any market concerns about overall exchange rate overvaluation (Goldstein
and Hawkins 1998, p. 4) and expectations of an imminent devaluation. As
Corsetti et al. put it, 'with the important exception of Korea, all the currencies
that crashed in 1997 had experienced a real appreciation' (1998a, p. 20).
Moreover, these overvaluations were accompanied by a large imbalance in
the balance of payments. As a group, the countries that came under attack in
1997 appear to have been those with large current account deficits throughout
the 1990s (ibid., p. 7).

However, the extent of any exchange rate misalignment was quite modest
in comparison with the size of the subsequent depreciations (ibid., p. 6). This
fact underlines the hypothesis that beyond speculative attacks against
overvalued currencies, important aspects of contagion have been at work.
The Thai crisis worked on the one hand as a 'conduit' to reveal fundamental
weaknesses among the other ASEAN countries (such as the sharp increases
in the incremental capital output ratio in the 1990s compared to the 1980s);
on the other hand 'wake-up' calls received by international fund managers
and the interdependency of the respective currencies because of competition
on third markets served to let the crisis spread, and, thereby, deepen.

NOTES

1.   See again Figure 3.4 for the size of expected losses in the domestic banking sector.
2.   Later on, we shall see, however, that this sequencing does not hold within the two-period
     decision problem!
3.   Figures 5.11–5.13 are courtesy of Peter Nunnenkamp.

6. The New International Financial Architecture

> Crises will occur again and the next one will be different in some dimension from the last – and it will also be unexpected. (Alexander Swoboda 1999, p. 4)

6.1 INTRODUCTION

The new international financial architecture (NIFA) – notwithstanding the fact that there is no common understanding about the meanings and the content of this term – should be built (remember that architecture is the art of construction) on three levels or 'floors'. These are (i) the national or domestic level, (ii) the international level and (iii) the supranational level. The supranational level goes beyond the international level in as much as – for example – the World Trade Organization (WTO) is not simply a successor of the General Agreement on Tariffs and Trade (GATT). It deals mainly with institutions, their instruments and the power to enforce them. On the international level, however, we are mainly concerned with bilateral and/or multilateral co-operation, and in the best of cases, co-ordination. In the following, this ordering gives a 'natural' structure to our chapter. Note that we shall not explore every angle of each level; our main aim is to detect *means of preventing and managing contagious financial crises* better than has obviously been possible in the past.

Note that we shall discuss for each level whether there is a need for new institutions or for a reform of existing institutions. This issue affects, more than other levels, the supranational level in form of the IMF and possibly other supranational organisations. We shall hence discuss, among other views, the relevant aspects of International Financial Institution Advisory Commission (IFIAC) report – also known as the 'Meltzer report' (2000) and other related reform proposals for the IMF. We shall see whether other, additional supranational institutions can come into play and co-operate with the IMF. If there is – on the respective level (national, international, supranational) – an 'impossible trinity', then we shall discuss which of the feasible solutions allows for a better prevention and management of contagious financial crises. On the international level, there are at least two 'impossible trinities' to take into account. One is the classical impossible trinity with regard to exchange rate regimes. Another, more recent one, is that relating to (international) financial market regimes (Frenkel and Menkhoff 2000). On the national level, we introduce as an innovation the 'domestic financial sector regime' as an impossible trinity within a single economy. In Figure 6.1, we give an overview of the main strands of discussion throughout this chapter.

Figure 6.1 The new international financial architecture: an overview

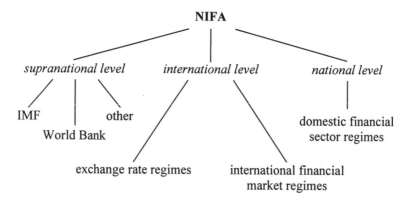

Source: Own compilation.

As Figure 6.1 shows, the NIFA must be built on three pillars: a national, an international and a supranational level. In this chapter, we shall first address the necessary reforms on the national level (organization of the domestic financial sector regime), then proceed to the international level (choose the appropriate exchange rate and sound international financial market regimes) and close with the supranational level (how to organize the IMF and the World Bank group in the future?).

At the end of 1999 the so-called G20 group was founded; this consortium comprises the G7 countries plus Russia and – for the first time – a number of emerging markets which experienced severe financial crises at the end of the last century. It is understood that the members of G20 should find a consensus on the future role (lender of last resort?) of the IMF (supranational level) and its instruments (contingent credit lines and so on), on discretionary or rule-orientated solutions (how much responsibility should be held by the creditors of emerging markets?) for the international financial markets (international level) and, last but not least, on guidelines for the individual financial market regimes in emerging markets (national level) and elsewhere.

6.2   REFORMS ON THE NATIONAL LEVEL

Risks are a natural ingredient in all capital market transactions. What is important is to take on bearable risks. As Dornbusch (1999, p. 291) has pointed out, several risks embedded in the balance sheets of financial institutions were beyond this criterion, for example in the Asian crisis. There was an excessive *liquidity risk* due to the mismatching of maturities, a *currency risk* because of large unhedged short positions, a *market* arising from investment in risky and volatile assets and a *national credit risk* because of the perception of accumulated individual risks associated with the country as a whole. *Controlling* risk is a means of avoiding unsustainable vulnerability of the domestic financial system. Dornbusch made two suggestions: (i) to set and enforce capital standards and (ii) to introduce sophisticated risk management (ibid., p. 294). We shall now pick up the issue of (regular) controls in the framework of an 'impossible trinity' for the domestic financial sector regime. In Figure 6.2, the three relevant goals which, following Jan Tinbergen (1964), cannot all be attained simultaneously, are depicted as circles.

Figure 6.2   The impossible trinity in the domestic financial sector regime

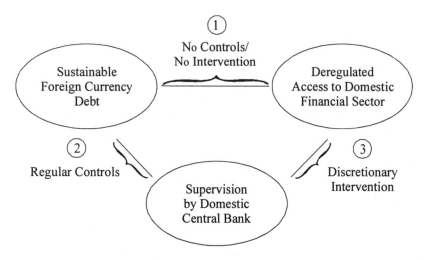

Source: Own compilation.

There are also three policy options. The first (1) is a world of no controls and no intervention which is compatible with attaining a sustainable foreign currency debt and, at the same time, having a deregulated access to the domestic financial sector. A sustainable foreign currency debt is an economic goal with its own merits as the inter-temporal theory of the balance of payments showed quite a while ago. A liberalized domestic capital market is also an economic goal for an emerging market as financial integration allows domestic savings and investment decisions to become separated (Kletzer 2000, p. 2) and because empirical investigations show that such liberalization tends to decrease the cost of capital where introduced (Bekaert and Harvey 2000, p. 565). This effect is due, primarily, to the fact that foreign speculators enhance domestic liquidity and increase the valuation of local companies (ibid., p. 567). No controls and no intervention in option (1) contains the implication that no policy distortions associated with government guarantees, limited liability schemes and so on can exist under this regime. Implicitly, this option rests upon the assumption of rational expectations, of undistorted international financial markets, of no policy distortions, including sovereign risk (Kletzer 2000, p. 3), of negligible information asymmetries and so on. In a less perfect world, additional issues come into play (see below).

A second option may consist of a world of strict regular controls (2) which is consistent with the goal of a sustainable foreign currency debt, but also with the goal of a supervision of financial transactions by the central bank or any other qualified agency. In this world, however, a fully deregulated access to the domestic financial sector is unavailable by definition.

What is the merit of a supervision of the domestic financial sector by the domestic central bank? For example, the lender of last resort issue. What about domestic central banks and their role as 'lender of last resort'? The monetarist view holds that 'if the central bank is able to keep monetary aggregates growing at appropriate rates, it is unlikely that a lender of last resort role is even needed to promote the health of the economy' (Mishkin 1994, p. 32). This position is fine in theory. But in practice it is like saying: 'If it stops raining, we'll go by foot and not by car'. But, possibly, if you wait long enough, you will be too late. 'To wait too long to implement a lender of last resort policy could be disastrous' (ibid., p. 35). The central bank should not pursue a policy of a 'too-big-to-fail proposition'. Instead, it can be reasonable to let the insolvent bank go under, but to announce, at the same time, that the central bank is ready to support the financial system as a whole with liquidity and hence prevent a bank panic from spreading to the rest of the banking system (ibid., p. 40). This policy of liquidity infusion also serves to give some hints on the regulatory oversight function a central bank should have; once a financial institution (bank, finance company and so on) is given access to the discount facilities of its respective central bank, the latter, in turn, may have access to information on the institution's risk-taking activities (ibid., p. 41). If such a case-by-case regulatory role is insufficient to prevent financial crises, periodic, and hence regular examinations of banks may be permitted to the monetary authorities.

The third option is a world of discretionary interventions (3); in this world, free access to the domestic financial sector goes along with a supervision by the central bank/qualified agencies. The supervision, however, is of a discretionary nature, similar to the interventions of central banks at the foreign exchange market during the Bretton Woods episode. Given the inability of single institutions to foresee market developments, this policy option is not consistent with a sustainable foreign currency debt. Obviously, this third, dangerous option was chosen by many of the emerging economies that ran into financial turmoil in the last decade of the last century. Hence, it seems that options (1) and (2) are the (only) alternatives which compete which each other *vis-à-vis* the goal of preventing and managing contagious financial crises.

But, if controlling risk in the sense chosen by Dornbusch (see above) and also by Mishkin makes sense in order to better prevent and manage contagious financial crises in emerging markets, it should be worthwhile to inspect in more detail those who are prepared to bear these risks and to talk about the risk premium that is to be found on financial markets. Talking about risks is almost the same as talking about speculation/speculators. It seems, however, that speculating is always accompanied by some sort of '*haut goût*'. 'In developing capital markets, the speculator, and in particular the international speculator, is looked upon with many reservations' (Bekaert and Harvey 2000, p. 565). This statement is somewhat opposed to the empirical observation that hazardous investment strategies are pursued in many cases in the first place by domestic agents and less so by foreign agents in the emerging market (see Chapter 3). Foreign speculators are attracted to emerging markets primarily for the diversification benefits they can reap.

If this is true, controlling risk in emerging markets is less a question of limiting the access of foreign investors to the domestic financial market, but rather of abolishing government guarantees/limited liability schemes on the one hand and introducing banking (supervisory and prudential) standards/ improve risk management at a given degree of foreign engagement in the domestic financial market on the other hand. A first step would be to announce target dates in the respective emerging markets for the implementation of the so-called 'Core Principles for Effective Banking Supervision' (BIS 1997). A main shortcoming of these standards, however, is that they were designed for international banks and the Basle Committee for Banking Supervision has no enforcement power (Eichengreen 1999a, p. 25).

Goldstein therefore asks for a sharpening and extending of the Core Principles in three directions: (i) to set out 'a tougher line on greater transparency for government involvement in the banking system' (1998,

p. 55), (ii) to impose much higher capital requirements than those set as the Basle Capital Accord minimum ('signatories agree to hold their banks to minimal capital requirements of 8 percent of risk-weighted assets', Eichengreen 1999a, p. 24) in emerging markets given their unstable environment and (iii) to add to the list of the Core Principles 'the elements of an efficient bankruptcy law' (Goldstein 1998, p. 56; Siebert 1999, p. 2). One may add that these efforts should be extended to the corporate sector (Eichengreen 1999a, pp. 28–30).

Recent empirical research demonstrates that the risk premium – that is, the expected excess return from holding a foreign currency deposit in an emerging market – can be attributed to country-specific fundamentals like per capita GNP, average inflation and credit risk (Bansal and Dahlquist 2000, p. 140). All of these factors are endogenous. While the first two items are usually highly influenced by domestic monetary and fiscal policy, the last item is, among other things, a function of a well-established surveillance of domestic financial agents by the respective central bank. It turns out, hence, that domestic financial stability in emerging markets, 'produced', among other things, by enforced standards and active surveillance of the monetary authorities, is a key element for the prevention of contagious financial crises.

6.3   REFORMS ON THE INTERNATIONAL LEVEL

On the international level, we have to appraise in the first place exchange rate regimes in countries 'susceptible' to financial crises. As Steven Hanke (1999) has pointed out several times, pseudo-fixed or semi-fixed exchange rate regimes are strong candidates for speculative attacks and can hence contribute to the onset of a contagious financial crisis. Before we turn to analyse those hybrids and their future role within a NIFA, it is worthwhile having a look at another 'impossible trinity'.

Figure 6.3 depicts the classical dilemma of stabilization policy. It is not feasible for a government to allow a free movement of capital, to pursue a strategy of a stable exchange rate and to pretend autonomy in its monetary policy simultaneously (Sell and Gehle 1996, pp. 48–9, 182–7; Frenkel and Menkhoff 2000, pp. 11–16).

The very first option (1) stands by and large for the 'mainstream' during the post-Bretton Woods era of 1973 to 1995. Before flexible exchange rates became a reality, many well-known economists, such as Milton Friedman, Egon Sohmen and Herbert Giersch, served as advocates of this regime in the late 1960s/early 1970s. It was argued that a free movement of capital would improve the world-wide allocation of capital and also help to let the banks better manage their transformation tasks (maturity transformation, risk transformation and so on). The first oil-price crisis of 1973–74 was a strong test of the capability of the international financial system to recycle the Organization of Petroleum-Exporting Countries' (OPEC) surpluses into the industrialized world without causing significant inflation. From today's point of view, we may say that the system passed the test. The autonomy of the respective monetary policies had been demanded vigorously, partly reflecting the frustration over the ultimate results of the Bretton Woods regime, when $n-1$ countries had no option but to face and then to react to the actions of the US Federal Reserve. At the same time, monetarists claimed that only in an environment of flexible exchange rates could a money supply strategy be implemented successfully.

Figure 6.3   The impossible trinity in exchange rate regimes

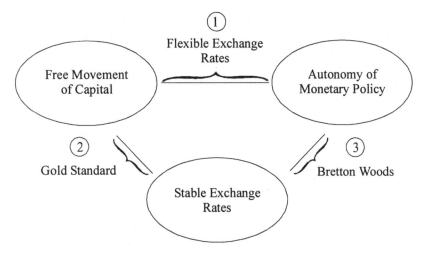

Source: Frenkel and Menkhoff (2000, p. 12).

As a matter of fact, many countries in the world economy did not introduce – or, once introduced, maintain – flexible exchange rates. In the industrialized world, European countries invented the 'snake in the tunnel' (1973–78) which became the predecessor of the EMS (1979–98). Developing countries opted in many cases for currency pegs (usually against the US dollar) organized as adjustable pegs, crawling pegs and so on or simply for some sort of 'managed floating'. These forms of exchange rate regimes in particular helped to create conditions favourable to speculative attacks (see Chapter 2 for more details) during the 1990s. Nevertheless, many govern-ments find it difficult 'to move from pegged exchange rates to greater exchange rate flexibility – what is known in the economic policy community as the "exit" problem' (Eichengreen 1999b, p. C1).

The reason for this reluctance has to do with the experiences countries have had in the past. As Eichengreen reports, 'typically growth has slowed in the period leading up to the exit. In the year the exit takes place, growth is negative and significantly below that in both the non-exit cases and in countries with lasting pegs. ... Subsequent to the exit, output and exports recover' (ibid., pp. C4–5). The best timing for the exit option seems to be a time of capital inflows, or at least when capital is not flowing out. Countries which ran into a deep crisis, like Thailand in 1997–98, missed the right point in time to introduce a greater exchange rate flexibility. As in the case of Mexico in 1994–95, politicians feared loss of face and negative reputational consequences of a devaluation as they were in the run-up to a presidential election. During the period of capital inflows preceding the crisis, the exchange rate peg was maintained and it motivated banks, corporates and other agents to accumulate unhedged foreign currency exposure (ibid., p. C8). In neither country did the pegging of the exchange rate prevent a speculative attack. On the contrary, when private investors suddenly came to believe that there was increased risk, this fact alone was able to produce a self-fulfilling speculative attack, once the economy's fundamentals had deteriorated sufficiently (Flood and Marion 2000, p. 262).

On a world economy scale, however, the 'partisans' of greater exchange rate flexibility are in a defence situation, so to speak. The crippling enthusiasm for flexible exchange rates must be largely attributed to the high volatility observed on the foreign exchange markets. The historical example of the gold standard – our option (2) in Figure 6.3 – has received a renewed interest in the last years, partly induced by the mentioned volatility on foreign exchange markets. This regime offers an alternative where it is not necessary to do without a free movement of capital when stable exchange rates are desired. In contrast to the historical episode of the gold standard, modern derivatives of this exchange rate regime – the currency board figuring prominently – do not hinge on the fluctuations of gold production, of price changes and arbitrage possibilities on the gold market and so on. Steven Hanke and others pushed the idea of currency boards in the early 1990s and by now a number of additional developing countries like Argentina or economies in transition like Estonia are operating this exchange rate regime successfully. Active monetary policy, under this regime, is no longer feasible. But, in contrast to the Bretton Woods regime, national governments may well change the foreign currency to which they choose to fix their domestic money. Hence, in principle, there is no key currency in the world economy.

Strong advocates of currency boards like George Soros or the economist Steven Hanke from Johns Hopkins University, however, have erroneously attributed to the currency board a capacity which it does not possess. A currency board is definitely not a perfect absorber/insulator against speculative attacks and hence against the onset and contagion of financial crises. While it is true that under this regime the domestic authorities cannot be forced to intervene on the foreign exchange market, it is unlikely that the system survives if strong capital outflows drive the domestic (nominal and real) interest rates up to critical levels. If at all, only balanced public budgets (or budgets in surplus) can afford temporarily high interest rate scenarios. Moreover, foreign exchange is not as perfect as gold as a means of backing domestic paper money. Foreign exchange is not held in cash or demand deposits by the respective currency board/central bank, but more likely as a portfolio of time deposits/bonds and so on. The corresponding different maturities make foreign exchange reserves less convertible and hence less liquid than gold was under the gold standard. If the maturity structure of foreign exchange reserves held by a currency board were known by speculators, these could bet against the board or at least force the board to incur expensive short-term credit to fulfil its conversion duties.

Let us end our discussion of Figure 6.3 with option (3). Despite the widespread disappointment with the results of the Bretton Woods example (1944–73), the financial crises of the last decade have revitalized some aspects of this regime. The optimists may go too far when they assign to this system a high autonomy of monetary policy for the participating countries on the one hand and a high degree of exchange rate stability on the other. The goal of free movement of capital – which was explicitly violated under the Bretton Woods regime – has come under severe criticism recently against the background of the financial turmoil observed in several countries in the last decade. Capital controls are widely discussed as a means of fighting or even avoiding financial crises, not to mention Malaysia's strong efforts to overcome its foreign exchange crisis (which began in 1997) mainly using this particular instrument.

Quantitative capital controls – whether organized as controls of capital imports or of capital exports – are, according to the overwhelming majority of empirical studies, the wrong instrument to prevent domestic financial crises. The results achieved by Nadem Ul Haque and Peter Montiel (1990) are still holding: in spite of severe capital controls, deviations from the uncovered interest parity were hard to detect in the vast majority of periods and countries (developed plus developing) investigated. These findings point at the lack of *effectiveness* of the instrument of capital controls. Moreover, Bacchetta (1990) has shown in a seminal paper that neither temporary nor permanent capital controls can help to avoid speculative attacks or the substitution of capital exports by imports of goods. In what concerns the *efficiency* of this instrument, the unanimous view is that capital controls are inefficient (Sell and Gehle 1996, pp. 98–129).

As Eichengreen correctly states, 'outflow controls ... attempt to contain instability in the banking system not by preventing bank owners and managers from levering up their bets but by preventing depositors fearful of the consequences from taking and bringing down the banking system' (1999a, p. 55). These controls hence only treat symptoms rather than the cause of the financial turmoil. A better cure will always consist in a thorough elimination of distortions in the domestic financial sector (government guarantees, insurance schemes) and in the credible intention to restrain any excessive monetary and fiscal policy (ibid., p. 57).

The experiences gained by *Malaysia* with its controls on capital flows since autumn 1997 seem to tell a different story. From a short-term point of view, the capital controls installed helped to bring interest rates down from a level of 11 to a level of 7 per cent in early 1998. The attractiveness of domestic shares traded on the Malaysian stock exchange was raised artificially while recorded foreign direct investment inflows to the industrial sector declined by 12 per cent (Frenkel and Menkhoff 2000, pp. 71–2). On the foreign exchange market, the Malaysian ringgit experienced some recovery in 1998 *vis-à-vis* 1997. But it remains to be seen whether the stabilization of the ringgit must be attributed to other, more significant factors.

Beyond quantitative restrictions on international capital transactions, the economics profession has put forward various schemes for a taxation of foreign exchange transactions. The most prominent is the idea launched by Nobel prize winner James Tobin in 1978. The Tobin tax is meant to tax all transactions with foreign exchange ('all spot conversions of one currency into another') world-wide. The tax rate should be in the interval of 0.1 and 0.5 per cent of the transactions' volume (ibid., p. 65) according to Tobin. Such a tax can in principle reduce the profit from speculation and thereby deter speculators from short-run transactions and hence reduce the volatility of exchange rates. To be effective, the tax rate must neutralize the gains from significant parity changes. It is unclear, however, how it is possible to convince all countries to participate in the system. If not, the tax will be to the detriment of those countries that have introduced the tax. In other words: there is need for international co-ordination if the tax is collected by the national tax authorities or possibly by a supranational institution responsible for the distribution of the tax revenues (ibid., pp. 65–6). Also, it remains to be seen how the proceeds of such a tax can be used efficiently.

A second proposal comes from the French economist Jacques Mélitz (1994). Instead of taxing transactions, Mélitz favours a direct taxation of the gains earned from short-term international financial transactions. All gains in foreign exchange stemming from sales of assets/repayment of debt and which are held for less than one year, should be subject to the tax. In principle, a Mélitz-type tax does not hinge upon the unanimous participation of all countries who are present at the world-wide foreign exchange markets. But, this advantage is reduced by the fact that the volatility of exchange rates will hardly be affected by such a tax: at best, gains from foreign exchange transactions are taxed and hence reduced, but they are not eliminated (ibid., p. 66).

A special tax on transactions in the capital account was introduced by Chile in 1991 and it has been said that these Chilean-type capital controls can be more effective and efficient than other, traditional means of controlling capital flows (Hoffmann 1999, p. 83). These controls consist in market-based measures to regulate capital inflows at the short end. More precisely, we are dealing here with taxes on short-term capital inflows in the form of unremunerated reserve requirements (URRs) on financial credits (Buch 1999, p. 3). 'Since 1991, foreign loans and deposits by non-residents in Chile have generally been subject to a 20% URR' (ibid., p. 6). That is, only capital imports, not capital outflows are affected by the tax.

After an introductory URR of 20 per cent, Chile has recently eased its controls by setting the URR to zero in autumn 1998. This is surprising from the point of view that the original intention of a tax on capital inflows was said to be the reduction in the volatility of capital transactions and exchange rates! Instead, the Chilean authorities decided – in the wake of the Asian crisis – that they wanted to 'attract more capital in order to support the currency and to prevent a further devaluation which could hurt firms with open foreign exchange liabilities' (ibid.). The idea, thus, was to support capital inflows as a means of avoiding a reversal of direction in capital flows. In the context of our subject, one may well ask the question whether the Chilean authorities assumed themselves to be already 'immune' against contagion. Can it have been the other way around, that is, that easing capital inflows helped to bring in the Asian Flu? According to Edwards (1998) the controls did not insulate Chile from the Asian financial crisis. He finds that the interest rate response was greater in Chile than in Hong Kong, so the controls can hardly have been effective.

The empirical evidence is mixed. With a view to the transactions, Buch finds that 'since 1996, the share of short-term lending to Chile has been below-average and on a decline' (1999, p. 11). Hence, we can observe a 'significant impact on the composition of inflows [in favour of medium and long term, to the detriment of short term], but not on the level' (Eichengreen 1999a, p. 53). One may attribute this outcome to the increase in the effective tax rate equivalent of the URR in 1996. Evidence, however, does not show a decline in the volatility of capital flows after the controls had been imposed

(1991–98). Yet, at the same time, a reduction in exchange rate volatility has been observed 'pursuant to the introduction of the URR' (ibid., p. 14). Summarizing, the overwhelming impression is that capital controls or taxes are insufficient means to insulate an economy from a contagious financial turmoil. Furthermore, the volatility of neither capital flows nor exchange rates is not necessarily dangerous *per se*. It is the sudden change in the direction of capital flows accompanied by a precipitous fall in the exchange rate which hits the economies, as we could observe in the cases of Mexico, Asia, Russia and Brazil.

The financial turmoil episodes in the last decade have increased the interest in broadening the scope of government action against the effects caused or at least triggered by international capital transactions. In Figure 6.4, the instruments to directly or indirectly control capital transactions, discussed above, are now supplemented by means of 'compensating' the effects of turbulent capital flows on the domestic economy: one additional option (1) lies in the explicit accumulation of foreign exchange reserves; a second one draws on the use of contingent credit lines (3).

Figure 6.4 Policy interventions as means to compensate/control capital transactions

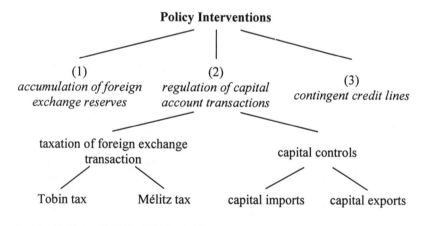

Sources: Frenkel and Menkhoff (2000, p. 64); own compilation.

The accumulation of reserves – equivalent to the amount of debt maturing within one year – as an instrument of isolation against turmoil on international financial markets or a speculative attack against one's own currency goes back to Alan Greenspan (Kletzer 2000, p. 15). A clue in this proposal, however, lies in governments' ability to raise reserves. As an increase in reserves cannot come as an exogenous event, the most likely strategy is that the domestic authorities borrow reserves abroad. The cost of raising these reserves is the difference between the interest rate paid on the country's external debt and the interest earned on foreign reserves (ibid., p. 16). With rational expectations of forward-looking agents, it is clear that the costs incurred by borrowed reserves have to be paid some time in the future. This can be done by 'current or future spending cuts, tax revenue increases or monetisation' (ibid., p. 17). With given fiscal policies, an increase in the growth rate of the monetary base is to be expected. If the exchange rate peg was consistent with current and future monetary policy before the increase in reserves, now it becomes unsustainable in the absence of fiscal adjustment. Hence, the accumulation of reserves can only help to defend a peg as long as fiscal policy is adjusted accordingly. Apart from these theoretical aspects, historical experiences with reserve accumulation are not encouraging: 'reserves have, in turn, been largely invested in low-yielding instruments, mostly treasury bills, in industrial-country markets' (Buira 1999, p. 11).

The last option available in Figure 6.4 makes reference to the so-called 'contingent (or precautionary) credit lines'. This idea was put forward in autumn 1998 by US President Bill Clinton. The IMF introduced this instrument in 1999 (Golder 1999, p. 14). We can deal with it in this section rather than in the next one as it enhances the battery of IMF facilities without affecting the IMF's nature or character as an institution. Under this facility, the IMF can commit resources on a contingency basis to countries that are under threat of contagion from crises in other emerging markets. As in the case of other facilities, conditionality[1] would be attached to the provision of funds. In the words of Stefan Golder:

> A precautionary credit line can therefore help to avoid such attacks by way of an IMF approval of its economic policy as well as the signalling of readily available resources. The essence of a precautionary credit line therefore is to protect 'innocent bystanders' from an indiscriminate loss of investors' confidence. (Golder 1999, pp. 14–15)

What makes contingent credit lines so appealing is that they explicitly make reference to the phenomenon of 'contagion' in financial markets – the main subject of this book.

Several problems, however, arise in conjunction with this new instrument. The first is the issue of *eligibility*. The new facility should be strictly 'reserved' for those countries with sound economic policies, high standards implemented in the respective financial system (including effective bankruptcy procedures) and good relationships with their foreign private creditors. But, when can we speak of 'innocent bystanders' affected by 'pure contagion'? In contrast, countries that are in need of policy adjustment/policy corrections would – *ceteris paribus* (!) – continue to apply for Fund support in the 'classical categories' of stabilization programmes of the IMF. It is most likely that the eligibility issue will flow into an adverse selection problem. To overcome this problem, a catalogue of indicators will be needed which is accepted internationally and which should be monitored by an independent institution such as the Bank for International Settlements in Basle.

A second problem or drawback of precautionary credit lines is related to the *setting of standards*. If a country receives good or even very good 'marks' along the indicators applied, this may give rise to feelings of an illusory security that could lead to a misallocation of funds by financial markets. On the other hand, if a country receives low marks and is hence 'downgraded', the scheme might trigger capital flight out of the respective country. This issue is intimately linked to the possible reactions of the market participants on the publication of 'leading indicators' on the status of emerging economies. We shall address this important question again in the last chapter of this book.

In principle, contingent credit lines can also be provided by private creditors ('bailing in private creditors'). The inherent problem, however, is that private creditors could reduce other loans to the country in question 'in an equal amount to the contingent credit when the contingency arises. This means that the contingent lines of credit need not increase the resources available to the government in the event of a crisis' (Kletzer 2000, p. 19). In fact, 'banks participating in a line of credit to the Mexican government resisted an increase in their country exposure by refusing to grant new credits to Mexican firms' (Buira 1999, p. 12). On the other hand, the fear that 'lenders could be tempted to take greater risks [when contingent credit lines exist], and thereby increase rather than decrease the stability of the international financial system' (Golder 1999, p. 16) is not well founded. Private lenders have been blamed for this attitude during periods when the IMF was playing its traditional role of designing rescue packages and the issue is not linked intrinsically to the instrument of contingent credit lines.

A third issue assigned to contingent credit lines is related to the *accentuation of the problem*: 'new risks, one being that the country applying for the credit line may signal to the market that a problem exists' (Siebert 1999, p. 7). This argument comes, on top of the rest, from economists who, in other circumstances, are the most vigorous advocates of the market economy. Would market participants not already be aware of these countries and their economies? If there does exist a distinction between well-informed investors (in emerging markets) and less well informed investors, is the IMF now going to 'take over' in the future the role of the well-informed investors *vis-à-vis* the less-informed investors? We believe, on the contrary, that contingent credit lines should encompass credible information to the investors on the soundness of the economic fundamentals of the economy in question. Also, this new instrument gives to the investors a hint about the costs/risks associated with a hypothetical speculative attack.

Despite the problems mentioned and discussed, the idea of contingent credit lines is in principle consistent with the insights gained from epidemiology. It seems that this scheme is concerned with countries that are 'susceptible' to a contagious virus and therefore, in positive terms, candidates for a 'vaccination programme'. As is well known from epidemiology, the success of vaccination hinges very much on the non-infection of the susceptibles *ex ante*. The indicators suggested for the classification of countries simply serve to identify candidates for vaccination that are most likely 'in good health'. In order to 'interrupt the spread of infection it is only necessary to reduce the ... number of susceptibles to below that which will enable each primary case to give rise to at least one secondary case' (Nokes and Anderson 1992, p. 189). As in epidemiology, the efficacy of contingent credit lines should be assessed according to the degree of prevention of infection they can provide. It should be clear, however, that the 'duration of protection' provided by contingent credit lines can never be compared to the corresponding duration in classical vaccination programmes against epidemic diseases (Anderson et al. 1997, p. 1467).

Vaccination in epidemiology has a *positive external effect*: for 'those individuals who miss vaccination there is a reduced risk of contracting infection ... susceptible individuals gain protection from the vaccinated proportion of the population' (Nokes and Anderson 1992, p. 190). This is so, because after vaccination the host population is now 'effectively smaller and transmission is correspondingly less efficient' (Anderson and May 1990, p. 642). On international financial markets, it may be just the other way around. Speculators possibly concentrate their attacks all the more against susceptible countries/markets which do not enjoy the benefit of contingent credit lines. And, there is a last important aspect. As in the case of mass vaccination destined to conserve and foster *public health*, contingent credit lines is an obligation, in the first place, for public agencies like the IMF.

Let us come back for a moment to the important issue of 'bailing in the private sector'. Private investors have been shielded by IMF rescue action in the Mexican, the Korean and the Russian cases. 'Official funds were used to repurchase and retire short-term debts' (Eichengreen 1999a, p. 59). As Siebert observes, '[f]or equity capital, private investors are bailed in automatically when stock prices fell' (1999, p. 11). For bonds and bank credits, the incorporation of new clauses (majority voting requirements for the modification of the terms of credit, sharing, minimum legal threshold, rules on collective representation and non-acceleration) into loan contracts, but also into international bonds, can help to address the responsibility of private creditors and to make it easier to renegotiate defaulted debts. '[C]reditors could assume some of the risks' (ibid.).

So far, the impossible trinity in the exchange rate regimes has helped us to think about more or less implicit policy co-ordination to prevent and manage contagious financial crises. The Bretton Woods system as well as the gold standard provided such co-ordination devices, be it in the form of the monetary policy of the leading currency or in the form of international price arbitrage through international trade. In a system of more or less flexible exchange rates, policy co-ordination, if it is wanted, has to be designed explicitly. As Mishkin puts it, 'international policy co-ordination to deal with financial crises is imperative' (1994, p. 42). This statement holds, if only for the reason that 'if a central bank does not feel that it has the resources to contain a financial crisis in its country, then it needs to be able to solicit the help of other central banks to keep the financial crisis from getting out of hand and spreading to other countries' (ibid., p. 43). Let us explore the relevant issues in detail.

Co-ordination can be understood as the explicit will of different countries to adopt common instruments and to organize their economic policy towards common goals. Co-ordination is helpful/necessary, *ceteris paribus*, when spill-over effects come into play such as in the case of contagious financial crises. Co-ordination, however, is risky or even harmful if there is (i) high insecurity about the reasons for the onset of a crisis and about the effects of policy instruments available to fight the crisis. The same applies when the (ii) costs of bargaining between the hypothetical partners and/or the (iii) incentives to cheat among the countries who underwrite an agreement or at least promise to co-operate are high. Assume away for a moment, for reasons of simplicity, the last two problems. Then we have to deal in essence with the size/significance of spill-over effects on the one hand and with the degree of insecurity among the policymakers with regard to appropriate policy intervention on the other, as depicted in Figure 6.5.

Most likely, the relevant quadrants for our subject, the occurrence of contagious financial crises in the world economy, are the northwest quadrant (optimistic case) and the northeast quadrant (pessimistic case). In the framework of Chapter 5, however, the incentive to cheat (one-period problem) or to opt for a compound strategy of either taking the medicine or regaining reputation after cheating in the previous period (two-period problem) seems to be the more relevant variable than the degree of insecurity about the cures of economic policy! The revised Figure 6.5 now reads as shown in Figure 6.6.

We refer the reader to Chapter 5 where we have deducted analytically those factors which tend to favour the mentioned strategies. The stronger (weaker) these factors are, the more likely it is that we find ourselves in the northeast (northwest) quadrant.

Figure 6.5   Costs and benefits of international policy co-ordination

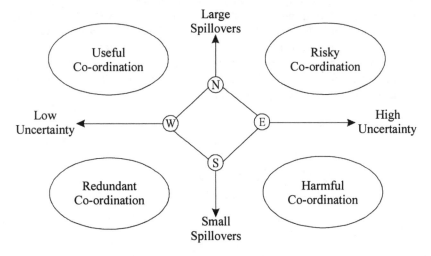

Sources: Klodt (2000, p. 2); own compilation.

Figure 6.6   Costs and benefits of policy co-ordination in the presence of contagion

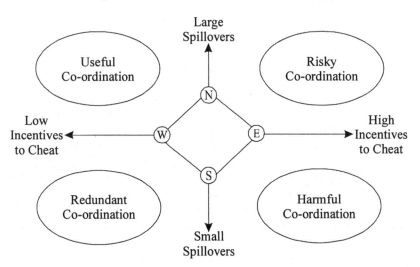

Source: Own compilation.

In the era of globalization, a sharp distinction between the order of exchange rates and the order of financial markets is neither possible nor useful. If there is another impossible trinity related to the order of financial markets – which we then have to take into account when dealing with the NIFA – this impossible trinity should be intimately linked to the order of exchange rates. A proposal made by Frenkel and Menkhoff (2000) is depicted in Figure 6.7. The three goals from Figure 6.3 now translate into 'global financial markets', 'national autonomy' and 'stable financial markets'. The last goal corresponds to the existence of 'stable exchange rates', the first one to the issue of 'free capital movements' and the one in between to the goal of 'autonomy of monetary policy'.

Figure 6.7   The impossible trinity in the international financial sector regime

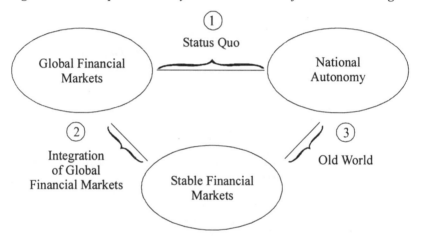

Sources: Frenkel and Menkhoff (2000, p.17); own compilation.

When opting for the first strategy (1), domestic authorities accept globalisation of international financial markets – as a part of the status quo – without renouncing on autonomy in setting and implementing national instruments to intervene on financial markets. In principle, no global rules are available under this scenario. This option seems to be difficult if not impossible to pursue for small open economies. These may be restricted to the task of supervising their own financial institutions (see above). Strategy (3) seems to be – by and large – obsolete as it is only conceivable in an environment of non-global financial markets. This environment, of course, will never come back.

Strategy (2) implies the integration of global financial markets. It presupposes that the already integrated international financial markets are supplemented by (i) widely accepted banking/capital standards, (ii) rules of harmonized/co-ordinated conduct and (iii) improved transparency and disclosure in international financial markets. As we shall see subsequently, there are at present a number of different strategies aiming at this goal.

The development of international banking standards is well advanced. The surveillance of banking systems must not only be strengthened, but enforcement mechanisms should follow. At present, a number of proposals are being discussed. The so-called 'Basle proposal' – put forward by the Basle Committee for Banking Supervision (whose members are the central bank governors of G10), an institution which was built upon the tradition of the Basle capital accord from 1988 (minimum capital requirements for international banks) – asks for new equity capital standards for European banks along the lines of US banks and the introduction of standardized, and hence *external* credit ratings applied to borrowers from industrialized countries, from emerging markets and from developing economies (Engelen 1999, p. 34). The ratings would be provided from widely accepted international rating agencies (Standard & Poor's, Moody's and so on).

In contrast, large European banks like the German Deutsche Bank and the Dutch ABN-Amro Bank have demanded throughout 1999 the acceptance and priority of internal credit ratings *vis-à-vis* external ratings (ibid.). Also, they are in favour of the newly installed European Central Bank becoming the banking supervision authority in Europe. To date, banking supervision is still the responsibility of national European agencies or central banks.

At the meeting (April 2000) of international banks from Europe, the US and emerging economies in The Hague, a paper devoted to the reform of the Basle capital accord (1988) was presented (*Handelsblatt* 2000a, p. 25). A working group of major banks agreed that external ratings as a method of evaluating credit risks should play only a minor role in the future. The group also suggested adopting the principle of equal treatment towards all financial intermediaries and applying the rules of equity capital not only to banks, but to all institutions involved in the business of credit extension. In the meantime, a revision of the 1988 Basle capital accord is in progress (Otto 2000, p. 46). Under the title 'Basle II', the amendment will be published probably in the end of 2001.

In 1999 the Financial Stability Forum (FSF) was founded with the purpose of achieving a higher degree of co-ordination between the G7 group, representatives from financial centres outside G7, the IMF, the BIS, the OECD and so on. It was agreed that the forum reports to the group of seven (Tietmeyer 1999, p. 5). The FSF, however, suffers from two major shortcomings. One is that a number of important emerging markets have been left out and a second one is that – in contrast to the IMF and to the WTO – this new institution has no means of enforcing sanctions (Frenkel and

Menkhoff 2000, p. 43). By definition, it is an international assembly of interested and affected groups, but not a supranational institution (see below).

Meanwhile, three groups of experts of the FSF have worked out proposals with regard to offshore financial centres, high-leverage institutions and the role of erratic capital flows in the world economy (Engelen 2000, p. 46). *Offshore centres* will have to accept an investigation of their surveillance rules and practices on financial markets by the IMF. If the IMF finds shortcomings, such as information sharing, these defects will have to be corrected quickly. Otherwise, the international community of banks and financial intermediaries under the auspices of the FSF is entitled to impose sanctions against the respective offshore centres. During the summer of 2000, a blacklist of offshore centres was published, which, according to the IMF do not meet the requirements set by the FSF. Hedge funds, as the most prominent representatives of high-leverage institutions, however, were not affected by new regulation proposals. The working group has urged that hedge funds should be subject to self-regulating measures. Otherwise, a scheme for the registration of credits could be installed in the future. As to the occurrence of *volatile capital flows* from and into emerging markets, the respective working group has designed new guidelines for the improvement of the existing financial infrastructure and the use of modern hedging instruments against the risk of exchange rate/interest rate changes.

As Goldstein puts it, 'all parties would profit from the availability of more comprehensive, more frequent and more timely data' (1998, p. 57) on a number of key financial variables such as the maturity and currency composition of external debt in emerging economies, the composition and maturity of net international reserves and estimates about the size and structure of non-performing loans in these countries. The last, however, would require an international harmonized definition of the term 'non-performing' to be agreed. Better information on the health of economies/ financial markets has its own merit for hypothetical investors and other market participants. In the last chapter we shall address the question – raised already in the introduction to this book – on the benefits and costs of 'leading' or 'early-warning' indicators with regard to contagious financial crises.

6.4 REFORMS ON THE SUPRANATIONAL LEVEL

6.4.1 Optimal Diversity of Multilateral Agencies

The reforms discussed so far must be implemented primarily on a national or international level. In some fields/areas the presence of supranational agencies, however, can be recommended. This applies when we are dealing with external effects whose internalization hinges upon the action of a multilateral agency or in the case of international public goods/bads and so on. For each individual agency, it is imperative to define 'a set of tasks ... that are distinct from the tasks of other multilateral agencies, to avoid counterproductive overlap' (IFIAC 2000, p. 21). Each agency should be responsible for one main area. These are trivial insights from the theory of economic policy. They deal with 'the assignment of policy areas to institutions' (Siebert 1999, p. 5). Assume for a moment a different scenario. If one agency had overlapping tasks with another agency, two principles of decision making would be in direct conflict: the 'hierarchy principle' (*within* any of the individual institutions) and the 'principle of equal partners' (applicable for the relations *between* autonomous agencies). Yet, these insights are often far from being understood by the relevant institutions.

6.4.2 The International Monetary Fund

The new mission
During the meetings of the IMF and the World Bank group in Washington, DC (September 1999) a key clue was claiming more *transparency* in NIFA. It was said that more transparency would help to 'bail in' the private sector in the prevention and 'solution' of financial crises. The IMF itself proposed the introduction of internationally accepted transparency codes and standards. This idea is not a new one: in 1998, the IMF had introduced its 'Special Data Dissemination Standard' and had asked its 182 members to submit accordingly the necessary statistical bases. The IFIAC has suggested, furthermore, that all IMF member countries should in future publish data on their economic performance (including the maturity structure of their outstanding sovereign debt) in a timely and uniform manner (IFIAC 2000, p. 22).

More controversial is the issue of the IMF's role as a lender (of last resort?) to countries in financial crisis. Traditional economists like Lutz Hoffmann (1999, p. 80) argue that the IMF should not be both a player *in* the crisis and a controller *of* the crisis. Hence, he suggests that the IMF should restrain itself to the task of designing programmes of stabilization and structural adjustment and that the role of an international policy surveillance institution should be passed on to the BIS or perhaps even to the World Bank. Moreover, according to Hoffmann, the IMF should continue to be involved in rescue actions, policy packages, debt rescheduling and so on.

We do not share his view, but we find more rationality in the arguments put forward by the IFIAC: against the background of the long history of IMF policy package failures, the Meltzer report has put forward two radical innovations. The IMF should (i) no longer impose any type of conditions, but provide only advice on economic policy as a part of regular consultations with its members (IFIAC 2000, p. 22) and (ii) give short-term liquidity loans to *emerging economies* in crisis 'that have preconditions that establish financial soundness' (ibid.). To be eligible, a member country should meet minimum prudential standards (capitalization of bank and so on) and 'would receive immediate assistance without further deliberation or negotiation' (ibid., p. 23). These 'rules' should define the future new role of the IMF, rather than continuing the unsuccessful 'discretionary' part played in the past. This aspect of IMF policy has been strongly demanded by many economists for some time: 'Automatic mechanisms rather than discretionary actions should play a more important role' (Siebert 1999, p. 4). In a way they correspond to the services provided by a sound health insurance and also to our main subject: contagion. A patient who cares about his/her own health status during the year(s) does not have to negotiate with his/her insurance company the conditions of financing the costs which accrue for the prevention or cure of an acute contagious disease.

Note that in the Meltzer report we find the explicit condition that recipient countries are not allowed to sponsor bailouts (IFIAC 2000, p. 22) – in favour of large uninsured foreign creditors and/or in favour of medium/small domestic debtors equipped with government guarantees – with the liquidity infusion provided by the IMF. Hence, the Meltzer commission is one of the very few attempts to address the moral hazard problem of the IMF directly. It is worth mentioning also that there is no room for 'conditionality' in the previous sense of this term as a part of IMF philosophy. Note also that the Meltzer commission no longer wants the IMF to be an unspecific agency, responsible for providing liquidity to all of the so-called 'third world'. Rather, as a global institution, it must help to overcome the global externalities 'produced' by emerging economies.

Yatrakis and Gart (2000) have recently reviewed the experiences of Thailand, Korea and Indonesia with the IMF and those of Malaysia – who eschewed the IMF – in 1997–98. They find that – along the lines of the Meltzer report – macroeconomic conditionality (tight monetary and fiscal policies to restore the confidence of foreign investors and to support the domestic currencies) resulted in 'yet higher interest rates, widespread corporate bankruptcies, negative real growth, rising unemployment and, particularly in Indonesia, extensive rioting and political unrest' (Yatrakis and Gart 2000, p. 17). Malaysia, as opposed to the three other countries mentioned, did better, but not so much because of imposing controls on short-term capital inflows and prohibiting a part of capital outflows. Following the advice of Paul Krugman, Steve Radelet and Jeffrey Sachs, the authorities launched a stimulating domestic monetary policy to restore economic growth (ibid., p. 18). This points at the obligation of the domestic central bank to provide liquidity on the terms laid down by Frederick Mishkin (see above). Yet, 'all theories would advise an expansionary fiscal stance at a time of recession' (Buira 1999, p. 5). The IMF, in its programmes, however, invariably required a pro-cyclical fiscal retrenchment (ibid.). Malaysia, in turn, will very soon have to think over its capital controls: 'temporary barriers put up to protect domestic financial institutions while they transform have a tendency to become permanent, impeding the country from realising the benefits of globalisation' (ibid., p. 23).

It is sometimes argued (Illing 2000, p. 11) that under these new auspices, the actions of the IMF would become (in the worst case) redundant. Why should the respective countries not prefer to apply for contingent credit lines from the private banking sector? As we have shown above, specific problems arise when contingent credit lines are organized privately. Another reason for not doing so, is the following. As opposed to private creditors, the IMF plays the role often played by the modern welfare state on the national level. One motivation for the existence of the modern welfare state is its capacity to sign insurance contracts with its citizens which no private insurance company would underwrite. The IMF as the prospective 'quasi lender of last resort' according to the Meltzer report, would fill a similar position towards emerging economies.

The IMF, however, cannot become a 'true' lender of last resort to the world economy. As Siebert puts it, there are at least two reasons for this. First, the IMF lends to national governments, and not to financial institutions. Second, the IMF has a limited amount of resources and cannot print money (1999, p. 5). As experiences in the last few years revealed, the IMF's resources were already stretched after several interventions (Jeanne and Wyplosz 1999, p. 16). 'If a systemic crisis for the world economy develops, the central bank will have to play the role of a lender of last resort in a co-ordinated action' (ibid.).

Supporting reforms on the national level

A number of emerging market economies were already or will be in the foreseeable future clients of the IMF. According to the IFIAC, the IMF should 'discourage excessive reliance on short-term borrowing and encourage financial institutions in the borrowing countries to adopt higher standards of safety and soundness' (IFIAC 2000, p. 17). We may add that such measures contribute to the construction of a 'national safety net' towards contagious financial crises – not to be confused with the widespread system of government guarantees in favour of the domestic financial system.

Supporting reforms on the international level

Based on the many bad experiences collected over decades, the Meltzer report concludes – and we agree – that 'countries should choose either firmly-fixed or fluctuating rates' (ibid., p. 25). Or, in the words of Barry Eichengreen:

> [T]he IMF needs to more forcefully encourage its members to policies of greater exchange rate flexibility, and the sooner the better. With few exceptions it should pressure its members ... to abandon simple pegs, crawling pegs, narrow bands and other mechanisms for limiting exchange rate flexibility before they are forced to do so by the markets. ... The only exception to this rule is countries that are prepared not just to fix the exchange rate but to lock it in for the foreseeable future. (Eichengreen 1999a, pp. 105–7)

Hence, in contrast to the past, the IMF should change its policy and no longer 'implicitly defend a pegged exchange rate' (Siebert 1999, p. 7), as happened, for instance, in the recent Brazilian and Russian crises (see above).

6.4.3 The Idea of an Asian Monetary Fund (AMF)

This idea was put forward for the first time, by Japan, at the September meeting of the IMF and the World Bank group in 1997 (*Handelsblatt* 2000b, p. 45). The European Union, but also the US, were strong opponents of this concept from the beginning. The ASEAN group, however, is still pursuing the idea. They argue that such an additional institution may help to intensify financial market co-operation in the region and so prevent the occurrence of another severe contagious financial crisis. Andrew K. Rose is a strong advocate of the AMF: 'Since trade is regional, the region loses disproportionately from trade disruptions which are caused by currency crises. Therefore, the region should try to prevent the spread of these crises' (Rose 1998, p. 8). And since 'currency crises create regional costs, the region has an incentive to create institutions to mitigate these costs by providing a financial safety net' (ibid., p. 17).

The argument is false for several reasons. First of all, as the cases of Russia and Brazil in 1998–99 have demonstrated, we know that currency crises are no longer a regional phenomenon. If this is true, the costs that accrue by contagion have to be borne not only by the region where the crisis began. Hence, there is need for a non-regional, preferably supranational agency to help the countries affected with contingent credit lines/short-term loans to avoid a liquidity crunch. Second, the implementation of such an AMF plan would undermine the existence of one single multilateral agency, the IMF, responsible for the surveillance of its 182 members and acting as a 'quasi lender of last resort'. The existence of various institutions with overlapping tasks violates the rule (see above) that specific policy areas are to be assigned to individual institutions.

Supachai Panitchpakdi, who will follow Mike Moore in 2002 as director general of the United Nations Conference on Trade and Development (UNCTAD), has pointed out that an AMF would better meet the requirement of subsidiarity than the IMF (Petersen 2000, p. 13). This argument is wrong, too. As contagion is rather a global than a regional phenomenon, the subsidiarity principle requires a global institution to take care of it. But, if this is true, then the recommendation of the Meltzer report that the IMF's liquidity loans should be extended exclusively to emerging economies, is valid, too. Only these countries 'produce' those negative externalities we are interested in (contagion) and they need a supranational agency like the IMF. So Weidemann's and others' critique against the Meltzer report – because the latter does not suggest that all developing countries become clients of the IMF – is erroneous (Weidemann 2000, p. 53).

6.4.4 The International Bank for Reconstruction and Development (IBRD) and Regional Development Banks

The IBRD should not be involved in the business of crisis lending, that is, in the prevention and management of contagious financial crises. This statement originates in two observations: in the first place, the development banks should not have overlapping tasks with the IMF (see above). Second, their original mission – and common goal – is to reduce poverty in the developing countries. This goal has a medium- and long-term perspective ('steady flow of official funding', IFIAC 2000, p. 32) in contrast to the short-term liquidity infusions in the wave of a contagious financial market crisis. Poverty, in terms of financial markets, is the lack of access to private sector resources. Third, this kind of momentum indicates that poor countries can hardly be the objective of a reverse in large capital flows and hence, of contagion. This observation points again at the conceptually incorrect criticism of Weidemann (2000, see above) against the Meltzer report.

If the ongoing 'systems competition' debate held in Germany – between Horst Siebert on the hand and Hans-Werner Sinn on the other – has demonstrated anything, then it is that countries which want to attract foreign private capital should be endowed with a modern and efficient infrastructure. Financing infrastructure projects in poor countries is where the development banks should have their main field of activity. As the Meltzer report states, this would be accompanied by additional benefits: 'when the banks financed mainly infrastructure, they could, at least, assess the project's success' (IFIAC 2000, p. 35).

6.4.5 The World Trade Organisation (WTO)

Since the WTO was set up (1995), world trade relations in general and specific forms of protectionism in particular have been under close scrutiny. Moreover, for the first time, we now have an institution which is able to enforce sanctions. This is also helpful with regard to the phenomenon of contagion. A number of respected economists have stressed the significance of 'contagion through trade' (see also Chapter 4). Trade links can in fact, if not cause, at least ease the occurrence of contagion. The existence of the WTO is then all the more important. Countries should not try – the attempt would be fruitless anyway, because trade contraction cannot do away with contagion – to isolate themselves from contagion through trade by means of renewed protection. But, if they do, the WTO is there to convince them to draw back.

The WTO is also beneficial to financial stability in emerging economies: 'the WTO's program of opening up financial services to foreign competition contributes to the growth of international trade and investment, world output and living standards, and economic stability' (ibid., p. 49). This does not mean, however, that the WTO should enter the field of regulation setting, accounting practices and financial standards, because then it would clearly violate the principle of subsidiarity and the optimal assignment of tasks to institutions.

6.4.6 The Bank for International Settlements

The BIS, as it now stands, has never received the same degree of public attention which the IMF and the World Bank Group have called forth. Perhaps the city of Basle alongside the river Rhine is less interesting to the media and therefore more secluded than New York. 'The success of the organisation, it is often said, derives from the secrecy of its meetings and the trust created among central bankers through their frank discussions at their frequent meetings' (ibid., p. 44). The modest public recognition of the BIS, however, does not tally with its increasing importance in the design of rules and standards for NIFA (see above).

Since March 1999, 45 central banks have been represented at the BIS and have access to general meetings. That means that the BIS is no longer an assembly of central bankers primarily from Europe, the US and Canada. Ironically, the Basle Committee on Banking Supervision (formed by the G10 central bank governors in 1974), which is one of the most important forums of the BIS, issued 25 core principles for effective banking supervision, 'applicable to all countries' (ibid., p. 46) in 1997. The year 1997, as is well known, was when the Asian Flu invaded Southeast and East Asia (see above). The financial standards set by the BIS or its committees will continue to exert great influence on national financial standards in emerging markets.

6.5 CONCLUSIONS

It seems that most of the proposals put forward on the road to NIFA, aim at two things. First, to reorganize the division of work between national, international and supranational agencies; and second, to redefine the tasks of each individual agency such that its effectiveness and efficiency can be enhanced. For the latter, the ongoing discussion very much emphasizes the importance of 'moral hazard' and the possible ways of avoiding it.

In Figure 6.8, we have depicted the hypothetical optimization task of a 'moral hazard averse' multilateral agency with regard to its presence on international financial markets. We assume in the first place – though the theoretical arguments do not convince fully and there is no clear-cut empirical evidence available so far – that there exists a positive linear relationship between the willingness of the multilateral agency to bail out foreign banks/funds/owners of bonds on the one hand and the amount of private capital flows which is steered into emerging market economies on the other. The multilateral agency has a positively sloped indifference curve. This represents the amount of compensation in terms of large net capital inflows that the agency is prepared to bail out foreign creditors in the case of a financial crisis in the emerging market.

Figure 6.8   Is there a dilemma for multilateral agencies on international financial markets?

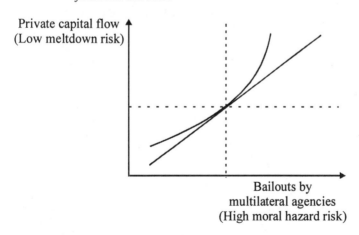

Source: Own compilation.

The extreme position held, for instance, by Anna J. Schwartz (1999) – that the IMF is by and large an institution which should be rejected – can be represented by the broken horizontal line. Irrespective of the existence of a multilateral bailing-out agency, private capital flows to emerging economies have a certain size or they have not. The other extreme position could be interpreted along the lines of a vertical Phillips curve. The advocates of this view may be traditionalists with regard to the role of the IMF who attribute to this institution the production of 'pure' international public goods: regardless of the size of capital flows to emerging economies, the IMF should always be prepared to finance rescue actions even if this implies strong bailing-out effects.

We do not share either view. Instead, we believe that Charles W. Calomiris is right, when he writes: 'without a reliable means of bringing credible market discipline to bear on banks, to provide strong incentives for prudent risk management, government deposit insurance and IMF lending will spur excessive risk taking, financial collapse, and its attendant costs' (1999, p. 380). The IMF and the other agencies reviewed in this chapter have a future role to play, which, however, can no longer be in the bailout, or more generally, in the moral hazard business. The IMF, for example, could charge higher interest/penalty rates to the clients of its new facilities. More convincing is to define clearly the categories/criteria under which an application for IMF funds is feasible. These should be linked to the occurrence of contagion.

NOTE

1.   The Meltzer report, however, seriously questions whether the IMF should continue with its
     old philosophy of conditionality (see below).

7. Final Remarks

Tomorrow it may be judged to be prospering. That is the nature of the current dispensation. It's tulip mania. It's epidemic suggestion. (Victor Quinn in David Hare's play, 'My Zinc Bed'; Faber and Faber 2000, p. 103)

7.1 CAN THE QUESTIONS RAISED IN THE INTRODUCTION TO THIS BOOK BE ANSWERED?

When introducing this book, we gave an overview of the forthcoming chapters on the one hand and questioned the validity, actuality and relevance of the so-called 'early warning indicators' which have been or still are being used in order to *predict* contagious financial crises, on the other. The end of this book is a good time to recapitulate this criticism. Our aim in the following should be to draw conclusions from the individual chapters – beyond the scope of simply giving another summary of contents – with regard to a sounder and more suitable concept of early warning indicators.

In principle, we depart from an easy rule of thinking. Long before getting into the business of collection, systematization and further analysis of numerical data to build 'indicators', every economist should be aware of the following fact. Once the data and hence the indicators are ready, this information comes too late to *predict* any contagious financial crisis. This point was raised several times in the 1980s by Herbert Giersch, the former president of the Kiel Institute of World Economics. Giersch blamed the macroeconomists for their 'belief' in data sets and in the improved techniques to speed up the availability of those data for economic policy advice. His main argument was always: in the race between (the occurrence of) important changes in the 'real economy' and (the struggle of) the economist to get information about 'what's going on' by looking at the data, the economist will necessarily always lose.

But, even if early signals are available in time, how can we 'read' and understand them adequately? The crisis of the Mexican peso in December 1994 serves as a good example. As Agénor and Masson report, 'markets appear to have seriously underestimated the risk of devaluation, despite early warning signals – such as the appreciation of the real exchange rate and, most importantly, the growing current account deficit' (1999, p. 83). The problem with the authors' conclusion is, however, that it was not clear what the signal(s) really meant and whether it was (they were) necessarily (a) warning signal(s) with regard to the exchange rate system. Let us make this point plain, taking the above example of a real exchange rate appreciation. To infer from an observed *real* exchange rate appreciation the most likely correction with a large *nominal* devaluation (Goldfajn and Valdés 1999, p. 231) implies denying further possibilities – such as a nominal price adjustment in the domestic economy – of correction or assigning them a rather low probability. In order to make such a strong judgement, however, additional information, for example concerning the credibility of the policy-makers, the price flexibility on the goods markets and so on, should be available. Domestic price adjustments are often 'accompanied by prolonged recessions, speculative attacks on the currency, or extremely high interest rates. [But], this does not mean that the nominal exchange rate must always be used to correct misalignments' (ibid., p. 256).

It requires – similar to Robert E. Lucas and the theory of rational expectations – an understanding of the structural model of a market, of an economy and so on. We need to identify who the agents are, what motivates them, what targets they pursue and what kind of constraints they have to respect. We have to investigate, for example, the extent to which instability in financial markets has its roots in macroeconomic phenomena or, conversely, whether macroeconomic imbalances affect the stability of financial markets (White 2000, p. 4). In this book on contagious financial crises, such a requirement will profit from insights gained in the earlier parts of the book (Chapters 2 to 5) in general and in the two core explanation models set up in Chapters 3 and 5 in particular. In other words, in the first place we have to put together a good deal of *qualitative* information. On the basis of this qualitative information, we may then proceed in some – not in all – areas to supplement this information with quantitative data, numerical indicators and so on. The outcome should be 'compatible', that is, it should fit nicely with the 'language' of NIFA discussed in the preceding chapter. The latter aims, as is well known, at the *prevention and management* of contagious financial crises. Early warning indicators should, at best, be able to help *predict* such crises.

Our procedure will follow the logic of 'looking forward and concluding backwards' which is the most familiar technique in game theory. Knowing how the IMF – in its most likely future role – will deal with the *prevention and management* of contagious financial crises imposes certain requirements on the design of early warning indicators. These requirements will then be fed back to the main results achieved in Chapters 2 to 5 of this book. At the end, we hope to come up with a set of qualitative and quantitative variables which, in our view, will reflect major insights on the onset and the contagious spread of financial crises, but also match the new semantics of the IMF. In this sense, we hope that the earlier chapters of the book can help to answer – as best as we can – questions raised in the introduction.

7.2 WHAT TYPE OF MINIMUM INFORMATION DOES THE IMF NEED FOR AN ADEQUATE PREDICTION OF A CONTAGIOUS FINANCIAL CRISIS?

If we identify the future IMF with two types of credit: (i) contingent credit lines without an explicit conditionality similar to past IMF programming and (ii) liquidity loans according to the proposal of the Meltzer commission, the following – by and large qualitative – information at least is needed to help predict imminent financial crises:

1. Are the countries in question really 'emerging markets'?[1]
2. Is the respective domestic financial sector in good shape or do we find institutional characteristics of weak banking systems? (Goldstein 1999, p. 327).
3. Have the countries already introduced capital standards, prudent regulations and so on along the lines of the Basle accord?
4. What about banking supervision by the central bank or any other agency?
5. What do we know about the quality of corporate governance (Berg and Pattillo 1999b, p. 365) in the respective country?
6. Is the specific country under consideration more a candidate for the 'onset' of a financial market crisis or for being affected by 'contagion'? In the latter case, the respective country should be able to qualify for the existing 'contingent credit lines'.
7. If we do find countries of both types: how are their economies inter-linked? By trade channels, by investment channels, financial sector channels (bank lending, diversified portfolios) and so on? Note that if bond and equity markets are still underdeveloped in the respective country, it is rather unlikely that portfolio channels of contagion can play any substantial role (Kaminsky and Reinhart 2000, p. 158). The same applies, *mutatis mutandis*, to the other categories.
8. What type of exchange rate regime has been installed? Remember that policies of maintaining predictable currency pegs contributed in the past to the onset and the subsequent spreading of financial crises (Blöndal and Christiansen 1999, p. 12).
9. Is the existing exchange rate regime susceptible to a speculative attack?

10. Will a hypothetical speculative attack primarily melt down domestic reserves or rather push up domestic interest rates?
11. Has the country in question already been a client of the IMF in the past and if so, to what extent did the IMF bail out domestic and foreign creditors (moral hazard likelihood)?
12. Has the World Bank been involved in the past in the business of financing 'structural adjustment programmes' or any other programmes beyond projects intimately linked to domestic infrastructure?

It is almost not worth mentioning that this set of information will not be sufficient for the more or less reliable prediction of a contagious financial crisis. Therefore, we should like to supplement these with key variables and parameters which have been shown to be important throughout this book.

7.3   WHAT SORT OF ADDITIONAL 'EARLY WARNING INDICATORS' EMERGE FROM THE RESULTS OF THIS BOOK?

And thus the native hue of resolution is sicklied o'er with the pale cast of thought. (Hamlet, Prince of Denmark, Thorndike 1973, p. 862)

In medicine, paleness, lack of appetite, sleeplessness and listlessness are taken as early warning signals for an imminent human disease. These indicators sometimes come as late and are as redundant as many of the alleged early warning indicators in economics. Often they can be observed long before we detect an unusual pulse, a rising temperature, a high blood pressure and so on. In principle, analogous observations should be available to predict the likely occurrence of an economic crisis. In the following, we aim to list – by and large according to the sequence of chapters in this book – additional qualitative and quantitative information which may be helpful in predicting a contagious financial crisis.

1. Do we find signals for an *expected* high share of non-performing loans in the financial sector accompanying a high share of short-term foreign capital on the liability side?
2. How relevant is the non-tradables sector as a recipient of (non-performing?) loans?
3. How severe is the maturity mismatch when comparing assets and liabilities in the domestic financial sector?
4. Is there a positive interest rate differential *vis-à-vis* the rest of the world?

5. What about the (absolute and relative) amount of foreign exchange reserves?
6. How large is the stock of latent capital outflows due to deposits/loans of foreign creditors?
7. What is the extent of the actual overvaluation of the domestic currency in relation to the long-term equilibrium exchange rate?
8. What types of government guarantees, implicit bailout clauses and so on exist in favour of domestic financial intermediaries (that is, including, but also beyond commercial banks)?
9. Do we observe the banks/investors/financiers in the emerging market 'to be overoptimistic' (see also Phelps 1999, p. 337)? The problem with exaggerated optimism is (see above) that once disillusion takes place, pessimism may go too far in the following (Agénor and Masson 1999, p. 83) and may end in financial panic.
10. Is there information available on the policy objective function of the respective government and the budget constraints it has to respect?
11. How much is the country dependent on trade? The more it is, the higher the gains it can reap from an unexpected devaluation.
12. If the government can choose between alternative strategies, which strategy (simple or compound) is most likely the dominant one?
13. How credible is the officially announced strategy *vis-à-vis* the exchange rate (see also Agénor and Masson 1999, p. 73)?
14. Under what circumstances is it likely that the second-victim country is pursuing an analogous strategy with regard to the first-victim country?

This list is far from being exhaustive, either. Therefore, we add briefly some additional criteria which do not 'naturally' emanate from our analysis, but still may have some significance for the prediction issue.

7.4   WHAT ELSE COULD BE USEFUL TO PREDICT CONTAGIOUS FINANCIAL CRISES MORE EFFECTIVELY?

1. How close are the relationships between the government on the one hand and large firms (*chaebols* in the case of Korea) in the respective emerging market on the other (Nam 2000, p. 38)?
2. How (under)developed are domestic bond markets? The less developed these are, the more is credit risk concentrated on banks and the higher is the maturity risk for banks because of limited availability of instruments for banks to hedge in local currency (Hawkins and Turner 2000, p. 20).

3. Do deposit insurance schemes exist in the banking sector? Any undifferentiated system of deposit insurance may give raise to moral hazard problems in the banking sector.
4. What about the reputation of the politicians in power? Macroeconomic policy announcements can be made by 'weak' or 'strong' politicians. Only the latter can be expected to implement a reform programme with rigour.
5. In which currency does the emerging market primarily invoice its exports? Asian countries affected by the contagious financial crisis origination in Thailand suffered from the fact that 'the appreciation of the US dollar *vis-à-vis* the yen started to erode their competitive position' (Blöndal and Christiansen 1999, p. 10). As this case demonstrates, it may be helpful to have predictions on the development of the exchange rate of the currency in which major exports are invoiced.

Unfortunately, even the most complete catalogue of indicators/variables is questioned from a rather fundamental methodological point of view. This aspect will be presented and discussed extensively in the next section.

7.5　HOW USEFUL/HARMFUL CAN EARLY WARNING INDICATORS BE?

A widespread hypothesis states that: if you ever have evidence from early warning indicators that a financial crisis is imminent in a country, do not publish it, because if you do so, you will herewith possibly accelerate and deepen the crisis. Phelps even argues that 'by publishing such information it might precipitate a crisis that the country might contend it would otherwise have escaped' (Phelps 1999, p. 336). In a discipline like medicine, this is nowadays an 'old-fashioned' view. In the past, doctors of medicine were afraid that cancer patients might collapse when confronted with their diagnosis. In the meantime, the conviction has grown that the opposite is true: only the 'whole truth' is capable of mobilizing all the forces of the patient to fight the disease, it is said. And this applies more so to highly contagious, epidemic diseases. Early warning and information supplement vaccination action and serve as a positive externality (see above).

The same reasoning applies, we believe, to contagious economic crises, too. For example, in the banking sector, the benefits of transparency and disclosure seem to exceed the costs: 'disclosure of problems can force banking consolidation, transfer of problem assets, and closure of insolvent institutions – necessary conditions for quick recovery of a troubled banking sector' (Rosengren 1999, p. 374). By contrast banks – like those in Japan – which failed to disclose their problems, exacerbated their difficulties (ibid.).

Yet, Phelps contradicts himself (see above) when he states that 'in the event of excessive or misdirected investment such that a crisis of some size or other is going to follow, it is good that the crisis comes soon – the sooner the better. Then internal balances will not build up to so large a size' (Phelps 1999, p. 334). Hence, there is a mutual understanding about the need for early recognition of financial problems. It is a mystery to me how this strategy can work when hidden from the public. Disclosure, transparency and early identification of financial problems seem to be just the two sides of the same coin and, most importantly, prerequisites for a regaining of confidence. Moreover, in an intensive investigation on the 'contagion', which the Mexican currency crisis of 1994–95 exerted on Argentina's banking sector, Schumacher (2000, p. 276) summarizes: 'findings support the asymmetry of information approach to bank runs and suggest that a policy of information disclosure might be effective as a deterrent to bank runs caused by exogenously generated shocks on bank solvency, such as an attack on the domestic currency'.

Once more: even it was true that early information on financial problems in one country can – in the first place – exacerbate this country's problems, this alone would be no reason to remain silent about these problems. This is because from a world's wealth point of view, transparency and disclosure are crucial standards that must be imposed. Why? Financial turmoil in one country can, as we have seen, cause 'contagion' to other, primarily emerging economies. In the words of the public finance language, we are dealing here with a strong *negative externality*. The sooner and the clearer the warnings are, the more likely it is that this externality can be evaded or internalized, *ceteris paribus*. And one may add that if candidates for 'contagion' are 'insured' *ex ante* by 'contingent credit lines', so much the better.

It is also maintained in the literature that 'the country's authorities may be impelled to freeze their policy stance for fear that any policy shift will be interpreted as an admission of weakness and will unleash or intensify a speculative attack' (Buira 1999, p. 20). The logic of this argument is far from being compelling: 'If their position were seen to be strong, however, because they were known to have ample support from the IMF or other sources, they would be able to adjust policy confidently in response to changing circumstances' (ibid.). Moreover, the position of the 'patient' is fostered by a firm and reliable new IMF with contingent credit lines for susceptible economies and liquidity loans for countries already hit by a financial crisis. This issue is related to the 'weak' or 'strong' policymaker problem raised by Drazen and Masson (1994). Contingent credit lines can be especially beneficial against the background of 'weak' policymakers in the domestic economy.

7.6   OPEN QUESTIONS FOR FUTURE RESEARCH

When reading a book – perhaps with the exception of the clear story in any 'whodunnit' novel – we are left in the end with open questions. This book will be no exception. Perhaps we can help the reader so far, in that we can ourselves address a number of seemingly unresolved issues.

It is well known that respected credit-rating agencies did not foresee the major financial crises in the last decade of the 20th century. However, they helped to aggravate some of the crises by downgrading the creditworthiness of the respective countries in the middle of the crisis (Hawkins and Turner 2000, p. 12). Hence, the agencies tended to work pro-cyclically, the main reason being a backward- rather than a forward-looking assessment of the countries in question. In order to avoid this outcome, forward-looking information must determine the ratings, at least in combination with actual information. Hawkins and Turner give an excellent example: until now, 'depreciation in the wake of a crisis typically leads to a downgrade – whereas a forward-looking approach ... would recognise a more competitive exchange rate as a source of medium-term strength, not weakness' (ibid., p. 13). The economics profession must do additional careful research to detect a more reliable basis for country ratings. Credit assessments should have a long-term focus and thereby exert a stabilizing influence (ibid.).

Can a dollarization of emerging markets' economies make these less vulnerable to capital flow reversals? The Thai crisis superseded the earlier experiences in Latin America: the financial turmoil resulted 'in a 26 percentage point swing in private capital flows (from inflows of about 18 percent of GDP in 1996 to outflows of more than 8 percent in 1997)' (Calvo and Reinhart 1999, p. 2). A full dollarization is accompanied by a number of severe shortcomings for the respective economy. If not agreed with the US authorities, the country in question would not even share the seigniorage revenues (ibid., p. 5). Also, the Federal Reserve will hardly take into account the pace of the economy in the emerging market when deciding on the course of US monetary policy and so on. But, we still do not know enough about the possible benefits of dollarization and their size. Calvo and Reinhart (1999), for example, argue that with large foreign exchange reserves, lender of last resort services could be provided to the domestic banking system, instead of firing the reserves in the battle against speculators at a peg regime.

Do increased international capital mobility and the quick reactions of investors to news make countries more susceptible to 'contagion' in the future? This question affects the relevance of herding behaviour on international financial markets. There is no serious paper which denies the existence and significance of herding behaviour. It is also an accepted view that herding causes negative externalities and is a signal for market failure, when the rush for the exit applies not only to investors in first-victim countries, but also to investors in second-tier countries. Yet, the pattern of herding behaviour is not homogeneous and it varies between different regions/crises and the associated type of capital flows. Foreign direct investment, for example, seems not to follow any herding patterns (Nunnenkamp 2000, p. 9).

Can long-term portfolio investment from the developed countries bring more stability and less volatility into the capital flows to emerging economies? Preliminary evidence seems to support this view. As Nunnenkamp reports, 'volatility was most pronounced with regard to bank lending ... portfolio investment comprises relatively stable elements such as investment by pension funds and life insurance companies, whereas volatility in portfolio investment is mainly due to the short-term profit orientation of managed investment funds (country funds and mutual funds)' (ibid., pp. 8–9). These findings, however, are based on experiences gained between 1996 and 1999 only. More empirical research is needed in the future to establish a stable relationship between volatility of flows to (and from!) emerging economies on the one hand and the source of funds (in the developed countries) on the other.

Can the long-term nature of pension fund engagements contribute to a reduction in the overall volatility of capital flows in the world economy? It is a fact that demographic developments and the reform of the pension systems in major developed countries (complementing the pay-as-you-go system with elements of a capital-based pension system) 'are expected to result in rapidly expanding pension fund assets' (ibid., p. 16). These assets, by virtue of portfolio equilibrium and world-wide savings–investment balance conditions, will, to a large part, have to be steered into emerging market economies. Note that developed economies have to 'achieve' surpluses in their current account balances in order to do so. We may expect that the savings accumulated in pension funds will contribute to a sustainable financing of productive investments in emerging market economies and, hence, help reduce the volatility of overall capital flows (ibid.).

Did the crises in Asia lead to the dismantling of a special sort of corporatism? There is some evidence that, for example in Korea, government interventions – be it in the form of implicit guarantees or in the form of directing the allocation of credits into 'priority' sectors – were also responsible for the strong incentives to undertake risky investments and to forget about hedging opportunities against the exchange rate risk. The

Korean *chaebols* are economic units which have perhaps no parallel in the world economy. Hence, we do need more 'institutional knowledge' in general and more knowledge about the links between public and private institutions in emerging market economies in particular. The IMF's call for more 'transparency and disclosure' may be helpful in this respect, as well.

Do we overlook country-specific weaknesses when we identify robust cross-country early warning indicators? As several chapters of this book have shown, it is worth looking at individual experiences in emerging market economies. The causes for the onset of a financial crisis were not the same in Mexico, Thailand or Russia. And yet, two important countries affected by contagion (Korea in the case of the Asian Flu and Brazil in the case of the Russian Virus) went through rather distinct crisis episodes. One of the most remarkable differences was that Korea liberalized its capital account in a rather unorthodox manner. Rather than the other way around, 'the Korean government lifted restrictions on short-term capital flows in the early 1990s, but kept limits on long-term investment (notably on FDI)' (ibid., p. 12). At the same time, Brazilian banks and enterprises – in contrast to Thailand, Korea (see above) and other affected Asian economies – 'had largely hedged the risk of devaluation' (ibid., p. 14).

The next contagious financial crisis is not around the next corner. This, however, does not mean that our subject is no longer 'in vogue'. The economics profession was not well prepared for the crises which occurred in the 1990s. We shall be better prepared for those to come in the future.

NOTE

1. This question points at a methodological weakness which in many studies is overlooked. Empirical research (see Kaminsky and Reinhart 2000) based on country samples that include developed industrialized countries like Finland, Norway and Sweden are biased. Notwithstanding the fact – which is reflected in Chapter 2 of this book – that these countries were indeed affected by contagious speculative attacks in the early 1990s, they are not really at the core of the contagion issue.

Bibliography

Agénor, P.-R. (1997), 'Borrowing Risk and the Tequila Effect', IMF Working Paper 86/97.

Agénor, P.-R. and J. Aizenman (1998), 'Contagion and Volatility with Imperfect Credit Markets', *IMF Staff Papers*, **45** (2), pp. 207–35.

Agénor, P.-R. and P.R. Masson (1999), 'Credibility, Reputation, and the Mexican Peso Crisis', *Journal of Money, Credit, and Banking*, **31** (1), pp. 70–84.

Aghion, P., P. Bacchetta and A. Banerjee (1999), 'Capital Markets and the Instability of Open Economies', CEPR Discussion Paper Series No. 2083.

Aghion, P., P. Bacchetta and A. Banerjee (2000), 'A Simple Model of Monetary Policy and Currency Crises', *European Economic Review*, **44**, pp. 728–38.

Ahluwalia, P. (2000), 'Discriminating Contagion: An Alternative Explanation of Contagious Currency Crises in Emerging Markets', IMF Working Paper 00/14.

Akerlof, G. and P. Romer (1993), 'Looting the Economic Underworld of Bankruptcy for Profit', *Brookings Papers on Economic Activity*, **24** (2), pp. 1–73.

Alba, P., A. Bhattachary, S. Claessens, S. Ghosh and L. Hernandez (1998), 'Volatility and Contagion in a Financially Integrated World. Lessons from East Asia's Recent Experience', World Bank Policy Research Working Paper No. 2008.

Anderson, R.M. (1994), 'The Croonian Lecture, 1994. Populations, Infectious Disease and Immunity: A Very Non-linear World', *Philosophical Transactions of the Royal Society London B*, **346**, pp. 457–505.

Anderson, R.M. (1998), 'Analytical Theory of Epidemics', in R. M. Krause (ed.), *Emerging Infections*, New York: Academic Press, Chapter 2, pp. 23–50.

Anderson, R.M., C. Donnelly and S. Gupta (1997), 'Vaccine Design, Evaluation, and Community-based Use for Antigenically Variable Infectious Agents', *The Lancet*, **350**, pp. 1466–70.

Anderson, R.M. and R.M. May (1990), 'Modern Vaccines', *The Lancet*, **335**, pp. 641–5.

Anderson, R. M. and R. M. May (1991), *Infectious Diseases of Humans. Dynamics and Control*, Oxford, New York, Tokyo: Oxford University Press.

Anderson, Roy M. and D. James Nokes (1996), 'Mathematical Models of Transmission and Control', in Roger Detels, Walter W. Holland, James McEwen, and Gilbert S. Omenn (eds), *Oxford Textbook of Public Health. Vol. 2: The Methods of Public Health*, Oxford, New York, Tokyo: Oxford University Press, Chapter 14, pp. 225–52.

Anderson, Roy M. and D. James Nokes (1997), 'Mathematical Models of Transmission and Control', in Roger Detels, Walter W. Holland, James McEwen, and Gilbert S. Omenn (eds), *Oxford Textbook of Public Health. Vol. 2: The Methods of Public Health*, third edition, Oxford, New York, Tokyo: Oxford University Press, Chapter 18, pp. 689–719.

Aschinger, Gerhard (1995), *Stock Exchange Crash and Speculation (Börsenkrach und Spekulation. Eine ökonomische Analyse)*, Munich: Vahlen-Verlag.

Aschinger, G. (1996), 'The Nature of Financial Crises', *Swiss Bank Corporation: Economic and Financial Prospects*, **3**, pp. 12–19.

Aschinger, G. (1998), 'An Analysis of the Hong Kong Crash', *Swiss Bank Corporation: Economic and Financial Prospects*, **1**, pp. 12–19.

Avery, C. and P. Zemsky (1998), 'Multidimensional Uncertainty and Herd Behavior in Financial Markets', *American Economic Review*, **88** (4), pp. 724–48.

Bacchetta, P. (1990), 'Temporary Capital Controls in a Balance of Payments Crisis', *Journal of International Money and Finance*, **9**, pp. 246–57.

Bacchetta, P. and E. van Wincoop (1998), 'Capital Flows to Emerging Markets: Liberalization, Overshooting and Volatility', CEPR Discussion Paper Series No. 1889.

Baig, T. and I. Goldfajn (1999), 'Financial Market Contagion in the Asian Crisis', *IMF Staff Papers*, **46** (2), pp. 167–95.

Bank for International Settlements (1997), *Core Principles for Effective Banking Supervision*, Basle: Basle Committee for Banking Supervision.

Bansal, R. and M. Dahlquist (2000), 'The Forward Premium Puzzle: Different Tales from Developed and Emerging Economies', *Journal of International Economics*, **51**, pp. 115–44.

Barro, R.J. and D.B. Gordon (1983), 'Rules, Discretion and Reputation in a Model of Monetary Policy', *Journal of Monetary Economics*, **12**, pp. 101–21.

Bekaert, G. and C.R. Harvey (2000), 'Foreign Speculators and Emerging Equity Markets', *Journal of Finance*, **40** (2), pp. 565–613.

Bensaid, B. and O. Jeanne (1997), 'The Instability of Fixed Exchange Rate Systems When Raising the Nominal Interest Rate Is Costly', *European*

Economic Review, **41**, pp. 1461–78.

Berg, A. and C. Pattillo (1999a), 'Predicting Currency Crises: The Indicators Approach and an Alternative', *Journal of International Money and Finance*, **18**, pp. 561–86.

Berg, Andrew and Catherine Pattillo (1999b), 'The Signals Approach to Early Currency Crisis: Does It Work and Is There a Better Way?', in William C. Hunter, George G. Kaufman and Thomas H. Krueger (eds), *The Asian Financial Crisis: Origins, Implications, and Solutions*, Boston, Dordrecht, London: Kluwer Academic Publishers, pp. 351–68.

Blanchard, O. (1979), 'Speculative Bubbles, Crashes and Rational Expectations, *Economics Letters*, **3**, pp. 387–9.

Blanchard, O. and M. Watson (1982), 'Bubbles, Rational Expectations and Financial Markets', in Paul Wachtel (ed.), *Crises in the Economic and Financial Structure*, Farnborough: Lexington Books, pp. 295–316.

Blejer, Mario I. (1984), 'Recent Economic Policies of the Southern Cone Countries and the Monetary Approach to the Balance of Payments', in Nicolas A. Barletta, Mario I. Blejer and Luis Landau (eds), *Economic Liberalization and Stabilization Policies in Argentina, Chile, and Uruguay. Applications of the Monetary Approach to the Balance of Payments*, Washington, DC: World Bank, pp. 3–11.

Blöndal, S. and H. Christiansen (1999), 'The Recent Experience with Capital Flows to Emerging Market Economies', OECD Economics Department Working Papers No. 211.

Bovespa (2000), 'Nominal IBOVESPA from 2 January 1998 to 30 December 1999', São Paulo: São Paulo Stock Exchange, Datasheet.

Buch, C.M. (1999), 'Chilean-type Capital Controls: A Building Block of the New International Financial Architecture?', Kiel Discussion Paper No. 350.

Buckberg, E. (1996), 'Institutional Investors and Asset Pricing in Emerging Markets', IMF Working Paper 2/96.

Buira, A. (1999), 'An Alternative Approach to Financial Crises', *Essays in International Finance*, No. 212, Princeton, NJ: International Finance Section, Department of Economics, Princeton University.

Buiter, Willem H., Giancarlo Corsetti and Paolo A. Pesenti (1998), *Financial Markets and European Monetary Cooperation*, Cambridge, MA: Cambridge University Press.

Burnside, C., M. Eichenbaum and S. Rebelo (1998), 'Prospective Deficits and the Asian Currency Crisis', NBER Working Paper Series No. 6758.

Calomiris, Charles W. (1999), 'Moral Hazard is Avoidable', in William C. Hunter, George G. Kaufman and Thomas H. Krueger (eds), *The Asian Financial Crisis: Origins, Implications, and Solutions*, Boston, Dordrecht, London: Kluwer Academic Publishers, pp. 379–84.

Calvo, G. A. (1998a), 'Understanding the Russian Virus. With Special Reference to Latin America', paper presented at the Deutsche Bank's Conference on 'Emerging Markets: Can They Be Crisis Free', Washington, DC, 13 October.

Calvo, Guillermo A. (1998b), 'Varieties of Capital Market Crises', in Guillermo A. Calvo and Mervyn A. King (eds), *The Debt Burden and Its Consequences for Monetary Policy: Proceedings of a Conference Held by the International Economic Association at the Deutsche Bundesbank, Frankfurt, Germany*, Basingstoke, Hampshire, London: Macmillan St Martin's Press, pp. 181–202.

Calvo, G.A. (1999), *Contagion in Emerging Markets: When Wall Street Is a Carrier*, Mimeo, College Park: University of Maryland.

Calvo, G.A. and E.G. Mendoza (1996), 'Mexico's Balance-of-Payments Crisis: A Chronicle of a Death Foretold', *Journal of International Economics,* **41**, pp. 235–64.

Calvo, G.A. and E.G. Mendoza (1997), 'Rational Herd Behavior and the Globalization of Securities Markets', Minneapolis: Institute for Empirical Macroeconomics, Federal Reserve Bank of Minneapolis, Discussion Paper No. 120.

Calvo, G.A. and E.G. Mendoza (1999), *Rational Contagion and the Globalization of Securities Markets*, Mimeo, College Park: University of Maryland.

Calvo, S. and C. Reinhart (1995), 'Capital Flows to Latin America: Is There Evidence of Contagious Effects?', World Bank Policy Research Working Paper 1619.

Calvo, Guillermo A. and Carmen M. Reinhart (1996), 'Capital Flows to Latin America: Is There Evidence of Contagious Effects?', in Guillermo A. Calvo, Morris Goldstein and Eduard Hochreither (eds), *Private Capital Flows to Emerging Markets After the Mexican Crisis*, Washington, DC: Institute for International Economics, pp. 151–84.

Calvo, G.A. and C.M. Reinhart (1999), 'Capital Flow Reversals, the Exchange Rate Debate, and Dollarization', *Finance & Development*, **36** (3), internet version http://www.imf.org/external/pubs/ft/fandd/1999/09/calvo.htm.

Canzoneri, Matthew B. and Dale W. Henderson (1991), *Monetary Policy in Interdependent Economies: a Game-theoretic Approach*, Cambridge, MA: MIT Press.

Caramazza, F., L. Ricci and R. Salgado (2000), 'Trade and Financial Contagion in Currency Crises', IMF Working Paper No. 00/55.

Central Bank of the Russian Federation (2000a), 'Exchange Rate of Currency', internet version http://www.cbr.ru/eng/markets/val2.htm, 22 August.

Central Bank of the Russian Federation (2000b), 'Moscow Inter Bank Actual Credit Rate', internet version http://www.cbr.ru/eng/markets/mkr.html, 22 August.

Chang, R. and A. Velasco (1998a), 'Financial Fragility and the Exchange Rate Regime', NBER Working Paper No. 6469.

Chang, R. and A. Velasco (1998b), 'Financial Crises in Emerging Markets: A Canonical Model', NBER Working Paper No. 6606.

Chang, R. and A. Velasco (1999), 'Liquidity Crises in Financial Markets: Theory and Policy', Federal Reserve Bank of Atlanta, Working Paper No. 99-15.

Choueiri, N. (1999), 'A Model of Contagious Currency Crises with Application to Argentina', IMF Working Paper No. 29/99.

Choueiri, N. and G. Kaminsky (1999), 'Has the Nature of Crises Changed? A Quarter Century of Currency Crises in Argentina', IMF Working Paper No. 99/152.

Corbo, Valverde (1984), 'Commentary on Recent Experience in the Southern Cone (Chile)', in Nicolas A. Barletta, Mario I. Blejer and Luis Landau (eds), *Economic Liberalization and Stabilization Policies in Argentina, Chile, and Uruguay. Applications of the Monetary Approach to the Balance of Payments*, Washington, DC: World Bank, pp. 56–63.

Corden, M. and J.P. Neary (1982), 'Booming Sector and De-industrialization in a Small Open Economy', *Economic Journal*, **92**, pp. 825–48.

Corsetti, G., P. Pesenti and N. Roubini (1998a), 'What Caused the Asian Currency and Financial Crisis? Part I: A Macroeconomic Overview', Mimeo, revised version, New York: Federal Reserve Bank of New York, September.

Corsetti, G., P. Pesenti and N. Roubini (1998b), 'Paper Tigers? A Model of the Asian Crisis', Mimeo, revised version, New York: Federal Reserve Bank of New York, December.

Corsetti, G., P. Pesenti and N. Roubini (1999), 'Paper Tigers? A Model of the Asian Crisis', *European Economic Review*, **43**, pp. 1211–36.

Crafts, N. (1999), 'East Asian Growth Before and After the Crisis', *IMF Staff Papers*, **46** (2), pp. 139–66.

Currie, David A. and Paul Levine (1993), *Rules, Reputation and Macroeconomic Policy Coordination*, Cambridge, MA: Cambridge University Press.

Dahlquist, M. and S.F. Gray (2000), 'Regime-Switching and Interest Rates in the European Monetary System', *Journal of International Economics*, **50**, pp. 399–419.

Davies, Stephen (1979), *The Diffusion of Process Innovations*, Cambridge: Cambridge University Press.

De Grauwe, Paul (1992), *The Economics of Monetary Integration*, Oxford:

Oxford University Press.

Devarajan, Shantayanan and Dani Rodrik (1992), 'Do the Benefits of Fixed Exchange Rates Outweigh Their Costs? The CFA Zone in Africa', in Ian Goldin and L. Alan Winters (eds), *Open Economies: Structural Adjustment and Agriculture [papers from a joint conference held by the Centre for Economic Policy Research and the OECD Development Centre in Paris in April 1991]*, Cambridge, MA: Cambridge University Press, pp. 66–85.

Diamond, D.W. and P.H. Dybvig (1983), 'Bank Runs, Deposit Insurance, and Liquidity', *Journal of Political Economy*, **91** (3), pp. 401–19.

Díaz-Alejandro, Carlos (1985, reprinted 1991), 'Goodbye Financial Repression, Hello Financial Crash' ('Adiós represión financiera. ¡Qué tal, crac financiero!'), reprinted in L. Bendesky (ed.), *The Role of the Central Bank Today (El Papel de la Banca Central en la Actualidad)*, Madrid: Banco de España, pp. 215–42.

Diwan, I. and B. Hoekman (1999), 'Competition, Complementarity and Contagion in East Asia', CEPR Discussion Paper Series No. 2112.

Donges, J.B. (1999), 'Global Finanical Market, Exchage Rate Crisis and Emerging Markets' ('Globale Finanzmärkte, Währungskrisen und aufstrebende Volkswirtschaften'), *Zeitschrift für Wirtschaftspolitik*, **48** (2), pp. 129–46.

Dornbusch, R. (1999), 'After Asia: New Directions for the International Financial System', *Journal of Policy Modeling*, **21** (3), pp. 289–99.

Dornbusch, R. and A. Werner (1994), 'Mexico, Stabilization, Reform, and No Growth', *Brookings Papers on Economic Activity*, 1, pp. 253–97.

Drazen, A. (1999), 'Political Contagion in Currency Crises', NBER Working Paper Series No. 7211.

Drazen, A. and P.R. Masson (1994), 'Credibility of Policies Versus Credibility of Policymakers', *The Quarterly Journal of Economics*, **109** (3), pp. 735–54.

Dunstan, R. (1982), 'The Rumour Process', *Journal of Applied Probability*, **19**, pp. 759–66.

Edison, H.J., P. Luangaram and M. Miller (1998), 'Asset Bubbles, Domino Effects and "Lifeboats": Elements of the East Asian Crisis', CEPR Discussion Paper Series No. 1866

Edwards, Sebastian (1984), 'Commentary on Recent Experience in the Southern Cone (Chile)', in Nicolas A. Barletta, Mario I. Blejer and Luis Landau (eds), *Economic Liberalization and Stabilization Policies in Argentina, Chile, and Uruguay. Applications of the Monetary Approach to the Balance of Payments*, Washington, DC: The World Bank, pp. 63–6.

Edwards, S. (1998), 'Interest Rate Volatility, Contagion and Convergence: An Empirical Investigation of the Cases of Argentina, Chile and Mexico',

Journal of Applied Economics, **1** (1), pp. 55–86.

Eichengreen, Barry (1999a), *Toward a New International Financial Architecture. A Practical Post-Asia Agenda*, Washington, DC: Institute for International Economics.

Eichengreen, B. (1999b), 'Kicking the Habit: Moving from Pegged Rates to Greater Exchange Rate Flexibility', *Economic Journal*, **103** (March), pp. C1–14.

Eichengreen, Barry and Andrew K. Rose (1997), 'Contagious Currency Crises: Channels of Conveyance', in Takatoshi Ito and Anne O. Krueger (eds), *Changes in Exchange Rates in Rapidly Developing Countries: Theory, Practice, and Policy Issues*, Chicago and London: University of Chicago Press, pp. 29–51.

Eichengreen, B. and A.K. Rose (1998), 'Staying Afloat When the Wind Shifts: External Factors and Emerging-market Banking Crises', NBER Working Paper Series No. 6370.

Eichengreen, B., A.K. Rose and C. Wyplosz (1995a), 'Contagious Currency Crises', NBER Working Paper Series No. 5681.

Eichengreen, B., A.K. Rose and C. Wyplosz (1995b), 'Exchange Market Mayhem. The Antecedents and Aftermath of Speculative Attacks', *Economic Policy: A European Forum*, **10** (21, October), pp. 251–312.

Eichengreen, B., A.K. Rose and C. Wyplosz (1996a), 'Contagious Currency Crises', NBER Working Paper Series No. 5681.

Eichengreen, B., A.K. Rose and C. Wyplosz (1996b), 'Contagious Currency Crises: First Tests', *Scandinavian Journal of Economics*, **98** (4), pp. 463–84.

Enders, K. (1983), 'Structural Consequences of a Resource Boom in an Industrialized Country: De-industrialization and Norwegian Experiences' ('Strukturelle Konsequenzen eines Rohstoffbooms in einem Industrieland: Deindustrialisierungsstrategie und norwegische Erfahrungen'), Kiel: University of Kiel, Diskussionsbeitrag aus dem Institut für Theoretische Volkswirtschaftslehre No. 52.

Engelen, K.C. (1999), 'Strong Resistance Against Basle Proposal' ('Heftiger Widerstand gegen Baseler Vorschläge'), *Handelsblatt*, 28 September, p. 34.

Engelen, K.C. (2000), 'Off-shore Centres with Loose Supervision of the Financial Sector May Be Sanctioned' ('Offshore-Zentren mit laxer Aufsicht drohen Sanktionen'), *Handelsblatt*, 6 April, p. 46.

Evans, D. Morier (1849), *The Commercial Crisis, 1847–48*, reprinted 1969, New York: Augustus M. Kelley.

Federal Reserve Board (2000), 'Spot Exchange Rate – Brazil', internet version http://www.federalreserve.gov/Releases/H10/hist/dat96_bz.txt, 22 August.

Flood, R.P. and N.P. Marion (2000), 'Self-Fulfilling Risk Predictions: An Application to Speculative Attacks', *Journal of International Economics*, **50**, pp. 245–68.

Forbes, K. and R. Rigobon (1999), 'No Contagion, Only Interdependence: Measuring Stock Market Co-Movements', NBER Working Paper Series No. 7267.

Frankel, Jeffrey A. and Sergio L. Schmukler (1998), 'Crises, Contagion, and Country Funds: Effects on East Asia and Latin America', in Reuven Glick (ed.), *Managing Capital Flows and Exchange Rate Perspectives from the Pacific Basin*, Cambridge, MA: Cambridge University Press, pp. 232–66.

Fratzscher, M. (1998), 'Why are Currency Crises Contagious? A Comparison of the Latin American Crisis of 1994–1995 and the Asian Crisis of 1997–1998, *Weltwirtschaftliches Archiv*, **134** (4), pp. 664–91.

Fratzscher, M. (1999), 'What Causes Currency Crises: Sunspots, Contagion or Fundamentals?', San Domenico: European University Institute, EUI Working Paper ECO No. 99/39.

Frenkel, Michael and Lukas Menkhoff (2000), *Stable World Financal Market? The Debate on a New International Financial Architecture (Stabile Weltfinanzen? Die Debatte um eine neue internationale Finanzarchitektur)*, Berlin, Heidelberg and New York: Springer.

Furman, J. and J.E. Stiglitz (1998), 'Economic Crises: Evidence and Insights from East Asia', *Brookings Papers on Economic Activity*, 2, pp. 1–135.

Gangopadhyay, S. and G. Singh (2000), 'Avoiding Bank Runs in Transition Economies: The Role of Risk Neutral Capital', *Journal of Banking & Finance*, **24**, pp. 625–42.

Garber, P. (1990), 'Famous First Bubbles', *Journal of Economic Perspectives*, **4**, pp. 35–54.

Gerlach, S. and F. Smets (1995), 'Contagious Speculative Attacks', *European Journal of Political Economy*, **11**, pp. 45–63.

Gibson, H.D. and E. Tsakalotos (2000), *ERM-II: Problems for the 'Outs' and Their Relationship with the 'Ins'*, Mimeo, Athens: Athens University of Economics and Business.

Girton, L. and D. Roper (1977), 'A Monetary Model of Exchange Market Pressure Applied to the Postwar Canadian Experience', *American Economic Review*, **67** (4), pp. 537–48.

Glick, R. and A.K. Rose (1998), 'Contagion and Trade: Why are Currency Crises Regional?', CEPR Discussion Paper, No. 1947.

Golder, S. (1999), 'Precautionary Credit Lines: A Means to Contain Contagion in Financial Markets?', Kiel Discussion Paper No. 341.

Goldfajn, I. and R.O. Valdés (1997), 'Capital Flows and the Twin Crises: The Role of Liquidity', IMF Working Paper No. 87/97.

Goldfajn, I. and R.O. Valdés (1998), 'Are Currency Crises Predictable?'

European Economic Review, **42** (3–5), pp. 873–85.

Goldfajn, I. and R.O. Valdés (1999), 'The Aftermath of Appreciations', *Quarterly Journal of Economics*, **114** (1), pp. 229–62.

Goldstein, Morris (1998), *The Asian Financial Crisis. Causes, Cures and Systemic Implications*, Washington, DC: Institute for International Economics.

Goldstein, Morris (1999), 'Early Warning Indicators of Financial Crises', in William C. Hunter, George G. Kaufman and Thomas H. Krueger (eds), *The Asian Financial Crisis: Origins, Implications, and Solutions*, Boston, Dordrecht, London: Kluwer Academic Publishers, pp. 321–30.

Goldstein, M. and J. Hawkins (1998), 'The Origin of the Asian Financial Turmoil', Melbourne: Reserve Bank of Australia, Economic Research Department Research, Discussion Paper No. 9805.

Goswamy, M. and A. Kumar (1990), 'Stochastic Model for Spread of Rumour Supported by a Leader Resulting in Collective Violence and Planning of Control Measures', *Mathematical Social Sciences*, **19**, pp. 23–36.

Griffith-Jones, S. (1996), 'The Mexican Peso Crisis', Mexico City: Institute of Development Studies, Discussion Paper 354.

Gruben, W.C. (1996), 'Policy Priorities and the Mexican Exchange Rate Crisis', *Federal Reserve Bank of Dallas Economic Review*, First Quarter, 19–29.

Haggard, Stephan and Sylvia Maxfield (1993), 'The Political Economy of Capital Account Liberalization', in Helmut Reisen and Bernhard Fischer (eds), *Financial Opening. Policy Issues and Experiences in Developing Countries*, Paris: OECD Development Centre, Documents du Centre de Développement, pp. 72–5.

Hamada, Koichi (1974), 'Alternative Exchange Rate Systems and the Interdependence of Monetary Policies', in Robert Z. Aliber (ed.), *National Monetary Policies and International Finance Systems*, Chicago: University of Chicago Press.

Handelsblatt (2000a), 'New Proposal for the Second Basle Accord' ('Neue Vorschläge für Basel'), 13 April, p. 25.

Handelsblatt (2000b), 'Looking for a New Financial Architecture' ('Auf der Suche nach neuer Finanzarchitektur'), 24–25 February, p. 45.

Hanke, S.H. (1999), 'The Case for Currency Boards', Mimeo, 1998 William S. Vickrey Distinguished Address given at the Boston Conference of International Atlantic Economic Society, Boston.

Hawkins, J. and P. Turner (2000), 'International Financial Reform: Regulatory and Other Issues', paper presented at Conference on 'International Financial Contagion: how it spreads and how it can be stopped', Washington, DC, 3–4 February.

Hoffmann, L. (1999), 'Exchange Rate Crises – Systematic Deficiencies of the Global Market Economy' ('Währungskrisen – Systemfehler der globalen Marktwirtschaft?'), *Zeitschrift für Wirtschaftspolitik*, **48** (1), pp. 72–84.

Horne, J. (1996), 'External Sustainability: The Mexican Peso Crisis', Sydney: Macquarie University, Macquarie Economics Research Papers.

Huang, H. and C. Xu (1999), 'Financial Institutions and the Financial Crisis in East Asia', *European Economic Review*, **43**, pp. 903–14.

Illing, G. (2000), 'The Proposals Made by the Meltzer-Report Can Lead into the Next Financial Crisis' ('Die Vorschläge des Meltzer-Reports wären der sichere Weg in die nächste Krise'), *IFO Schnelldienst*, **53** (24), pp. 9–12.

International Monetary Fund (2000), *International Financial Statistics*, Washington, DC: IMF.

International Financial Institution Advisory Commission (2000), 'The I.F.I.A.C. Report', internet version http://phantom-x.gsia.cmu.edu/IFIAC/Report.html.

Irvin, G. and D. Vines (1999), 'A Krugman–Dooley–Sachs Third Generation Model of the Asian Financial Crisis', CEPR Discussion Paper Series No. 2149.

Ito, T. (1997), 'Comment on Eichengreen and Rose', in Takatoshi Ito and Anne O. Krueger (eds), *Changes in Exchange Rates in Rapidly Developing Countries: Theory, Practice, and Policy Issues*, Chicago and London: University of Chicago Press, pp. 51–5.

Jeanne, O. and P.R. Masson (2000), 'Currency Crises, Sunspots and Markov-switching Regimes', *Journal of International Economics*, **50**, pp. 327–50.

Jeanne, O. and C. Wyplosz (1999), 'The International Lender of Last Resort: How Large Is Large Enough?', Mimeo, Washington, DC, September.

Kaminsky, G., S. Lizondo and C.M. Reinhart. (1998), 'Leading Indicators of Currency Crises', *IMF Staff Papers*, **45** (1), pp. 1–48.

Kaminsky, G. and C. Reinhart (1996), 'The Twin Crises: The Causes of Banking and Balance-of-payments Problems', Washington, DC: Board of Governors of the Federal Reserve System, International Finance Discussion Papers No. 544.

Kaminsky, G. and C.M. Reinhart (1998), 'On Crises, Contagion, and Confusion', Mimeo, College Park: University of Maryland, Department of Economics, December.

Kaminsky, G. and C.M. Reinhart (1999), 'Bank Lending and Contagion: Evidence from the Asian Crisis', Mimeo, College Park: University of Maryland, Department of Economics, September.

Kaminsky, G. and C.M. Reinhart (2000), 'On Crises, Contagion and Confusion', *Journal of International Economics*, **51**, pp. 145–68.

Karmann, A. (1999), 'Immune to Contagion or Favourable Events? Comment on Polanski's "Poland and International Financial Turbulence of the Second Half of the 1990s"', Mimeo, Dresden: University of Technology.

Kenen, P.B. (1995), 'Capital Controls, the EMS and EMU', *Economic Journal*, **105** (January), pp. 181–92.

Kindleberger, Charles P. (1978), *Manias, Panics, and Crashes*, New York: Basic Books.

Kletzer, K. (2000), 'The Effectiveness of Self-protection Policies for Safeguarding Emerging Market Economies from Crises', Bonn: Rheinische Friedrich-Wihlems-University, Center for European Integration Studies, ZEI Working Paper No. B8.

Klodt, H. (2000), 'Criteria and Guidelines for International Policy Coordination' ('Kriterien und Leitlinien für die internationale Politikkoordination') *Volkswirtschaftliche Korrespondenz der Adolf-Weber-Stiftung*, **39** (5), pp. 1–4.

Kodres, L.E. and M. Pritsker (1999), 'A Rational Expectations Model of Financial Contagion', Mimeo, Washington, DC: Federal Reserve Board, March.

Komulainen, T. (1999), 'Currency Crisis Theories – Some Explanations for the Russian Case', Helsinki: Bank of Finland, Institute for Economies in Transition, Bofit Discussion Paper No. 1.

Kornai, J. (1986), 'The Soft Budget Constraint', *Kyklos*, **39** (1), pp. 3–30.

Krugman, P. (1979), 'A Model of Balance of Payments Crises', *Journal of Money, Credit, and Banking*, **11** (3), pp. 311–25.

Krugman, P. (1991), 'Target Zones and Exchange Rate Dynamics', *Quarterly Journal of Economics*, **106** (3), pp. 669–82.

Krugman, P. (1994), 'The Myth of Asia's Miracle', *Foreign Affairs*, **73**, November–December, pp. 62–78.

Krugman, P. (1998a), 'What Happened to Asia?', Mimeo, internet version http://web.mit.edu/Krugman/www/disinter.html, January.

Krugman, P. (1998b), 'Currency Crises', Mimeo, internet version http://web.mit.edu/krugman/www/crises.html, prepared for NBER conference, October 1997.

Krzak, M. (1998), 'Contagion Effects of the Russian Financial Crisis on Central and Eastern Europe: The Case of Poland', *Focus in Transition*, No. 2, pp. 21–34.

Kydland, F.E. and E.C. Prescott, (1977), 'Rules Rather Than Discretion: The Inconsistency of Optimal Plans', *Journal of Political Economy*, **85** (3), pp. 473–92.

Lane, T. (1999), 'The Asian Financial Crisis. What Have we Learned?', *Finance & Development*, **36** (3), internet version http://www.imf.org/external/pubs/ft/fandd/1999/09/lane.htm.

Lefevre, C. and P. Picard (1994), 'Distribution of the Final Extent of a Rumour Process', *Journal of Applied Probability*, **30**, pp. 244–9.

Levy-Yeyati, E. and A. Ubide (1998), 'Crises, Contagion, and the Closed-end Country Fund Puzzle. IMF Working Paper Series No. 143/98.

Loisel, O. and P. Martin (1999), 'Coordination, Cooperation, Contagion and Currency Crises', CEPR Discussion Paper Series No. 2075.

Lowell, J., C.R. Neu and D. Tang (1998), 'Financial Crises and Contagion in Emerging Markets Countries', Rand Working Paper No. MR 962.

Lücke, M. (1992), 'The Diffusion of Process Innovations in Industrialized and Developing Countries: A Case Study of the World Textile and Steel Industries', *World Development*, **21** (7), pp. 1225–38.

Lücke, M. (1993), *Technical Progress and the Division of Labour Between Industrialized and Developing Countries (Technischer Fortschritt und die Arbeitsteilung zwischen Industrie- und Entwicklungsländern. Eine empirische Analyse)*, Tübingen: Tübingen Mohr, Kieler Studien No. 247.

Lüders, Rolf (1983), 'Commentary on Recent Experience in the Southern Cone (Chile)', in Nicolas A. Barletta, Mario I. Blejer and Luis Landau (eds), *Economic Liberalization and Stabilization Policies in Argentina, Chile, and Uruguay. Applications of the Monetary Approach to the Balance of Payments*, Washington, DC: World Bank, pp. 66–9.

Lunar Finance (2000), 'SELIC from 2 January 1998 to 31 December 1999', São Paulo: Lunar Finance, Datasheet.

Maaß, H. and F.L. Sell (1998), 'Confident Expectations, Rational Expectations and the Optimal Conduct of Monetary Policy', *Economic Modelling*, **15** (4), pp. 519–41.

Mansfield, Edwin W. (1968), *Industrial Research and Technical Innovation: An Econometric Analysis*, New York: Norton.

Masera, R.S. (1994), 'Single Market, Exchange Rates and Monetary Unification', *The World Economy*, **17** (3), pp. 249–79.

Masson, P. (1998), 'Contagion: Monsoonal Effects, Spillovers, and Jumps Between Multiple Equilibria', IMF Working Paper No. 142/98.

Masson, P. (1999), 'Multiple Equilibria, Contagion, and the Emerging Market Crises', IMF Working Paper No. 164/99.

McKinnon, Ronald I. (1973), *Money and Capital in Economic Development*, Washington, DC: Brookings Institution.

McKinnon, R.I. and H. Pill (1997), 'Credible Economic Liberalizations and Overborrowing', *American Economic Review, Papers and Proceedings*, **87** (2), pp. 189–93.

McKinnon, R.I. and H. Pill (1998a), 'International Overborrowing. A Decomposition of Credit and Currency Risks', Stanford: Stanford University, Department of Economics, Working Paper 98-004.

McKinnon, Roland I. and Huw Pill (1998b), 'The Overborrowing Syndrome:

Are East Asian Economies Different?', in Reuven Glick (ed.), *Managing Capital Flows and Exchange Rates: Perspectives from the Pacific Basin*, Cambridge: Cambridge University Press, pp. 322–55.

Mélitz, J. (1994), 'Comment on the Tobin Tax', paper presented at Conference of Globalization of Markets CIDEI, Rome: Università di Roma, 27–28 October.

Miller, M. and L. Zhang (1997), 'Sovereign Liquidity Crises: The Strategic Case for a Payments Standstill', Mimeo, Warwick: University of Warwick, Department of Economics, November.

Miller, V. (1998), 'The Double Drain with a Cross-border Twist: More on the Relationship Between Banking and Currency Crises', *American Economic Review, Papers and Proceedings*, **88** (2), pp. 439–43.

Minnitti, M. (1998), 'The Dynamics of Crime: A Study of Social Contagion', Mimeo, Babson Park: Babson College.

Mishkin, F.S. (1994), 'Preventing Financial Crises: An International Perspective', NBER Working Paper Series No. 4636.

Moreno, R. and B. Trehan (2000), 'Common Shocks and Currency Crisis', Mimeo, San Francisco: Federal Reserve Bank of San Francisco, April.

Morris, S. and H.S. Shin (1998a), 'A Theory of the Onset of Currency Attacks', CEPR Discussion Paper Series No. 2025.

Morris, S. and H.S. Shin (1998b), 'Unique Equilibrium in a Model of Self-fulfilling Attacks', *American Economic Review*, **88** (3), pp. 587–97.

Mundell, R.A. (1961), 'A Theory of Optimum Currency Areas', *American Economic Review*, **51** (3), pp. 657–65.

Muns, Joaquim (1997), 'From the Werner Plan to the Euro, or the History of the Long March Toward European Monetary Union', in Joaquim Muns (ed.), *Spain and The Euro: Risks and Opportunities*, Barcelona: Caja de Ahorro y Pensiones de Barcelona, Research Department, Studies and Report Series, pp. 11–49.

Mussa, M., A. Swoboda, J. Zettelmayer and O. Jeanne (1999), 'Moderating Fluctuations in Capital Flows to Emerging Market Economies', *Finance & Development*, **36** (3), internet version http://www.imf.org/external/pubs/ft/fandd/1999/09/mussa.htm.

Nam, C.W. (2000), 'Some Western Misunderstandings Surrounding the Origin of the Korean and Asian Economic Crises', *Review of Asian and Pacific Studies*, **19**, pp. 21–44.

Nofsinger, J.R. and R.W. Sias (1999), 'Herding and Feedback Trading by Institutional and Individual Investors', *Journal of Finance*, **54** (6), pp. 2263–95.

Nokes, D.J. and R.M. Anderson (1992), 'Mathematical Models of Infectious Agent Transmission and the Impact of Mass Vaccination', *Reviews in Medical Microbiology*, **3**, pp. 187–95.

Noorlander, J. (1992), 'Lessons from the EMS Crisis', *Swiss Bank Corporation: Economic and Financial Prospects*, No. 6, pp. 4–8.

Nunnenkamp, P. (1999), 'Latin America after the Currency Crash in Brazil. Why the Optimists May Be Wrong', Kiel Discussion Papers No. 337.

Nunnenkamp, P. (2000), 'Boom, Bust, Recovery – What Next in Private Capital Flows to Emerging Economies?' Kiel Discussion Paper No. 362.

Obstfeld, M. (1986), 'Rational and Self-fulfilling Balance of Payments Crises', *American Economic Review*, 76 (4), pp. 72–81.

Obstfeld, M. (1996), 'Models of Currency Crises With Self-fulfilling Features', *European Economic Review*, 40, 1037–47.

Organization for Economic Cooperation and Development (1996), *Economic Outlook No. 59*, Paris: OECD, June.

Osei, G.K. and J.W. Thompson (1977), 'The Supersession of one Rumour by Another', *Journal of Applied Probability*, 14, pp. 122–34.

Ötker, I. and C. Pazarbasioglu (1996), 'Speculative Attacks and Currency Crises: The Mexican Experience', *Open Economies Review*, 7, 535–52.

Otto, P. (2000), 'Meister Warns Against Time Pressure for New Basle Accord' ('Meister warnt vor Termindruck bei neuem Baseler Akkord'), *Handelsblatt*, 21 September, p. 46.

Ozkan, F.G. and A. Sutherland (1998), 'A Currency Crisis Model with an Optimising Policymaker', *Journal of International Economics*, 44, pp. 339–64.

Palma, G. (1998), 'Three and a Half Cycles of Mania, Panic and (Asymmetric) Crash: East Asia and Latin America Compared', *Cambridge Journal of Economics*, 22, pp. 789–808.

Petersen, D. (2000), 'Thailand Aims at an Early-warning System in Asia' ('Thailand will Frühwarnsystem in Asien'), *Handelsblatt*, 14 February, p. 13.

Phelps, E.S. (1999), 'Lessons from the Corporatist Crisis in Some Asian Nations', *Journal of Policy Modeling*, 21 (3), pp. 331–9.

Pinto, Brain (1991), 'Unification of Official and Black Market Exchange Rates in Sub-Saharan Africa', in Emil Maria Claassen (ed.), *Exchange Rate Policies in Developing and Post-socialist Countries*, pp. 327–51.

Radelet, S. (1998), 'Comment on: Furman, J. and J.E. Stiglitz: Economic Crises: Evidence and Insights from East Asia', *Brookings Papers on Economic Activity*, 2, pp. 118–23.

Radelet, S. and J. Sachs (1998a), 'The East Asian Financial Crisis: Diagnosis, Remedies, Prospects', *Brookings Papers on Economic Activity*, 1, pp. 1–90.

Radelet, S. and J. Sachs (1998b), 'The Onset of the East Asian Financial Crisis', Mimeo, Cambridge, MA: Harvard Institute for International Development, March.

Rogoff, K. (1985), 'Can International Monetary Policy Coordination be Counterproductive?', *Journal of International Economics*, **49** (5), pp. 199–217.

Rose, A.K. (1998), 'Limiting Currency Crises and Contagion: Is There a Case for an Asian Monetary Fund?', Mimeo, Berkeley: University of California, December.

Rosengren, Eric (1999), 'Will Greater Disclosure and Transparency Prevent the Next Banking Crisis', in William C. Hunter, George G. Kaufman and Thomas H. Krueger (eds), *The Asian Financial Crisis: Origins, Implications, and Solutions*, Boston, Dordrecht, London: Kluwer Academic Publishers, pp. 369–76.

Russian Trading System (2000), 'RTS Interfax Index', internet version http://www.rtsnet.ru/scripts/engl/index.idc?, 22 August.

Sachs, J. (1994a), 'Russia's Struggle with Stabilization: Conceptual Issues and Evidence', in Michael Bruno and Boris Pleskovic (eds), *Proceedings of the Annual Conference on Development Economics 1993*, Washington, DC: World Bank, pp. 57–80.

Sachs, J. (1994b), 'Beyond Bretton Woods: A New Blueprint', *The Economist* (UK), 333: 1–7 October, pp. 27–8.

Sachs, J., A. Tornell and A. Velasco (1996a), 'Financial Crises in Emerging Markets: The Lessons from 1995', *Brookings Papers on Economic Activity*, 1, pp. 147–215.

Sachs, J., A. Tornell and A. Velasco (1996b), 'The Mexican Peso Crisis: Sudden Death or Death Foretold?', *Journal of International Economics*, **41**, pp. 265–83.

Sachverständigenrat (SVR) zur Begutachtung der gesamtwirtschaftlichen Entwicklung (1993), *Time for Action – Fostering the Power of Motivation (Zeit zum Handeln – Antriebskräfte stärken. Jahresgutachten 1993/94)*, Stuttgart: Metzler-Poeschel Verlag.

Salvatore, D. (1996), 'The European Monetary System: Crisis and Future', *Open Economies Review*, 7, pp. 601–23.

Schinasi, G.J. and R.T. Smith (1999), 'Portfolio Diversification, Leverage, and Financial Contagion', IMF Working Paper No. 136/99.

Schneider, M. and A. Tornell (1999), 'Lending Booms and Speculative Crises', Mimeo, Rochester: University of Rochester, July.

Schumacher, L. (2000), 'Bank Runs and Currency Run in a System Without a Safety Net: Argentina and the "Tequila" Shock', *Journal of Monetary Economics*, **46**, pp. 257–77.

Schumpeter, Joseph A. (1934), *The Theory of Economic Development*, Cambridge, MA: Harvard University Press.

Schwarz, A.J. (1999), 'Assessing IMF's Crisis Prevention and Management Record', in William C. Hunter, George G. Kaufman and Thomas H.

Krueger (eds), *The Asian Financial Crisis: Origins, Implications, and Solutions*, Boston, Dordrecht, London: Kluwer Academic Publishers, pp. 453–7.

Sell, F.L. (1988a), 'The Dutch Disease: Adjustment Process as a Consequence of a Resource Boom' ('The Dutch Disease: Anpassungsprozesse als Folge eines Ressourcenbooms'), *WISU*, **17** (5), pp. 289–94.

Sell, Friedrich L. (1988b), *Monetary and Exchange Rate Policy in Emerging Market Economies (Geld- und Währungspolitik in Schwellenländern, am Beispiel der ASEAN-Staaten)*, Berlin: Duncker & Humblot.

Sell, F.L. (1993a), 'Liberalization of the Capital Account and Macroeconomic Stabilization' ('Liberalisierung des Kapitalverkehrs und makroökonomische Stabilisierung'), *List Forum für Wirtschafts- und Finanzpolitik*, **19** (1), pp. 64–75.

Sell, F.L. (1993b), *Development Economics (Ökonomik der Entwicklungsländer)*, Berlin, Heidelberg and New York: Peter Lang Verlag.

Sell, F.L. (1998), 'Issues in Monetary and Exchange Rate Policy of Developing Countries', in Helmut Wagner (ed.), *Current Issues in Monetary Economics*, Heidelberg: Physica, pp. 289–306.

Sell, F.L. (2000), 'On the Diagnosis of Financial Crises', *The Opening Bell, A Business and Economics Newsletter from the Sigmund Weis School of Business of Susquehanna University*, **2** (2), pp. 2–3.

Sell, Friedrich. L. and Silke Gehle (1996), *Reform Policy in Developing Countries and in Emerging Market Economies (Reformpolitik in Transformations- und Entwicklungsländern)*, Munich: Vahlen.

Shaw, Edward S. (1973), *Financial Deepening in Economic Development*, New York: Oxford University Press.

Siebert, H. (1999), 'Improving the World's Financial Architecture. The Role of the IMF', Kiel Discussion Paper No. 351.

Silverberg, G., G. Dosi and L. Orsenigo (1988), 'Innovation, Diversity and Diffusion: A Self-Organisation Model', *Economic Journal*, **98**, pp. 1032–54.

Sinn, Hans-Werner (1980), *Economic Decisions Under Uncertainty (Ökonomische Entscheidungen bei Ungewißheit)*, Tübingen: J.C.B. Mohr.

Sinn, H.-W. (1982), 'Human Wealth and Liability Insurance', *European Economic Review*, **17**, pp. 149–62.

Sinn, Hans-Werner (1997), *The Role of the State in the Banking Sector. The Example of the German 'Landesbanken' (Der Staat im Bankwesen. Zur Rolle der Landesbanken in Deutschland)*, München: Verlag C.H. Beck.

Sjaastad, Larry A. (1983), 'Liberalization and Stabilization. Experiences in the Southern Cone', in Nicolas A. Barletta, Mario I. Blejer and Luis Landau (eds), *Economic Liberalization and Stabilization Policies in Argentina, Chile, and Uruguay. Applications of the Monetary Approach to the Balance of Payments*, Washington, DC: World Bank, pp. 83–103.

Stiglitz, J.A. and A. Weiss (1981), 'Credit Rationing in Markets with Imperfect Information', *American Economic Review*, **71** (3), pp. 393–410.

Sudbury, A. (1985), 'The Proportion of the Population Never Hearing a Rumour', *Journal of Applied Probability*, **22**, pp. 443–6.

Swoboda, A. (1999), 'Reforming the International Financial Architecture', *Finance & Development*, **36** (3), internet version http://www.imf.org/external/pubs/ft/fandd/1999/09/swoboda.htm.

Tan, III, J.A.R. (1998), 'Contagion Effects During the Asian Financial Crisis: Some Evidence from Stock Price Data', San Francisco, CA: Federal Reserve Bank of San Francisco, Center for Pacific Basin Studies Working Paper PB 98–06.

Thorndike, S. (ed.) (1973), *The Complete Works of William Shakespeare*, London: Murray Sales & Service Co. Cresta House.

Tietmayer, H. (1999), 'Evolving Cooperation and Coordination in Financial Market Surveillance', *Finance & Development*, **36** (3), internet version http://www.imf.org/external/pubs/ft/fandd/1999/09/tietmaye.htm.

Tinbergen, Jan (1964), *Economic Policy: Principles and Design*, Amsterdam: North Holland.

Tobin, J. (1978), 'A Proposal for International Monetary Reform', *Eastern Economic Journal*, **4**, pp. 153–9.

Tornell, A. (1999), 'Common Fundamentals in the Tequila and Asian Crises', NBER Working Paper Series No. 7139.

Tuteja, R. and K. Gupta (1992), 'Diffusion of News and Rumours in Stochastic and Deterministic Approach with Pro-rumour and Anti-rumour Operators', *Journal of the Indian Society of Statistical Operations Research*, **13** (1–4), pp. 23–33.

Ul Haque, N. and P. Montiel (1990), 'Capital Mobility in Developing Countries – Some Empirical Tests', IMF Working Paper No. 90/117.

United Nations (1998), *Economic Survey of Europe, No. 1*, Geneva: United Nations, Economic Commission for Europe.

Uribe, M. (1996), 'The Tequila Effect: Theory and Evidence from Argentina', Washington, DC: International Finance Discussion Papers No. 552.

Velasco, A. (1996), 'Fixed Exchange Rates: Credibility, Flexibility and Multiplicity', *European Economic Review*, **40**, pp. 1023–35.

Weidemann, J. (2000), 'Reform Proposals for the IMF' ('Reformen für den Währungsfonds'), *Handelsblatt*, 4 November, p. 53.

White, W.R. (2000), 'What Have We Learned From Recent Crises and Policy Responses?', Basle: Bank of International Settlements, BIS Working Paper No. 84.

World Bank (1998), *Global Economic Prospects 1998/99: Beyond Financial*

Crises, Washington, DC: World Bank.

Xie, X. (1999), 'Contagion Through Interactive Production and Dynamic Effects of Trade', *International Economic Review*, **40** (1), pp. 165–86.

Yan, H.-D. (1998), 'Intertemporal Current Account Balance and the South-East Asian Currency Crises', Mimeo, Taichung, Taiwan: Feng-Chia University, Department of Economics, March.

Yatrakis, P. G. and A. Gart (2000), 'Asia's Financial Crisis and the Role of the IMF', Mimeo, Fort Lauderdale: Nova Southeastern University, Wayne Huizenga Graduate School of Business and Entrepreneurship, March.

Index